The Russian Autocracy in Crisis

1905-1907

The Russian Autocracy in Crisis

1905-1907

by
Ann Erickson Healy

Archon Books
1976

© 1976 by Ann Erickson Healy
First published 1976 as an Archon Book,
an imprint of The Shoe String Press, Inc.,
Hamden, Connecticut 06514

Printed in the United States of America

Library of Congress Cataloging in Publication Data

Healy, Ann Erickson, 1930-
    The Russian autocracy in crisis, 1905-1907.

    Bibliography: p.
    Includes index.
    1. Russia—Politics and government—1904-1914.
2. Russia. Gosudarstvennaia Duma. 1st, 1906 3.
Nicholas II, Emperor of Russia, 1868-1918. I. Title.
DK262.H36   320.9'47'08   75-41331
ISBN 0-208-01577-9

To
Matthew,
Ellen,
and Jon
for sharing their mother with Clio

Contents

PART I. The Background

PART II. Administration versus Opposition:

The Era of the First Duma

Preface

The years 1905 and 1906 saw the most momentous changes in Russia between the emancipation of the serfs and the other reforms of Alexander II in the middle of the nineteenth century, and the revolution of 1917. That winter marked the end of the old autocratic system, when in the midst of mass revolts, Tsar Nicholas II granted his subjects a popularly elected legislative assembly, the State Duma. During subsequent months his administration hammered out the 1906 version of the Fundamental Laws of the Russian Empire. The new statutes retained many key powers for the executive. Tsarist Russia never had a ministry responsible to the legislature, although the demand for such a ministry was a major cry of the opposition. The executive branch regularly used its powers, sometimes in direct violation of the Fundamental Laws, to inaugurate measures which the Duma would not approve. However attenuated its powers, between 1906 and the fall of the Tsar, the State Duma was a permanent branch of the Russian government. The first two Dumas were very radical and each lasted only a few months before the Tsar dissolved it. Their successor, elected under a more restricted franchise, had considerable legislative achievements to its credit, such as a bill inaugurating a compulsory free school system. Beyond that, for the first time in Russian history, there existed a forum where it was legally possible to subject the Tsar's administration to regular and extensive criticism. Furthermore, with the Duma came political parties across a wide spectrum—from the Bolsheviks to the right wing Union of the Russia People, both radical groups dedicated to the destruction of the quasi-constitutional system which replaced the old autocracy. Most other parties were less extremist, but all of them—and there were far too many for an effectively functioning legislature—suffered from political inexperience and lack of unity.

Frequently horrified by the proceedings on the Duma floor, Nicholas II and many of his key advisors were never comfortable with the new system. To them, the Russian Empire had many severe problems which could better be handled through executive measures. If the legislature did not give its approval to these measures, then the administration must operate without that approval.

Few students of the Russian revolution of 1905 have shown much interest in the problems of those responsible at the time for governing Russia, and even the First Duma awaits adequate study. The present work began as an investigation of the struggle between the First Duma and the administration of Nicholas II. Not surprisingly, it was soon apparent that the main lines of battle were laid out before the fledgling assembly convened. The unwanted child of an anxious and uncertain monarch who had been steeped in the traditions of autocracy, the First Duma was born at the peak of a widespread revolt. Passions ran high throughout 1905 and the demands had escalated regularly. The response from a frightened administration had been hesitant, at times contradictory, and always unsatisfactory to the angry populace. Finally on October 17, 1905, the Tsar granted a popularly elected legislative assembly. Flushed with initial success against the monarch, a large segment of the opposition immediately regarded that assembly as an opportunity to push for additional concessions, as well as to provide legislative guarantees for the civil rights which had also been mentioned in the October 17 announcement. Nicholas and most of his advisors, on the other hand, believed that he had already made more concessions than was advisable. They awaited the arrival of the representatives of the populace with fear, not at all confident that these men could, or would, work with the administration to solve the many problems which beset their troubled country.

Once it convened on April 27, 1906, the proceedings in the First Duma convinced the men in the Tsar's administration that their fears were well founded. From the start the over-optimistic and inexperienced legislators pushed for broad reform programs which went much beyond the monarch's concessions of October, 1905. Moreover, with one exception, the chamber gave no consideration to legislative proposals which arrived from the administration. The result was an impasse with neither side willing to make the compromises necessary for an effective parliamentary system. Finally, Nicholas II opted to end that impasse with his July 8, 1906, decree dissolving the new chamber.

The present study is an attempt to recapture the main events in the dramatic and bitter struggle between the Tsar's administration and its opposition during the critical period of 1905 and 1906. The chief editors of my manuscript were Professor Michael B. Petrovich of the University of Wisconsin, and my husband, Professor David F. Healy. I owe them both many thanks for constant encouragement and sound advice. My final version benefitted from the suggestions of Professors Keith L. Bryant and Alfred Levin, from the former because he is a perceptive historian with no special knowledge of this field, from the latter because he knows it so well. My typists, Patricia Checkvala and Rosanne Jacobson, also deserve special thanks for their intelligent and efficient services.

The dates in the text are all in accord with the Julian calendar, then in use in the Russian Empire. Add thirteen days to determine the corresponding date under the Gregorian calendar which was then employed in the west. The transliteration is according to J. Thomas Shaw's IInd system, without diacritical marks. Exceptions occur in the case of names which have a commonly accepted English spelling, such as Alexander.

ABBREVIATIONS USED FOR
FREQUENTLY USED TITLES

Bing, *Secret Letters*	Bing, Edward J., ed. *The Secret Letters of the Last Tsar.* New York, 1938.
Nicholas, *Dnevnik.*	Nicholas II. *Dnevnik Imperatora Nikolaia II: 1890-1906.* Berlin, 1923.
PSRI	*Polnoe sobranie zakonov Rossiskoi Imperii.* (All the references are to the Third Series) St. Petersburg, 1885-1916.
	Revoliutsiia 1905-1907 gg. v Rossi: Dokumenty i materialy. This is a series under the editorship of Anna M. Pankratova and includes the following:
VPS	*Vserossiiskaia politicheskaia stachka v Oktiabre 1905 goda.* 2 vols. Moscow-Leningrad, 1955.
VPR	*Vysshii podem revoliutsii 1905-1907 gg: Vooruzhennye vosstaniia.* 3 vols. Moscow-Leningrad, 1955-1956.
Vtoroi period revoliutsii, January-April, 1906.	*Vtoroi period revoliutsii: 1906-1907 gody.* January-April, 1906. Vol. I, Parts I and II. Moscow, 1957-59.
Vtoroi period revoliutsii, May-September, 1906.	*Vtoroi period revoliutsii: 1906-1907 gody.* May-September, 1906. Vol. II, Parts I, II, III. Moscow, 1961-1963.
SO	*Russia: Gosudarstvennia Duma. Stenograficheskie otchety 1906 god: sessia pervaia.* St. Petersburg, 1907.
Witte, TN I, TN II	Witte, Sergei Iu. *Vospominaniia: Tsarstvovanie Nikolaia II.* 2 vols. Berlin, 1922.

PART I
The Background

CHAPTER I

A Manifesto and Its Reception

On the evening of October 17, 1905, Nicholas II, Tsar and Autocrat of all the Russias, published a manifesto which promised his "loyal subjects" some of the reforms they were demanding in a virtual mass revolt.[1] He assured them of his "inflexible will" to grant the basic civil liberties—personal inviolability, freedom of conscience, speech, association, and assembly. Henceforth, no law would become effective in his empire without the sanction of a popular assembly (Duma), soon to be elected. The monarch guaranteed the Duma's "participation in supervising the legality of the government authorities," but referred specifically to a ministry appointed "by Us." In other words, the future ministers would be the choice of the Tsar, responsible to him and not to the assembly.

Like all great reforms in Tsarist Russia, the October Manifesto came down from the throne, and then only after great hesitation. Wrung from Nicholas when he saw no other answer to the disorders sweeping his empire, it remained to be seen how much real change would ensue. And as they had received Tsarist promises in the past, Nicholas's subjects greeted the manifesto with varied, vocal, and sometimes ominous reactions. Maurice Baring of London *Morning Post* found the Moscow streets decorated with flags the next morning. Everyone was in a "state of frantic and effervescing enthusiasm. . . . Old men were embracing each other and drinking the first glass of vodka to free Russia." An orator on Theater Square, however, was less enthusiastic: "We are all too much used to the rascality of the Autocracy to believe this; away with the Autocracy," he cried. Evidently expecting a eulogy, his listeners responded, "Away with you," and ran from the speaker.[2]

The mixed reaction in the Moscow streets had its counterpart in the varied responses of Russian political figures. Writing in the United States many years later, Alexander Kerensky could still recall his emotions when a friend brought word of the Tsar's surprise announcement. "Constitution" no longer seemed an empty slogan. "The age long bitter struggle of the people for freedom and the right to participate in the affairs of state seemed to be over. . . . My childhood adoration for the Tsar revived." The young lawyer spent a long sleepless night waiting to join the victory celebration on the morning following the manifesto's publication. Yet, to Kerensky's disappointment, the Nevskii Prospect was deserted in the early hours, aside from a handful of people carrying "Long live anarchy" banners.[3]

A few hours later, however, the St. Petersburg streets were far from empty. S. R. Mintslov, the well known museum curator and historical bibliographer, spent most of the dim, grey October day milling among the city crowds. By his own account he never joined a political party or participated actively in politics, but his vivid interest in his fellow man and in the situation in his troubled country are borne out by his lively diary.[4] A lengthy entry for October 18, 1905, that "greatest moment in Russian history," began on an enthusiastic note: "Hurrah! We are a free people." He and his "small circle" generally agreed that a great step had been taken, although even in his group there were a few skeptics. His own initial response was purely optimistic. "How strange and joyful it was to see red flags; only yesterday they were illegal," he exclaimed at one point. But like M. Baring he discovered a very mixed reception of the Tsar's promises. "No! This is not yet what we need. We must carry the revolution to its end," yelled one streetcorner orator. Another speaker shouted down the administration for giving with one hand, while taking with the other. Later a third harangued his listeners not to believe the government, and to demand an amnesty of all political prisoners. Frequent rumors that the Tsar would leave his estate outside the city and come to the Winter Palace prompted Mintslov to hasten to the monarch's St. Petersburg residence. As he approached the palace he glimpsed a crowd of supporters, pressing against the palace gates as they eagerly awaited their sovereign. "A stout bearded old man wept while singing from his heart" the words "Lord save your people." But Nicholas did not appear before the expectant crowd: "He is his own worst enemy, Tsar Nicholas," Mintslov observed cryptically.

On the same day that the Tsar issued the October Manifesto, the Union of Liberation, a loose alliance of left *zemstvo* (rural elected local councils) and city *duma* leaders, liberal intellectuals and professional men, was holding a conference in Moscow. Of mixed opinions, these men were united in their demands for civil liberties and basic reforms of the arbitrary autocracy. Most of them wanted a constitutional monarchy with a legislative assembly. It was at this meeting that the Constitutional Democratic Party (Kadets) was founded under the leadership of Paul Miliukov, famous historian and liberal political leader. Miliukov later recalled the group's complete surprise when a friendly journalist brought in a crumpled proof sheet, still wet with ink, which contained the text of the manifesto. The document created a vague, unsatisfactory sensation: the concessions seemed significant, but on careful examination they proved ambiguous. Later that evening the future Kadet leader ended a talk on a pessimistic note: "Nothing has changed; the struggle goes on."[5]

Political figures to the left of Kerensky and Miliukov had more expressive reservations. Leon Trotsky tore up a copy of the manifesto before a celebrating crowd of thousands in St. Petersburg. "So a constitution is granted," Trotsky wrote, "but the autocracy remains. Everything is given— and nothing is given. The proletariat wants neither the police hooligan Trepov nor the liberal broker Witte—it wants neither the wolf's snout nor the fox's tail. It does not want the police whip wrapped up in a constitution."[6] While Trotsky was in St. Petersburg at the center of the excitement, his more famous colleague, Vladimir Lenin, did not make it in time. Lenin left Geneva for Russia only to be met by enormously frustrating delays; storms at sea and difficulties over obtaining a false passport held him up in Stockholm, and he reached St. Petersburg only on November 8. His words from Geneva on October 19, however, were succinct and prophetic: "Tsarism is no longer strong enough to crush the revolution; the revolution is not yet strong enough to destroy tsarism."[7]

One of Lenin's agrarian socialist rivals, Vladimir Zenzinov, who was active in the terrorist wing of the Social Revolutionaries, also saw the news of the manifesto in a Geneva paper. After a comrade read it aloud, Zenzinov, to his own surprise, exclaimed: "Well! We will now soon see the barricades!" He felt mixed emotions—elation at a partial victory coupled with distrust of the government. To him the situation remained basically the same, since it was still *we*, the people, versus *they* the government.[8]

Among the most vocal centers of reform agitation in 1905 were the Russian universities. The economist, Vladimir Woytinsky, then a student and Social Democratic agitator in St. Petersburg, reacted much like his mentors, Lenin and Trotsky. "Newsboys ran by shouting '*Ukase* (decree) of the Tsar,'" he recalled. He acquired a copy and before his *droshky* (cab) reached the Neva quay his mind was made up: the manifesto was a fraud. He must help unmask it and carry on the offensive. At the university Woytinsky listened to a liberal professor tell his audience not to be discouraged by the vague promises of the document. "This is how great constitutions are born," the professor argued. Taking his place, Woytinsky demanded who shared the professor's illusions about the "Tsar and his gang." He then led a group of his peers to the Kazan Plaza, a semicircle off the Nevskii Prospect used frequently for demonstrations. En route the students met another procession carrying tricolor flags and singing "God Save the Tsar"; strangely enough this crowd greeted the students with a friendly "Hurrah."[9]

Hence, the other side of the political spectrum also had its representatives on the streets that day. Nor were they all as friendly as the group Woytinsky met. Along with loyal monarchists, sincerely reluctant to see the Tsar relinquish any of his power, were extreme right reactionaries. To them, all strikers, Jews, students, and revolutionaries were against the Tsar and the common people, and it was a matter of patriotism to defend the monarch. A host of patriotic demonstrations occurred throughout the empire.

These were similar in pattern: a group of marchers carried flags and Nicholas's portrait to the residences of the local governor and the mayor. Sometimes those dignitaries joined the procession, which then preceeded to the public square, where the local bishop frequently said a prayer. Often drunkards brought up the rear crying for "annihilation of the traitors."[10] Violence frequently erupted when rightist patriots met reformers or revolutionaries. Such excesses took place in Rostov-on-Don: "Neither the government, nor the population was prepared" for the October Manifesto, the governor wrote in November. "The whole city was in the streets." One delegation insisted that he free the local political prisoners, while their supporters went to the jail and demanded immediate amnesty. Some crowds appeared with national flags and portraits; others held up red flags, and clashes occurred in the most crowded streets. Sometimes the bloodshed was between demonstrators and the police, or the army, as in St. Petersburg when a company from the famous Semenovskii Regiment blockaded a crowd bearing red flags. The crowd took another route, stopped, and a revolutionary orator began a speech; at this point the troops let fly a volley of shots, killed the speaker, and wounded several others. Simon Kaplan, in 1905 a young member of the Marxist Jewish Bund, described bloody events in Minsk where soldiers fired into a crowd listening to a speaker at the railroad station. Kaplan claimed that over 100 deaths ensued, including 33 Bund members. The next day mounted police broke up a mass funeral with whips.[11]

The October Manifesto also led to a barrage of revolutionary literature. The Central Committee of the Social Democrats warned readers not to trust a Tsar of "bullets and whips, prisons and gallows, spies and hangmen," who was merely trying to calm the nation with a paper constitution he would not carry out. "Away with privileges, phoney elections, and phoney representatives." On to the armed uprising! A resolution of the First All-Russian Railroad Workers' Congress vitriolically denounced Nicholas's concessions. Russian citizens were still at the mercy of the police and gendarmes. The possibility of arbitrary death sentences remained, and many citizens lived with their civil rights greatly restricted in areas declared under special emergency legislation. The Social Democrats of Samara claimed the manifesto as a victory to "breathe new strength into our ranks" for the final battle with the autocrat. "We don't want peace" with Nicholas, since his "white flag, his October Manifesto, showed that the fortress of autocracy had lost its last means of struggle."[12]

In the midst of all this violent reaction from the left and the right, the feeble voices of a few political moderates urged the acceptance of the sudden concessions as the basis for a reformed monarchy. Many of these men soon banded together in a political party, the Union of October 17, 1905 (Octobrists), dedicated to this goal. They even took their title from the October Manifesto. One of the party's founders, Alexander Guchkov, scion of a prominent Moscow industrial family, financeer, and political leader, later described Nicholas's promises as "an act of confidence in the nation on the part of the Sovereign; Octobrism was the nation's answer; it was an act of faith in the Sovereign." Guchkov's first public response to the document came at a meeting of the Moscow municipal *duma*. Following a "hurrah" for the newly promised reforms, Kadet Party leader S. A. Muromtsev, soon to be elected president of the promised popular assembly, asked that the city council members rise in memory of those who had died in the freedom struggle. He suggested further that they press the administration for more concessions—the abolition of all state-of-emergency legislation and complete amnesty for political prisoners. A. Guchkov and his two brothers objected to these two proposals, but they carried. Alexander then proposed that the Moscow Duma send a congratulatory telegram to the Tsar, describing the "profound gratification" of the city council for the October concessions. For this "great act," with its guarantees for the "free development and full renewal" of the life of the whole populace, the representatives of the "henceforward free population" of Moscow sent their grateful thanks.[13]

Local officials and the public were not the only people caught unawares by the October Manifesto, since it also came as a total surprise to many individuals high up in government circles. Sergei Kryzhanovskii, a functionary in the Ministry of Internal Affairs, who was responsible for drafting many of Nicholas's decrees, had been very busy that fall. Since he had worked at home, he had seen almost no one and he was out of touch with major happenings in the administration. On October 17 his wife brought rumors of some kind of manifesto, but she had no details. That evening Kryzhanovskii received a telephone call asking that he report to Sergei Witte, newly appointed chief minister to the Tsar. Upon his arrival at Witte's home, Kryzhanovskii learned about the concessions from the former's subordinate. He then entered the chief minister's office and discovered Witte "pacing from corner to corner in worried fashion." Witte launched into a vacillating conversation about the effect the concessions would have on Duma statutes which Kryzhanovskii must draft. The latter left his interview at Witte's home in a dejected mood. As he walked away he met his "first group" of manifesto demonstrators, and a "vague premonition, a kind of anguish" filled his heart. "It was as if something had cracked in our life, which was being filled by an avalanche, moved by an intangible, outside force," he wrote later, recalling how the words "I am sorry Holy Russia . . ." had involuntarily leapt into his mind.

At three o'clock that same morning Kryzhanovskii was at the home of his direct superior, Minister of Internal Affairs Alexander Bulygin. The latter was in a dressing gown reading a galley proof from *Pravitelstvennyi Vestnik* (Government Messenger), the official administration daily. It seemed that Bulygin, the head of a major ministry, had learned about the manifesto from the newspaper. Calm as usual, Bulygin expressed surprise and indignation that he had not at least been warned in advance. The provincial governors, his subordinates in charge of administering and maintaining order in the geographic subdivisions of that sprawling empire, should also have received adequate notification about the concessions, Bulygin complained. As it was, Kryzhanovskii reminisced, most of the governors learned about the manifesto from their own sources, the morning after it appeared. They had received no instructions on "how to speak or act" in regard to this hastily conceived and hastily issued document.[14]

CHAPTER II

"All Over Russia They Cried for It"

Nicholas's reluctant decision to sign the October Manifesto had come only after great soul searching. Shortly
afterwards, he poured out his feelings in a letter to his
mother, the Dowager Empress Marie Feodorovna, who was
visiting relatives in Denmark that fall:

> My dear Mama, you can't imagine what I went through
> before that moment. . . . From all over Russia they
> cried for it, they begged for it, and around me many—very
> many—held the same views. . . . There was no other
> way out than to cross oneself and give what everyone
> was asking for.

Even Nicholas's diary entry on the evening of the signing
was an outburst of emotion in that ordinarily bland document: "After such a day the head is heavy and one's thoughts
are confused. God help us, pacify Russia."[1]

The concessions in the October Manifesto went against
all the deep and basic convictions held by the last Romanov
Tsar, and he granted them solely as an attempt to calm the
worst disturbances to date in that dynasty's three century
rule. On October 19, in an effort to explain his momentous
decision to the Dowager Empress, he described some of the
pressures surrounding him:

> We have been through such grave and unprecedented
> events that I feel as if the last time I wrote to you was a

year ago. . . . It makes me sick to read the news!
Nothing but new strikes in schools and factories, mur-
dered policemen, Cossacks and soldiers, riots, disorder,
mutinies. But the ministers, instead of acting with
quick decision, only assemble in council like a lot of
frightened hens, and cackle about providing united
ministerial action.[2]

The outburst of early October was actually the peak of a
mass revolt which had been shaking the weak foundations
of the Tsarist regime throughout the previous year. Petitions, protest groups, bomb-throwing assassins, peasant
riots, and strikes were certainly not new to Nicholas and
his officials, but this time it was different. The 1905 revolution embraced all layers of the population and broke out in
widespread areas of that vast empire. Furthermore, the
disturbances just would not peter out, nor had the time
honored repressive measures proved effective. On the other
hand, the August promise of a consultative elected national
assembly, the so-called Bulygin Duma, had been equally
ineffective. The August concession failed to placate the
opposition, the revolts mounted after it was announced,
and they swelled to fever pitch by late September.

The dissatisfaction of the empire's population with an
antiquated regime had deep roots. The discontent had
finally exploded in 1905, in part because the unpopular and
disastrous Russo-Japanese War had so clearly pointed up
the shortcomings of the system. The disorders were soon
out of hand, and, with large numbers of his troops off in
the Far East, Nicholas lacked the men to quell them. In
addition, the loyalty of those troops still at home was often
doubtful; at any rate many officers were afraid to test it.

One of the focal points of the reform movement was the
universities. In January 1905, almost every institution of
higher learning had been on strike, or closed by the authorities as a precaution. Many remained centers of agitation,
leaving higher education virtually neglected for the rest of
the year. In late August the Tsar suddenly conferred
autonomy on the universities, hoping to appease the aca-

demic community, and reopen them under peaceful conditions. Henceforth, the university staff could choose its own rectors, and official inspectors from the Ministry of Education would be subordinate to the former. The police could no longer enter the universities and the faculties would be responsible for student discipline. The attempt backfired and no one was appeased. The lecture halls merely became public forums immune from the police, while the faculties could not restrain student activists. Vladimir Woytinsky, who had joined the student branch of the Social Democrats earlier in 1905, has left a vivid recollection of the University of St. Petersburg that fall: "Suddenly, and to our surprise, the University became the center of workers' gatherings." Since the workers had not come to hear academic debates, the students decided to hold meetings twice a day. A new university regime developed— academic affairs until four or five o'clock, while in the evening the university belonged to the "revolutionary crowds that converged from all parts of the city." Mass meetings were also held in Jewish synagogues, the majority of which were located in the western border regions. Sometimes people arriving to worship for the Sabbath were surprised to find themselves listening to Jews who belonged to revolutionary socialist groups. Dedicated to the removal of legal discriminations levied against Jews, as well as to socialist goals, these agitators often failed to obtain prior consent for their appearance from synagogue authorities.[3]

Provincial institutions of higher learning were also used for meetings. A police report from Kazan described daily political gatherings at that university, where students openly collected money for a strike fund, the purchase of arms, and establishing peasant libraries; cries of "away with the autocracy" resounded through the halls. In Yaroslavl, the middle schools, including the female gymnasia and the ecclesiastical seminary, struck in mid-October. Along with characteristic student demands for an improved attitude of the faculty toward the students, they recommended basic changes in Russian political institutions. The strike at the Yaroslavl seminary was not unique, since

25

disturbances occurred at forty-eight of the fifty-eight Orthodox seminaries that fall. While the students may have been up in arms, an anecdote recalled by V. Gurko, a high level official in the Ministry of Internal Affairs, indicates that there was at least some respect left for tradition that October. Enraged at the lack of discipline, the madame of a local institution in the capital reputedly told her turbulent charges: "This is not a university, thank heaven; this is an establishment."[4]

Speeches against the administration drew workers to the universities, while students and other agitators poured into the factory districts seeking support for the freedom movement. The conditions under which these laborers lived and worked made many a receptive listener.[5] They dwelt in terrible slums, crowded into filthy rooms, moldy dank cellars, or barracks provided by the factories. Most worked long hours for low pay. Many came reluctantly to the city only to escape the awful poverty of the country-side, leaving their families in the villages and returning home for part of the year. City life was a new and frightening experience, its impersonal nature a grim contrast to closely knit village society.

Only a small percent of these peasants ever made enough money to bring their families to the city, hence many remained tied to the village by family and emotional ties, and also legal status. In the event of a factory shut-down the village hut, however crowded, was an emergency haven. These displaced peasants had very little chance to reestablish social ties in the factory environment. Trade unions were illegal; friendly societies were rare and not under worker control; and even the worker tearooms and libraries were established for them by others—civic groups or the government.

In the city social contrasts seemed harsher than in the village, where the individual had some status as an individual, in spite of his poverty. To these alienated workers, the factory owners seemed to have unlimited wealth for very little effort; their entrepreneurial skills counted as nothing to their employees. The broader causes of Russian poverty, as well as the frequently precarious financial state of Russian industrialists, were beyond the grasp of these workers, interested only in their own downtrodden lot.

However, beginning in 1898 increasing numbers of Russian industrialists had been suffering from a crisis, which stemmed in part from a shortage of capital on the international money market, to which the Russian economy was so closely linked. Overproduction in a country with a very limited internal market, provided another explanation for the slump which followed the industrial spurt of the nineties. To complicate the problem, the "exhaustion of the taxpaying capacity of the peasantry" resulted in more serious revenue problems for the administration than in previous years.[6] Then the poor harvest of 1901 led to a shortage of grain for export, traditionally the major source of foreign capital for the imperial budget. In 1902 the important iron and steel industry in the Ukraine was hit by depression. Throughout these depression years some 2,400 enterprises closed and nearly 90,000 workers lost their jobs.

While the financial status varied from plant to plant, the workers had no understanding of these differences. In 1905 a manager at the large Knoop's cotton works in Moscow told the British scholar, Bernard Pares, that the workers still thought that they could demand anything of the capitalists. Yet this man found his workers much less efficient than healthier and more intelligent workers in more advanced industrial nations. According to Pares, complaints of low productivity came to him from factory inspectors and zemstvo employees, not only from plant managers. Some critics pointed out that Russian workers did not understand the need for a profit, nor did they realize that capital was transferable, giving the owner the ultimate option of a permanent shutdown of a plant.[7]

Most Russian reformers, both liberal and radical, sympathized with the hostility of the workers toward their employers. Frequently anti-business, indifferent to economics, they tended to see only the lot of the employees, and refused to grant that an owner could be in financial trouble. They took this line in their publications and in speeches delivered in the factory districts and the workers listened eagerly. The manager of the Zindel textile works admitted to Pares in July of 1905 that the majority of his 2,400 workers were hostile, while those few who might support the management were afraid to speak out. On the other hand Pares learned from a factory inspector that the workers in Russia had a real basis for their complaints, since their food supply was often bad and their pay was low, even if one allowed for the generally low Russian standard of living. Thus, there were grievances on both sides, many of which were not amenable to immediate improvement, given the economic situation in a newly industrializing poor country.

Because it was against the law to strike, the workers in Russia had no suitable legal outlet for airing their grievances. Collective bargaining became illegal activity, and the labor movement tended to go underground where revolutionaries frequently assumed the leadership posts. During 1905 a fledgling union movement came out into the open in spite of the law. For example, by late summer trades unions such as those of the printers and bakers visibly functioned in several cities.[8]

The early months of 1905 were also marked by a rash of strikes which neither plant management nor the government could control. By the end of that year Tsarist Russia had witnessed more strikes, involving greater numbers of participants than in all previous years of its history. These strikes were frequently spontaneous and unorganized; during the early months of the year the workers stressed economic issues and in some cases won concessions from their employers. As the movement spread it became more radical and the use of force to back up demands was more prevalent. Also the workers showed an increasing interest in the political issues drilled into them by agitators.

By fall the idea of a general strike filled the air. Leftist propaganda screeched with calls for a nationwide strike to tie up the economy and lead to the overthrow of the autocracy. Elections to a constituent assembly which would set up a democratic republic were to follow. "Acquire your rights with arms in hands," urged the Social Democrats of Moscow; support the general strike, only the first step in the mighty struggle. They sought the support of the troops: "Don't shoot at your brothers, shoot at the Tsarist minions—the officers who order you to shoot the people." Even sleepy provincial Minsk pulsed with excitement; the ordinarily quiet streets were filled with workers, unmolested by the police. Rumors spread about a general strike and local revolutionaries eagerly prepared to support it.[9]

The great strike began at a press in Moscow where the printers struck for a small wage increase; the next day the Moscow Printers' Union urged its ranks to support them. The movement spread to other plants and industries and then out of the city. By October 8 all the railroad lines leading to Moscow, the nation's rail hub, were idle. The Central Bureau of the Union of Railway Workers, founded in April 1905 and the most important labor group in the country, called for general support of the strike until the administration would recognize its right to bargain. Line after line went out, until, when the Finnish lines joined on October 16, the entire imperial network was shut down: the government was not to regain complete control of the railroads until late January 1906.

While specific economic grievances varied from plant to plant, most lists of demands included pay raises, improved sanitary conditions, sick pay, civil treatment by their employers, and sometimes the eight- or nine-hour day. An insight into the conditions under which these men frequently existed is reflected in the request at one Moscow textile factory for individual cots to replace wooden planks in the plant dormitories.[10] Many lists requested the right to elect deputies to bargain with their employers, while others insisted on the right to strike. Not all of the workers mentioned political reforms, although demands for a constituent assembly, universal direct suffrage, and an amnesty for political prisoners appeared frequently in the grievance lists; the demand for a democratic republic was much less common.

The bureaucrat Vladimir Gurko left a vivid account of St. Petersburg that October: factories shut down, food deliveries ceased, presses and bakeries closed. The proprietors of banks and stores lowered metal screens or hastily boarded their windows. Crowds of strikers roamed the city, using benches and boilers as rostrums, from which they urged fellow workers to join them. The Cossacks and police were powerless to control the mobs; if they dispersed a meeting at one corner, the crowd merely moved to another. The workers at the electric power stations walked out and the capital was in darkness. On October 15 a strike of the typesetters cut off news from the rest of the empire. Business activity in the country met a virtual standstill with the entire rail system on strike.

Nor was the general strike confined to the working class. Intellectuals, professional men, even some industrialists, supported the mass strike. Lawyers refused to go to court and white collar workers in hospitals, offices, banks and schools failed to appear at their jobs. All the urban population was not involved, however, and some joined only from fear or momentary excitement.[11] Nevertheless, there was an impressive number of participants—about one million factory workers, over seven hundred thousand railroadmen, about fifty thousand government employees, plus tens of thousands of retail clerks, office workers, professional men and students. The result seemed "a union of forces in a general display of contempt for the regime."[12] Contempt they shared, but unity they had not, as subsequent events demonstrated.

Along with the mushrooming strike movement arose a peculiarly Russian institution, the *soviets* (Councils) of Workers' Deputies. The nucleii of these *soviets* were the committees which had organized the strikes. Of non-party origin, they sprang up all over Russia, and eventually spread to the troops and the villages. Leadership positions in them soon went to Social Revolutionary and Social Democrat agitators, especially the less radical Menshevik faction, most of whom belonged to the intelligentsia.

Most famous was the St. Petersburg Soviet, which held its initial session on October 13, 1905. Its first president, George Khrustalev-Nosar, was a lawyer and revolutionary orator, who had been released from the fortress-prison of St. Peter and St. Paul in mid-October, under orders to remain in Kharkov under police surveillance. When his guard fell asleep en route to Kharkov, he jumped from the train and promptly reappeared in the capital. A pale man with grey eyes and long hair, Khrustalev-Nosar was soon exhausted from excitement and lack of sleep; the "edge of his collar . . . crumpled like an old rag," his was an unkempt appearance as he presided over this unique assembly until his arrest in late November. The deputies varied from meeting to meeting, but on any night one might see factory workers, government employees, even an occasional professional man representing the Union of Unions, arguing into the late hours.[13] After Khrustalev-Nosar's arrest the deputies elected a three-man executive committee to replace him. Leon Trotsky, one of the world's masters of fiery polemical oratory, soon dominated this triumvirate.

The St. Petersburg Soviet became the revolutionary center of the mass strike movement, although it had not planned it, nor could it dominate or control it. The strike did bring the temporary paralysis of the government and the economy which its advocates had desired, however, and Nicholas found his government barraged with pessimistic reports from all sides. On October 10 the Governor-General of the city of Moscow wired: "The situation in Moscow and Moscow *guberniia* remains so serious that only the introduction of martial law will restore order." From Ivanovo-Vosnesensk, the historic textile center northeast of Moscow, came word of a "very threatening situation": presentations of demands accompanied by threats from angry workers interrupted factory schedules, while officials at the state bank and other government offices demanded protection from idle workers." "A hundred cossacks can't keep control . . . send two more companies," the governor pleaded.[14]

It was not only urban Russia that saw huge disturbances that year. In 1905 the Russian countryside was also ablaze

31

with riots, a serious situation where peasants still made up some eighty percent of the country's population. Traditionally land hungry, eking out a living on small plots with primitive methods, Tsarist Russian villages were famous for their squalor. Population pressure on the land had increased throughout the last half of the nineteenth century; the prices for land purchases and rentals had also risen sharply. To help relieve their situation, the peasants coveted the large estates, often mortgaged to the hilt, but nevertheless still in the hands of the gentry, or investors to whom they had sold out. The peasants were especially anxious to retrieve the "cut-offs," lands formerly used in common with the landlords, which had been assigned to the latter by the emancipation act. They also deeply resented their numerous burdensome tax obligations, as well as their inferior legal status.

That year misery in the countryside was worse than usual, especially in the southern and central black earth provinces, where a drought had brought a poor harvest, famine, and terrible sufferings to these regions where agriculture was virtually the only income source. Furthermore, by 1905, many of the peasants were somewhat shaken from their traditional rut. Those in the army, others who worked part of the year in the city, had heard many new and startling ideas. Political agitators had been coming in increasing numbers to the villages, trumpeting various schemes to take the land from the gentry, and opening up vistas of a new and prosperous life for the oppressed villagers.

As always the agrarian riots were elemental and disorganized. A modern Soviet historian has created a prototype: a burning haystack or the ring of a tocsin might provide the signal. Hundreds of peasants, on foot or in wagons, armed with axes, pitchforks, or knives suddenly converged on the landlord's property, where they razed his supply barns, ruined his crops, stole or killed his livestock. The mob then rushed to the estate office, where they burned or grabbed the records of peasant obligations to the landlord and the government. Sometimes they wrecked or burned the farm buildings, and much less often the manor house, forcing the owner and family to flee for their lives.[15]

That fall village disturbances became more frequent and violent; during the last four months of 1905 estate robberies or fires were reported in about one-quarter of the *uezds* (districts) of European Russia, while timber theft occurred in even more. In areas like the Baltic provinces, where most peasants were propertyless farm hands, they struck against the land barons. There were numerous instances of refusal to pay dues or taxes. In fact, officials recorded some type of agrarian disturbance in over half the European *uezds* of the Empire. Those areas hit worst by the poor harvest—Saratov, Kursk, and Chernigov—incurred the greatest losses from the rioting.[16]

Peasant discontent was also reflected in the uprisings in the army and navy, which caused such grave fears in the administration. The bulk of the lower ranks were peasants in uniform, who added gripes about harsh military life to their grievances as peasants. The slow demobilization after the Russo-Japanese War, slowed even more by the rail strike, added another irritant. Minister of War A. F. Rediger, a bespectacled general with a bulging waist, received many reports daily about outbreaks in military units. He attributed them not only to the general mood in the empire, but also to conditions in the army. A staunch proponent of pay raises for the ranks, Rediger called their pay so low as to be "almost ludicrous." Rations and gear were also inadequate and, "without aid from home, the soldiers were not only in dire straits, they could barely exist."[17]

These conditions made the inhabitants of the barracks a receptive audience for the mounting flood of anti-Tsarist propaganda aimed in their direction. Most of it was written by members of the Russian middle class. Only a small minority of the population, that group played a major role in establishing the mental climate essential for the widespread reform movement.[18] In comparison with their counterparts in the West, members of the Russian intelligentsia tended toward extremist positions. In large measure this reflected the unavailability of adequate legal productive outlets for their ideas and efforts. Nicholas's government consistently opposed any public participation in, or indeed even open discussion of, government affairs. Yet throughout his reign a host of legal and semilegal societies sprang up. Organizations of doctors, lawyers, teachers, *zemstvo* employees, and so forth tried to form central bodies to discuss common problems, but the government forbade this. Purely local meetings were sometimes banned or subjected to police surveillance, and it was illegal to indulge in any discussion of political issues at these gatherings.

Zemstvo leaders evaded the ban by meeting in private homes, where discussions soon ranged beyond agrarian problems to the need for some form of constitutional government. *Zemstvo* activists smuggled in literature from abroad which advocated reform of the autocracy. The government stepped up its repressive measures against these organizations. For instance, in 1904 it suspended the entire board of the Tver *zemstvo*, that same body whose leaders had been chided by Nicholas in 1895 for their "vain dreams" of public participation in the central government; the Tsar also assured them that he intended to preserve the autocracy as "firmly and undeviatingly" as his father. By late 1904 many of these organizations came out into the open in spite of the government. In May 1905 fourteen professional unions established a central body, the Union of Unions, under the chairmanship of Paul Miliukov. This body supported the general strike of the fall.

National and regional associations of businessmen, merchants, manufacturers, and bankers, previously a dormant element, came into existence and added their voices to the reform movement. Business leaders, increasingly disturbed by the widespread strikes, flooded the administration with reports demanding political concessions. Many expressed the fear that without constitutional change the labor unrest would continue.[19] After all, it was their employees who had walked out and their profits which were at stake. The burgeoning strike movement of 1905 shook many of them from their former indifference to political questions which did not touch them directly. Interested first in the labor issue, business organizations broadened their study into an analysis of the shortcomings of Russian society, government, and economy.

In January 1905 a statement from the Advisory Bureau of Iron Industrialists stressed that industry alone could not solve the problem of labor unrest, since it was but one manifestation of a general failure of Russian society. The empire lacked the proper climate for modern development and industrial progress. Low profits, the lack of a wide consumer market, too much government meddling in industrial and labor issues, the failure to provide universal education were all immediate problems, but basic political reforms were essential to solve them. Only with quality before the law, inviolability of person and domicile, freedom of speech and the press—the latter necessary if capital and labor were to air their needs—could a normal relationship among the basic groups in society be maintained. To allow industry to flourish, new legislation must be drawn up, with the participation of all sections of the public. A statement from a group of Moscow manufacturers the same month criticized Russian society and institutions for not having a firm basis in equally enforced law. According to their view, the tutelage of the bureaucracy held back Russia's economic development. It was useless to blame agitators for popular discontent, since the absence of basic civil rights and a freely elected representative body to defend popular interests, were the real cause of the disturbances. A group of manufacturers' representatives, who met at the home of the prominent Moscow banker and textile manufacturer, P. P. Ryabushinskii, announced flatly to the authorities in July of 1905 that "the subsequent economic development of the nation without putting its political life in order was impossible."[20]

Since January 1905, when the efforts of Minister of Finance V. Kokovtsov to goad factory workers into economic concessions to weaken the strike movement met a negative response, the business community had thrown the problem into the political arena. They insisted that they were powerless to handle the issues in the factories, and throughout the year they stressed political, rather than economic reforms. Under a modernized political system more responsive to the needs of its citizens, industry, and consequently labor and the whole of society, would prosper.

Many of these business leaders also sat on their municipal councils along with men from other elements of urban society. Like its rural counterpart, the *zemstvo*, the elected urban *duma* took care of local needs not handled by the central administration, such as sanitation, transportation, elementary education, and medical services. The city *dumas* had joined the liberal reform movement later than the rural councils, but by mid-1905 the national *zemstvo* congresses also included representatives from the cities. Furthermore, throughout 1905, many town councils had debated national political issues at their local meetings and sent petitions demanding reforms to the administration. Delegates from about a hundred cities met in Moscow in June, for the first Congress of town representatives. Along with adopting a ringing declaration that the time for petitions was past, they came out for the rapid convocation of a popularly elected assembly with decisive legislative powers, decentralization of the administration, and the instant bestowal of basic civil rights. Among those who suffered the most from the lack of civil liberties were the Jews, virtually all of whom were urban dwellers. Many Jewish organizations forwarded petitions to the administration demanding equal rights for religious minorities, as well as other basic reforms.[21]

The swell of protests from virtually all segments of society culminated in the great strike movement of October of 1905. By then the issues were no longer debated in orderly, often clandestine, meetings held in private homes of prominent and patriotic Russians sincerely seeking reforms in their troubled society. By then large crowds of angry protestors filled the streets of cities throughout the huge empire, the countryside was in turmoil, and to add to the difficulty the bulk of the Tsar's troops were still in the Far East, themselves in a mutinous mood.

The Tsar and his family spent these fearsome days at Peterhof, the beautiful Romanov estate frequently compared with Versailles. Like its French model, the magnificent grounds at Peterhof held several palatial buildings plus an elaborate network of waterfalls and fountains, lakes and canals. Located on the southern shore of the Gulf of Finland, about twenty miles southwest of the capital, during the October strike Peterhof was completely cut off from the rest of the empire except by water. With the local railroad out on strike, Nicholas ordered the crew on the imperial yacht, Polar Star, to stand by in the Peterhof harbor in case he should have to flee.

When in residence at Peterhof, the royal family always lived in the smaller Alexandra Cottage. Nestled in the center of a wooded park, the privacy and relative simplicity of the dwelling had much more appeal for Nicholas and his wife than the larger palaces on the grounds. Each summer the Tsar brought his family to this choice spot, its "splendid forests and delicious fresh breezes" providing a welcome haven from the season's heat.[22]

The physical isolation of the royal family during the terrible events of 1905 may be seen as symbolic of a much more important mental and spiritual gulf between Tsar and subjects. Nicholas simply did not understand the modern forces and ideas which had been churning in his country throughout his reign. He could not grasp the difficulties Russia faced as a backward empire, striving to retain big power status in a world of increasingly competitive modern industrial states. The enormous complexity of her domestic problems, and the plethora of solutions he heard advanced from all sides, served only to further confuse this troubled monarch.

There had been nothing in Nicholas's background or experiences that would have helped him to deal with these issues, and he lacked that rare ability, sometimes found in political figures, to rise above a limited background and adapt to new pressures. Since his early years he had been embued with the glorious traditions of the Romanov autocracy, and he came to the throne determined to preserve that system. By nature hesitant and conservative, he was not the man to cope well with a state undergoing rapid change, much less a country in the throes of revolution.

Nicholas was essentially a man of simple tastes, and he preferred the comfortable intimacy of a truly devoted family life above all else; from the start he found the position of Tsar a terrible burden, and he gained little satisfaction from wielding the powers of his exalted post. His preference for simplicity was reflected in his relations with virtually everyone who came in contact with him. The result was almost universal agreement about the Tsar's personal charm, and even his harshest critics could attest to that: "I do not know anyone, who, upon first meeting the Tsar, was not charmed by him; he charms with his cordial way, his manners, and especially with his evident breeding." The secret of this charm lay in a simple unaffected manner. It was strongest at an initial meeting, but persons who had continual contact with Nicholas often became immune to it.[23] Along with being well bred, Nicholas was intelligent and grasped the essence of specific issues quickly.

Charm and intelligence notwithstanding, this tragic man was not endowed by nature or experience for the huge tasks which ultimately fell on his weak shoulders. When he came to the throne at twenty-six, his only contacts with the world beyond the palace were a trip to the Far East and short stays with army regiments. And throughout his life he knew little about the people he governed, since his circle included only his family and the members of the court, a few courtiers, and upper level bureaucrats. In his diary Nicholas often mentioned people he had seen on a particular day. Any direct contacts he had with ordinary Russians were limited to occasional rare delegations of citizen's organizations and his frequent visits to wounded troops to thank them for their services. Of more significance, he had no meaningful or productive contact with those political figures who maintained influence with the public.

Even the ministers who reported personally, sometimes daily, to the Tsar, were unable to penetrate the intimate circle at the Romanov court. They felt that they were held by an invisible barrier from that private artificial world. In the court itself Nicholas did not want his intimates to discuss politics. Only persons of ultra-conservative views were welcome there, and as a result he and his wife viewed Russia from a narrow detached environment, firm in their faith that the Russian populace remained loyal to the autocracy.[24] Along with that conviction went the opinion that those people agitating for reforms were merely a vocal minority.

In a word, Nicholas's ideas and attitudes were completely out of touch with his twentieth-century country. He sincerely believed that the Almighty had entrusted him with the throne he inherited from his father, and that it was his duty to pass it on to his heir with its powers intact. Thus, he clung tenaciously to that throne, all the while considering it an onerous burden, for which he was unprepared. After his father's sudden death in 1894, he told his boyhood companion, Grand Duke Alexander Mikhailovich: "I am not prepared to be a Czar. I never wanted to become one. I know nothing of the business of ruling. I have no idea of even how to talk to the ministers." In 1916 Nicholas's wife confided to her children's tutor that throughout his reign her spouse had suffered from "his natural timidity," and from the fact that "he had been kept too much in the background" before his father died.[25]

Once he assumed office, Nicholas thoroughly disliked the duties it entailed. "Again those loathsome telegrams took up the whole day" he complained in his diary. In 1898 he wrote from the Crimea: "Twice a week the couriers bring piles of papers; on those days I get rather short tempered." This attitude did not disappear, and the Tsar continued to complain in his diary about meetings that dragged on, leaving little time for walking or reading to the family. July 27, 1905, on the other hand, was a splendid exception: "Happily the day was free—without tiresome meetings," leaving ample time for tennis and reading.[26] Yet, in spite of this aversion to his duties, he tried to keep the affairs of state in his own hands. He never had a private secretary, and sometimes even sealed the envelopes containing decrees himself. Close associates at the court never felt that they had his confidence. He usually preferred to consult his own conscience and then make a decision.[27]

Numerous of Nicholas's subordinates testified to his vexing habit of refusing to express his displeasure or disagreement directly to them. Always courteous, he would seem to accept a minister's proposals, or at least not comment on them; the next day the surprised minister might find a dismissal notice on his desk. Mosolov saw the explanation for this apparently devious conduct in the Tsar's aversion to arguments and a lack of combative spirit. A. P. Izvolskii, Minister of Foreign Affairs from 1906 to 1910, suggested that Nicholas lacked the moral courage to disagree face to face with his subordinates.

In addition to an archaic attitude toward his powers, Nicholas's comments conveyed an extreme religious fatalism. After he signed the October Manifesto he wrote: "My only consolation is that such is the will of God, and this grave decision will lead my dear Russia out of the intolerable chaos she has been in for nearly a year." Shortly afterwards, he expressed shame that "poor Russia has to go through a crisis like this before the eyes of the whole world," adding that it was "God's will, and we have to submit to our ordeal patiently to the end."[28]

Nicholas' concept of his office was in accord with the traditional official view. In 1895 the School Committee of the Holy Synod, the bureaucratic agency which controlled the state church, prepared a catechism for use by teachers of the Orthodox faith which contained the following precepts:

Q. What says the Fifth Commandment?
    A. Honor thy father and thy mother. . . .
Q. Should we honor only our parents?
    A. Beside our parents, we should respect all those who in any way fill their places for us.
Q. Whom, then, should we honor?
    A. 1. First and most of all, the Tsar.
       2. Pastors and spiritual teachers.

     3. Kindly persons, our superiors, and teachers.

     4. Our elders.

Q. Why should we especially respect the Tsar above all others?

  A. Because he is the father of the whole people and the anointed of God.

Q. What does the Word of God teach concerning respect for the Sovereign?

  A. "Fear God. Honor the king" (in the Russian version, Tsar) (Pet. 2:17). "My son, fear thou the Lord and the king; and meddle not with them" (Prov. 24:21). "Render therefore unto Caesar the things which are Caesar's and unto God the things that are God's" (Matt. 22:21).

Q. How should we show our respect for the Tsar?

  A. 1. We should feel complete loyalty to the Tsar and be prepared to lay down our lives for him.

    2. We should without objection fulfill his commands and be obedient to the authorities appointed by him.

    3. We should pray for his health and salvation, and also for that of all the Ruling House.

Q. With what spiritual feelings should we fulfill these commands?

  A. According to the words of the apostle Paul, "Not only for wrath, but also for conscience sake" (Rom. 13:5), with sincere esteem and love toward the father of our land.

Q. What should we think of those who violate their duty toward their Sovereign?

  A. They are guilty not only before the Sovereign, but also before God. The Word of God says, "Whosoever therefore resisteth the power, resisteth the ordinance of God" (Rom. 13:2).[29]

Not only were the duties of his weighty office a chore, the Tsar also disliked formal court functions. He did, however, derive sincere pleasure from attending military reviews, and he loved to spend time with individual units, or visiting wounded troops. He considered these experiences a contact with the "real Russia," the Russia of the loyal *narod* (people). Frequently the only happy note in a disconsolate letter described his joy and pride while watching a unit parade before him.

Because of his deep conviction that the bulk of the Russian population was loyal to the autocracy, Nicholas tended to minimize the discontent manifested by his subjects in the protest movement which swept his country in 1905. On June 6, 1905, he received a delegation of *zemstvo* and city officials, who told him of the current lack of faith in the government and urged him to allow public participation in state affairs. Assuring the delegates that he firmly intended to call for elected representatives of the populace, he then spoke to these men in outmoded unrealistic terms: "Let us restore both the ancient unity between the Tsar and all of Russia and the communication between me and the *zemstvo* people. . . . I hope that you will help me in this task."[30] It was as though he had not heard their warnings of the grave situation in his realm. He certainly had no comprehension of what the opposition political leaders actually meant by popular participation in government.

Aside from visits in the barracks, Nicholas was only comfortable with his family. A devoted father and husband, his tendency to remain aloof, even from court society, was increased by the wishes of his wife, Alexandra Feodorovna. Tsaritsa Alexandra, born Princess Alix Victoria of Hesse-Darmstadt, was the granddaughter of Queen Victoria of England. She met Nicholas in 1884 at the wedding of her sister, Ella, and his uncle, the Grand Duke Sergei, younger brother of Alexander III. Five years later, when she was seventeen, Alix visited Ella in St. Petersburg, where she saw a great deal of the young Tsarevich. Their romance blossomed and eventually she agreed to marry him. To do so she had to give up her Lutheran faith and join the Orthodox Church; once she made this decision, Alix became a zealous, and later fanatical convert. She took the name Alexandra Feodorovna, and on November 26, 1894, a week after the funeral of Alexander III, she married the young Tsar.

42

The new Tsaritsa was a shy, sensitive girl, unfamiliar with her adopted country and its language. She did not fit well into court society, which soon considered her snobbish. The balls and receptions she had to attend became a horror to her, and she began to avoid them whenever possible. During Alexandra's first years of marriage she devoted herself almost entirely to her rapidly growing family—four healthy girls, and at long last, on August 19, 1904, the long awaited heir, Tsarevich Alexis. By the time he was six weeks old the family began to suspect that Alexis was a victim of the dread disease, hemophilia. A closely guarded secret, this tragedy dominated the lives of the royal family thenceforth.

Alexandra was a strong-willed woman, who exerted considerable influence on her husband, especially during the latter part of his reign. Given a tendency toward religious mysticism, her understandable fears for the health of her son greatly accentuated this trait. While obsessed with the desire that he inherit his powers intact, and violently opposed to any concessions which would lessen them, Alexandra cannot be said to have had any political philosophy or acumen. Her central role in Russian history began after 1905, but she had definite ideas by then. In January she wrote one of her sisters in Battenburg:

> Things are in a bad state and it's abominably unpatriotic at the time when we are plunged into war to break forth with revolutionary ideas.
>
> Petersburg is a rotten town, not an atom Russian. The Russian people are deeply and truly devoted to their sovereign. . . . How I wish I were clever and could be of real use! I love my new country. It's so young, powerful, and has so much good in it, only utterly unbalanced and childlike. Poor Nicky, he has a bitter, hard life to lead. Had his father seen more people, drawn them around him, we should have had lots to fill the necessary posts.[31]

So, in 1905, the Tsaritsa shared her husband's conviction that the bulk of his subjects were devoted to the autocracy.

Thus, she saw no reason why he should concede any of his royal prerogatives and she never forgave those advisors who urged Nicholas to sign the October Manifesto. Until the end of the dynasty, her letters to her spouse were full of exhortations to be resolute, to stand up to the ministers, and to rule like a true monarch.

Alexandra was right in her fears that Nicholas was not a strong individual. He was, however, an unfortunate combination of weak-willed, and stubborn. He frequently vacillated on policy decisions, and at times changed his mind at the last minute, without telling the appropriate minister of a new decision. He never had a set of clear policies he wanted carried out. Yet, underneath these fluctuating policies was a basic stubbornness, which made his role an essentially negative factor in the destinies of his empire. For example, there were certain royal prerogatives, which his outdated mental framework told him he had no right to give up. And, while the pressures of the revolution of 1905 forced him to relinquish some of these powers, he remained convinced that the concessions of October 17, 1905, were detrimental to the state he ruled.

CHAPTER III

Sergei Witte and the October Manifesto

Nicholas issued the October Manifesto largely as a result of the urgings of Sergei Witte, his former Minister of Finance. By then, Witte had also agreed to accept what was to prove his most difficult assignment in a long and influential career in the upper echelons of the Tsarist bureaucracy, namely the post of chairman of the ministerial council from mid-October, 1905, to mid-April, 1906. Undoubtedly the most able and foresighted man in Nicholas' government, Witte had few friends and many enemies. His efforts to modernize the Russian economy had alienated his more tradition-bound contemporaries, many of whom had great influence in court circles. His emphasis on industrial development, coupled with a neglect of the enormous problems of Russian agriculture, had brought the wrath of many landowners and intellectuals upon him.

Nicholas inherited Witte from his father, Alexander III. As Minister of Finance under father and son, he originated many economic measures which aided Russia along its path towards becoming a modern industrial society. Dismissed from that post in 1903, he became President of the Committee of Ministers. In his memoirs he scorned the latter as a position "completely without function," which took care of a mass of "administrative rubbish."[1]

Hardly a tactful man, Witte's gruff, unpolished manner often made him a most difficult associate. He had the burly physique to go with this manner—massive head, long heavy torso on top of small oddly short legs, and enormous long arms. Half a head higher than most of his contemporaries, his large size and rough bearing combined with great talents to make an "impression of force and originality" even on his critics.[2]

Although of aristocratic background and upbringing, Witte was a businessman by training and outlook. He entered government service after a successful career as manager of the Southwestern Railroad, which he made one of the most profitable in Russia. His claim that he knew railroads from the bottom up was accurate, since he started in the ticket office of the Odessa Railway, where he was soon traffic office supervisor. Fittingly enough, it was under his ministry that the great Trans-Siberian Railroad was built.

When he came to St. Petersburg, Witte did not fit into its society. Not only was he business oriented, but he lacked polish and style and spoke plain Russian with an Odessa accent. He was not particularly cultured or well-bred and seemed a rough diamond in that social world with its fixed standards. Witte in turn loathed those courtiers who spent all their time on intrigue and in seeking government subsidies. He especially despised the Grand Dukes of the imperial family, because he thought that they squandered the family fortunes while giving bad advice to the Tsar. Yet, he sometimes bowed to the pretensions of their titles. Eventually he suffered from a secret snobbishness, and while calling himself a "plebean," he craved titles and decorations.[3]

Witte's memoirs reflect a great deal about this remarkable man. They are a curious amalgam of penetrating observations and analysis, combined with boasting, constant complaints—frequently justified—and repetitious diatribes against his political enemies. Even making allowance for the bitterness to be expected from such a capable man, whose career was to end in failure and ostracism, these memoirs still portray an unusually spiteful and arrogant nature. For instance, Witte ascribed the Tsar's bitter hostility toward him, not to his own sharp manner or to court intrigue alone: rather, "in the depths of his soul he could not but recognize that everything I told him, or about which I warned him, happened, and happened mainly because he had not listened to me."[4]

One of the main reasons Nicholas dismissed Witte from the Ministry of Finance in 1903 was the latter's increasing hostility toward the direction of Tsarist policy in the Far East. Under Witte, the empire had undergone considerable economic expansion, including the obtaining of railroad concessions in Manchuria; gradually, however, the Ministry of Finance lost control of Far Eastern policy. As friction between Russia and Japan mounted, Witte believed that it was to Russia's interest to avoid war with Japan at all costs, even if it meant turning Korea over to Japan temporarily.[5]

The war Witte feared broke out in February of 1904, and as he predicted, his country was totally unprepared and suffered a series of disastrous defeats. In the summer of 1905 the two rivals came to the conference table under the auspices of United States President Theodore Roosevelt. Ironically, after refusals from several professional diplomats, Nicholas had turned to Witte to lead the Russian delegation to Portsmouth, New Hampshire. Witte had little reason to feel flattered at the appointment; he, himself, observed ruefully that "when a sewer needs to be cleaned, they send Witte; but as soon as work of a cleaner type and nicer kind appears, plenty of other candidates spring up."[6]

Upon his return from Portsmouth, the Tsar conferred the title of count upon Witte, an honor customarily granted to the negotiator of a peace treaty.[7] The Russian public had never been enthusiastic about the war, fought in a faraway land over issues which hardly seemed vital to its interest. In general they were glad it was over. Witte had done an able job in a difficult situation and the concessions he made—loss of southern Sakhalin, Port Arthur, and a piece of the Southern Manchurian Railroad—seemed worth the price of ending the costly struggle. He and his fellow compatriots could now turn to more pressing domestic affairs.

Witte returned from Portsmouth in mid-September of 1905 in a "depressed and nervous condition," greatly in need of rest.[8] The situation which greeted him was far from restful: "From the day of my return from America I clearly saw that the revolution swelled not by the day, but by the hour. . . . In a word, complete chaos ensued." The widespread disorders had virtually called a halt to the operations of the central administration, recalled V. Gurko. It seemed suddenly to have lost the reason for its existence, and while publishing "thundering orders which it was powerless to enforce . . . feverishly looked about for a way out of its embarrassment."[9] At a meeting of several highly placed bureaucrats that September, one commented that after spending several months in the country, he was convinced that "in the provinces no one believed the government anymore, because it did not fulfill its proclamations and promises."[10]

The most important of these proclamations was the August 6, 1905, announcement promising a national consultative assembly which would be responsible for the "preliminary elaboration and discussion of legislative proposals." Generally referred to as the Bulygin Duma since Minister of the Interior A. F. Bulygin held the overall responsibility for drafting the decree, the new assembly was to be elected by a very small percent of the populace in multistaged elections.[11] To Nicholas the Bulygin Duma law represented an enormous concession because it would have given elected representatives of his subjects their first opportunity to participate in the central administration. Announced only after several months of violent outbursts against the autocratic system, the August 6 decree did not placate the angry populace: in fact, as Witte aptly put it, the concession "calmed no one." The Bulygin Duma was a stillborn chamber, and the revolutionary tide rose rapidly in the weeks following its pronouncement.

It was soon evident to everyone in the harrassed administration that the situation called for a more drastic response than the Bulygin consultative assembly. Newly decorated Count Witte found himself in the midst of the domestic turmoil, while the rest he so sorely needed had to wait. By Witte's own account, Count Dimitri Solskii, Chairman of the State Council, the main advisory body to the sovereign, came to him with the plea that he was the empire's only hope in the chaos. On October 9, Witte had the first of several meetings with his sovereign about the crisis, and ten days later Nicholas was to announce his appointment as chief minister. Once again Witte accepted responsibility when he had the opportunity: "as soon as the situation becomes critical, they begin to talk about me . . .," he later wrote, noting that Nicholas had again overcome his hostility and turned to him when everyone else refused.[12]

Witte obviously loved government office and the power it conferred. This is not to imply that he was not a patriotic Russian, who used that power to achieve what he considered essential reforms, often against enormous resistance. Yet, in spite of constant frustrations and failures, he always seemed to be available at the Tsar's call, however onerous the mission. Furthermore, after his dismissal as Minister of Finance in 1903, he had hung about the capital in a post with little function; surely his great abilities, along with his connections in financial circles at home and abroad, would have presented other attractive options, had he sought them.

During Nicholas's and Witte's first meeting about the crisis, Witte presented a lengthy memorandum to the Tsar. "There is no choice," Witte told him. "Either get at the head of the movement sweeping the country or give it up to elemental forces." Noting that further executions and bloodshed would only make matters worse, he advised the Tsar to consider the well-being of the realm and not stubbornly seek to preserve a system. "Constitution" need not be a frightening word, since one could be drawn up which assured Nicholas a "deciding voice."[13] Witte's recommendation went against one of the most deeply held convictions of his sovereign. Just about a year before, in December of 1904, Nicholas had told Witte: "I will never, in any event, agree to a representative form of government, because I consider it harmful for the state entrusted to me by God. . . ."[14]

Nor should Witte be considered a proponent of representative government. He criticized constitutional government in his memoirs, adding ruefully that it was an inevitable change, sooner or later, since all civilized countries were coming to it. His ideal was a modern, efficient, unlimited autocracy, dedicated to the public welfare, but he was too perceptive to hope to achieve such a system in his Russia of 1905. Nicholas simply could not fulfill all the requirements Witte deemed essential for a monarch: an autocrat needed a strong will and character, lofty ideals, and good breeding. Intelligence he regarded as a less basic requirement. It was also essential that the throne have an heir on which to center the people's hope and thus help to preserve the system. Witte idealized and overestimated the capabilities of his former sovereign, Alexander III, while being very much aware of the shortcomings of his son. If Alexander III "had not died so early, or if his son had possessed some of his ability as an autocrat, then of course nothing like what happened could have happened."[15]

These then, were the two men who met in lengthy, exhausting sessions in October, 1905, to try to find a solution to the crisis that wracked the Russian state. Witte, the proponent of an efficient modern autocracy, clearly saw that Nicholas was a weak Tsar and that concessions were the only possible answer to the protest movement. Nicholas, all the while convinced that he was betraying a God-given trust, finally accepted Witte's advice. At the time neither regarded the concessions as anything but a necessary evil, and a few years later Witte was most graphic about them during an interview with Bernard Pares. Readily admitting that he was the author of the October Manifesto, Witte then remarked: "I have a constitution in my head, but as to my heart, I spit on it!" Whereupon he spat on the floor in front of an amazed Pares![16]

Actually during their first meeting, Witte had told Nicholas that he must choose one of two options—either grant a constitution or declare a military dictatorship. Nicholas's reaction was characteristic: "He listened politely . . . but did not express his opinion." Witte further suggested that the Tsar consult with his other advisors and the imperial family before making a decision.[17] For the next few days the palace buzzed with rumors that Witte had come out in favor of the first option. Meanwhile, a still undecided Nicholas summoned his father's cousin, the Grand Duke Nicholas Nikolaievich, then off hunting on his Tula estate, for consultation. Momentarily the diehards were exultant as they envisioned a dictator ending the disorders. As Baron Vladimir Fredericks, Minister of the Court, put it: he hoped that the Grand Duke would "bring the revolution to heel" and then think about political liberties. The Grand Duke, a six-foot six-inch nephew of Alexander II, arrived at Peterhof on October 15. A professional soldier and poor politician, given to mysticism and fits of temper, he and the Tsar had a stormy interview on the same day. Baron Fredericks's assistant, A. Mosolov, who was in an adjoining room at the time, wrote that he heard raised voices, then shouting, after which the Grand Duke suddenly emerged and drove off in his car. Minister of War Rediger also heard the shouting, and when he was finally admitted to the Tsar's presence an hour later he found the usually composed monarch in a terrible state—nervous, flushed, and speaking with a quavering voice.[18] Accounts of what transpired during the Grand Duke's visit vary in detail, but several claim that at one point the flamboyant Nicholas N. pulled out a revolver and threatened suicide if Witte's advice to grant a constitution were ignored.

Two more days were to elapse between the Grand Duke's hasty exit and that moment, at six o'clock on the evening of October 17, when the Tsar finally put his signature to the document Witte presented. Shortly afterwards, Nicholas attempted to explain the momentous decision to his mother. If a soldier crushed the revolt, we would have found time to breathe, he wrote, but "likely as not, one would have to use force again in a few months. That would mean rivers of blood . . . government authority would be vindicated, but there would be no positive result. . . ." The other alternative was to accept Witte's proposal; he made doing so a contingency for his acceptance of the chairmanship of the ministerial council. "While not without risk," and Witte himself admitted that, it seemed the "only way out at present," so, after two long days of discussion, "in the end, invoking God's help, I signed." The Tsar's mother replied to her son's moving letter in characteristically sympathetic fashion:

> How terrible it must have been for you and how you must have suffered when confronted with such tremendous decisions—I felt all this in my heart and suffered with you. . . . It is still hard for me to believe that all this has been happening in Russia, but, in the end, I am sure you could not act otherwise than you have done. Our Lord has helped you to solve this terrible problem. . . . It's your great faith that helped you. He will reward you and I am sure help you to continue on the right path.

In the same letter Marie Feodorovna encouraged her son to show confidence in Witte and "let him act according to his program," reminding Nicholas that the chief minister also had "his measure of terrible difficulties" in his new post.[19]

The public announcement of Witte's appointment as the chief minister in a reorganized executive body, the Council of Ministers (*Soviet Ministrov*) appeared two days after Nicholas signed the October Manifesto. Henceforth, said the announcement, the chairman of this council would preside over a unified ministry with a single policy. He had the right to recommend ministerial appointments; the sovereign, however, reserved full control over the ministries of foreign affairs, the military, and the court: he also retained the right to appoint certain high civil officials, such as the Governor-General of Moscow.[20]

Witte refused to accept his new appointment without a guarantee of authority over his future colleagues. From his previous experience in Nicholas's government, he was all too familiar with the lack of coordination, indeed even the competition, between the ministries. Each man had directed his own affairs independently, and was individually

responsible to the Tsar. Any preliminary discussion between ministers took place mainly to seek support, win over
an opponent, or learn another's views. Each minister relied
on his own forcefulness, or access to the Tsar, to get his
policies accepted. The dominant position in the government shifted from one minister to another, or even outside
the ministry in some cases. There was no such thing as a
joint policy supported by the whole group.[21]

Witte realized that his was no easy assignment and that a
hard road lay ahead for himself and his weak-willed
sovereign. He complained about the terrible difficulties of
his situation to the prominent Kadet journalist, I. V. Gessen,
in a private talk between the two which had been "arranged,
indeed almost ordered" by the chief minister, shortly after
issuance of the October Manifesto. Gessen found Witte in
an agitated state, pacing from corner to corner of his office
with customary long strides; he had littered the carpet of
the huge room with large torn envelopes. Gessen's request
that the hated General D. F. Trepov, who was in charge of
restoring order to the country, be removed from office, led
to an outburst: "You imagine everything can be done
simply."[22]

Even before actually taking office, Witte had warned his
sovereign about the "incredibly difficult task" which lay
before the government. To accomplish what was essential,
he further wrote in his memorandum of October 9, the
administration had to put itself back in control, adopt a
consistent program, and carry it out. And in his memoirs
Witte recalled his warning to Grand Duke Nicholas during
the boat ride back to St. Petersburg on October 17—more
disorders would surely erupt, he predicted, hence the
military must have troops ready to quell them.

Force alone was not enough and Witte knew it. The
Tsarist government was completely discredited with the
public, and confidence had to be restored. One of the new
chairman's first moves was to hold a press conference, to
which he invited some thirty St. Petersburg newspaper
editors. After a series of hard exchanges with these editors,
who put forth the usual demands for instant amnesty, a

national militia, removal of the troops from the cities and an end to special emergency situations, Witte virtually pleaded for their support as molders of public opinion: "Help me, give me a few weeks . . . all disorders and revolutions always come from misunderstandings. . . . An endless mass of questions arises . . . only gradually will we come to that. . . ." But he met only interruptions and reiteration of the demands. Finally, to an editor's claim that the troops caused the disorders, Witte retorted that only after calm was restored could he remove them. Years later, Witte still rankled at the "insolent tone" adopted by the editor of *Birzhevye vedomosti* (The Stock Market Journal), whose comments had dominated the press interview, while the rest of the capital press corps, including men from conservative papers, either "indulged him or remained silent." The press conference had simply revealed the "kind of mass mental dementia" which had swept Russia that fall.[23]

Shortly after seeking the support of the capital press corps, Witte made a direct appeal to the city's working class. In a telegram of November 3 he urged his "little brother workers" to remain on the job and avoid trouble, while awaiting the aid of the government, which would do all that was possible for them if given adequate time. The telegram, which was widely available throughout factory districts, must have sounded strangely out of character with its author. It met with sneers and derision from the city's Soviet of Workers' Deputies, which categorically rejected the appeal and rebuked the chief minister for his "impertinent familiarity in addressing the workers as his brothers."[24]

Witte also attempted to include men in the cabinet who had the respect of the public.[25] These efforts failed. He could not meet the demands of left liberals that he guarantee the convocation of a constituent assembly elected by universal suffrage, and that a total amnesty and promised civil rights be put into effect at once. Three influential representatives of the moderate wing of the liberal movement claimed that they could do more to help Witte by

staying outside of the government, although they empha-
sized their agreement with his main program. According to
Witte, some of the liberals refused to serve in a cabinet with
Peter N. Durnovo, recently chosen to direct the all-important Ministry of the Interior. An experienced police official
with distinct capabilities, Durnovo was identified with
repressive measures and the old regime in the minds of the
opposition. Witte's arguments that only a man with police
experience could calm the rioting failed to convince them
of the wisdom of his choice. Eventually he had to select
all of Durnovo's colleagues from the old bureaucracy, since
the liberals remained stalwart in their refusal to accept
portfolios. Had they done so, they would have been forced
either to resign, or give up the above demands, since Nicholas would never have agreed to them.

Durnovo may be regarded simply as a symbol of more
fundamental differences between the upper bureaucracy
and its opposition. It was clear that Witte only sought
public support for his program, and that those few liberals
he might include in the ministry would have no important
role in making policy. Beyond that, the liberals realized
that Witte was not his own master, and they had considerable reason to suspect that the promises of the October
Manifesto would not be put into effect. It was also evident
that restoration of public order was going to require harsh
measures, and they were hesitant to associate themselves
with any government which would need to use them.

The Tsar and many in his entourage disapproved of this
unprecedented spectacle of a chief minister in the imperial
government actually courting public support. In a discussion of Witte's efforts to form a ministry, Nicholas complained to his mother: "I do not quite like his way of getting
in touch with various extremists, especially as all these
talks appear in the press next day, and as often as not are
distorted."[26]

During the first few weeks he was in office, Witte also
put through several measures designed to appease the
public. First of these, on October 21, 1905, was the announcement of a partial amnesty of political prisoners.

"In my soul I was a little afraid of the amnesty," Witte later wrote, "but I considered it necessary once we entered the path of the seventeenth of October." This law pardoned many strikers, and reduced the sentences of many others who had been convicted of crimes against the state. In addition, considerable numbers of those who had been punished by administrative order were released. Although many political prisoners were freed, the opposition press still attacked the bill as inadequate.[27] Indeed, in the months that followed, the issue of a complete political amnesty was one of the major rallying points of all opposition groups.

In an attempt to alleviate the discontent in the country-side, on November 3, 1905, Nicholas announced the reduction of all redemption dues by half after January 1, 1906, to be followed by their complete abolition the next year. The communal peasants owed these annual dues to the state, as payment for the former noble lands that their communes had received after the emancipation of the serfs in 1861. All the land was declared the property of the land-lords; the government had paid off the owners and in turn required the peasants to repay this amount, plus interest, in annual redemption payments over a forty-nine year period. Since 1886 state peasants had also paid redemption dues, instead of annual rent, for the use of state property; after a forty-four year period of payment, their so-called allotment lands would be redeemed and the obligation cancelled. Until 1903 the village commune was jointly responsible for these redemption debts, while over the years the peasants had gone into increasing arrears on these bur-densome payments. Another November 3, 1905, decree promised to increase the resources of the Peasant Land Bank to enable it to offer easier terms for land purchased under its auspices. Henceforth, landless or land poor peasants could buy land without down payments. A decree of November 25 released fifty million rubles of 4-1/2 percent certificates for the Peasant Land Bank. In spite of the financial loss these concessions would entail for the government, they were looked upon by most reformers as quite natural. After prevailing over considerable opposi-tion from some of his relatives, Nicholas eventually

56

transferred four million acres of Romanov land to the Peasant Land Bank for resale on easy terms. None of the other landed nobles followed the royal example.[28]

On November 24, a new press law, described in Witte's memoirs as a temporary measure until the Duma could replace it, abolished precensorship of periodicals; before that to be "legal" meant that a publication had been passed by censors. Discussions of problems of the state were no longer beyond the rights of the press, and violators of press regulations were to be punished only through proper judicial proceedings.[29] Actually through various devices such as literary criticism, satire, abstract and supposedly academic discussions, critics of the system had long successfully evaded Tsarist press regulations, which were always capriciously enforced. Since 1904 open attacks on the government had been a commonplace, while before that many publications of emigres and the underground press circulated widely in spite of the authorities.

Witte's new law did not provide complete freedom of the press; the government could still close newspapers and arrest editors, supposedly only through the courts. Examples of arbitrary suppression of publications still occurred, however, but frequently a closed publication reappeared in a few days under a new masthead. And as Maurice Baring, the English observer of the Russian scene in 1905, observed: "If the Press is not free it is certainly more explicit and more unrestrained in its violence than the Press of any European country. . . ." The writer Mintslov supported this observation: "The newspapers of all camps are now generally savage and bold," he wrote on October 31. In addition, the sudden airing of political issues in the press was creating a kind of generation, nay cultural, gap. The regular press was full of terms like "SR's," "SD's," and "autonomy," and some aristocratic ladies found it difficult to read the papers "since they understood almost nothing in them." An acquaintance of Mintslov's wife suggested that the ladies meet in their homes to hold discussions of current events to help them overcome their problem.[30]

Witte's efforts to calm his fellow citizens with specific

measures did not achieve the desired results, and his fear that more disruptions would occur proved accurate. He undoubtedly had not foreseen the extent of the disturbances, however. The six weeks following the October Manifesto, the so-called days of freedom, were marked by considerable violence, since instead of encouraging the public to settle down and await enactment of the reforms, the document served as a stimulus for further protests. Spurred on by partial success and the indecisiveness of the authorities, left liberals and revolutionaries pressed for additional concessions, with the latter frequently threatening armed rebellion to achieve their goals. Members of some minorities in the empire became increasingly restive of the Russian yoke, stimulated in part by a manifesto of October 22, 1905, which restored Finland to the special autonomous position it held before 1899.[31] Peasant disorders continued: "We shall work," said one group, busy looting and burning a manor, "while there is freedom. After New Year's there won't be any freedom any more." From talking with officers just back from the Far East, Mintslov gathered that the mood in the army remained bitter and volatile.[32]

Police recorded many marches to local prisons to support the mounting demand for complete amnesty for political prisoners. There were cases of success, as in Nizhnyi Novgorod where a gendarme officer reported that the court prosecutor had emptied the jails. A news reporter on the spot left a vivid account of the victory celebration: "A sea of up to 10,000" gathered at the female prison. Already empty but for a sole survivor, she was released to the screaming crowd. Proceeding to the male prison, the group learned that the sole remaining inmate therein would also be freed. A delegation from the crowd shortly inspected both jails and declared them empty, amidst the cheers of their audience. From Tver, however, the governor wrote that the police had turned back, without disorders, a crowd of about 2,000 on a similar march to the prison there.[33]

Hence confusion and excesses continued after October 17 as many of Nicholas's subjects interpreted the hard won concessions to suit their individual demands. The sudden announcement of the manifesto without any clear directives, coupled with the vague nature of its promises, presented serious problems to Tsarist authorities. They were left in a dilemma—should they enforce existing laws, many of which were in conflict with the manifesto? If they did not do so, how would order be restored? Alternative legislation could not be enacted in time to meet the immediate crisis, while many critics insisted that such enactments must be made only with the cooperation of the promised assembly, yet to be elected. "The result was a complete lack of legality and an unbelievable muddle throughout the country," wrote the Minister of War. Meanwhile, pressures mounted and it is hardly surprising that harrassed officials resorted to increased force, as they had in the past. Punitive detachments, the evoking of special emergency legislation which displaced regular laws and protections to citizens in a given area, arrests and sentences, handed down in or out of the courts—it was a familiar pattern. It is equally unsurprising that the public continued to criticize the authorities for resorting to these familiar methods. The main argument employed by agitators among servicemen, wired one general, was the contrast between the promises of the October Manifesto and the methods used to maintain discipline and restore order in the country.[34]

One of the most perplexing problems for local authorities was how to handle the hosts of meetings being called in their areas. For the first time in Russian history various political pressure groups came out into the open and formed political parties, liberally interpreting the promise of the right of association and assembly. This concession also seemed to legalize what had already been a significant labor union movement, which was spreading from the major industrial cities into the provinces, and into formerly untouched occupations. Even employees of the central government had begun to organize, in part for political purposes, much to the horror of the administration. In response, the head of the Department of Posts and Telegraphs announced that individuals in government service did not have the right to join unions agitating against the established order.

Since the grievances of the Postal-Telegraph Union were political as well as economic, employees who joined it would lose their jobs.[35] The communique added cryptically that the right to association promised in the October Manifesto "bore no relation" to this issue. In spite of this order, the union held its first congress on November 15 and demanded that the state rehire those employees who had been discharged.

Its request ignored, the congress called for a strike and insisted that postal employees should have the right to organize; they sought reinstatement of discharged coworkers, as well as specific economic improvements and basic political reforms. In the face of such open defiance by the state's own employees, Durnovo issued orders for the arrest of strike agitators and the dismissal of all participants. The union retaliated by calling for Durnovo's removal from office. On November 25 the government responded by arresting the Central Bureau of the Postal-Telegraph Union. On December 15 the Union conceded and told their members to go back to work. By then, however, it had obtained an agreement granting a cost of living bonus, plus wage and housing allotment increases. Penitent workers who had been fired could return to their jobs.

Thus, in this case the government ultimately used force, along with economic concessions, to get the union to capitulate. Victory over its own employees occurred, however, only after a month-long exchange of demands and counter-demands. This case was but one example of the hesitation and indecision of the Witte government as it sought to reestablish effective control during the "days of freedom." Floundering in its new role, the government seemed momentarily paralyzed; the populace sensed this and pushed for further concessions. On October 27 a troubled Nicholas described the situation as "difficult and serious," and by November 10 he was very impatient: "Everybody is afraid of taking courageous action: I keep on trying to force them—even Witte himself—to behave more energetically. . . ." Adding that the authorities in St. Petersburg seemed "to have less courage than anywhere else," with a rare insight into popular opinion, he commented that this deepened the public impression that the government was uncertain and afraid to "state openly what is permitted and what is not."[36]

Unlike his chief ministers, who realized that it was essential to conciliate the public if possible, Nicholas still thought primarily in terms of traditional force. Furthermore, he mentally divided his subjects into "good people" versus "subversive elements." Blind to the widespread support for the protest movement, Nicholas retained his firm belief that the masses, angered by the "impertinence of the socialists and revolutionaries," were still loyal to the autocracy. Consequently, the Tsar underestimated the discontent of the Russian masses with their oppressed and poor status, and he blamed the troubles of 1905 on that small minority of his subjects who were actively involved in the opposition political movements. In addition, Nicholas lumped the whole opposition together and he never really distinguished between those demanding constitutional reform, and those agitating for social revolution. To his eyes the entire country seemed suddenly to have gone mad.

The St. Petersburg Soviet became the focal center of the agitation. After considerable deliberation, its leaders had decided to reject the October Manifesto and to continue the general strike, threatening ultimate armed revolt if their demands for a democratic republic were not met. This time, however, the workers did not rally to the suggestion. In the flush of initial victory "we did not notice that the revolutionary wave began to recede," Woytinsky recalled. Unable to support themselves on meager strike funds, the workers began to return to their jobs. The Soviet leaders faced reality and called for an end of the strike at noon on October 21, making clear that this was only a tactical retreat, and that they were beginning to plan for the future armed uprising.

In the meantime, owing to the indecisiveness of the authorities, some *soviets* briefly took upon themselves certain government functions, usually with the support of the workers' militias which hastily formed. In St. Petersburg, for example, armed workers guarded the buildings of the Free Economic Society, where the Soviet met almost daily. In some areas armed bands of workers patrolled the streets. Police reports of the time contained frequent references to workers making their own weapons in factories. In one establishment in the capital they even requested the owner's permission to use factory materials to make knives for self defense![37] Understandably, the request was denied.

The claim that they needed weapons for self defense frequently had some validity, however. In the days immediately following the October Manifesto many pogroms took place throughout the empire. The main target was the familiar scapegoat, the Jews, but revolutionaries, strikers, intellectuals, and members of minority groups also bore the brunt of some of the attacks. For instance, in the Caucasus violence occurred when Tatars raided Armenian homes and shops. Frequently the pogroms followed a bloody clash between crowds celebrating the Tsar's concessions and portrait-bearing monarchists, when gangs of toughs known as "Black Hundreds" raced to the Jewish sections of the cities, destroyed business establishments and even set fire to occupied houses. The houses of suspected revolutionaries were also frequent targets of these extremists. While the incidents which set off each pogrom are frequently lost in a maze of conflicting testimony, many reports indicated that the police and the Cossacks sometimes incited, aided, or at least permitted these excesses. To cite but one example: the head of a government bank in Voronezh reported that he saw police and Cossacks accompany a "rampaging crowd," while making no effort to stop the destruction. Testimony of other witnesses at a meeting in Voronezh that evening pointed to the conclusion that the police "undoubtedly assisted in the pogrom."[38] Nicholas, on the other hand, had his own explanation, which needs no comment: "The impertinence of the Socialists and revolutionaries had angered the people once more; and, because nine-tenths of the troublemakers are Jews, the People's whole anger turned against them. That's how the pogroms happened."[39]

Since at times strikers as well as suspected revolutionaries were victims of these mobs, revolutionary agitators
were able to play on the laborers' understandable fears to
get them to form "armed brotherhoods." Eva Broido, then
a Menshevik organizer at the huge Putilov ironworks,
claimed that their "main worry" was not the police, but the
Black Hundreds, with their many sympathizers among the
workers. With the decline of revolutionary fervor, radicals
distributing propaganda were sometimes beaten up and
turned over to the police by patriotic workers. There were
excesses from the other side as well, as in Kazan, where
revolutionaries took arms and uniforms from policemen on
duty to form their people's militia.[40]

The capital Soviet also took the role of revolutionary
censor upon itself for a brief time. Before Witte published
the law abolishing precensorship of periodicals, in a
unique example of censorship in reverse, the Soviet instructed the typesetters to print only publications whose
editors refused to submit their copy to the government
censors. It threatened to confiscate and destroy the presses
of newspapers not submitting to this decision, while typesetters not adhering to it would be boycotted. Some one
thousand typesetters met on October 20 and supported the
Soviet request to print only uncensored publications.[41]

One of the main reasons why Witte tolerated the St.
Petersburg Soviet as long as he did, much to the dismay
of his sovereign, was the lack of troops in the populated
western section of the empire. Witte considered getting the
army back from Transbaikal as one of his major objectives.
The fate of the throne hung on these million plus troops, he
wrote. Not only were they needed to restore order, but they
were themselves rioting out in Siberia, while the railroad
strike held up their demobilization. On December 21 he
lamented that efforts to achieve a quick return of the troops
had failed. There was still a shortage in European Russia,
and only rarely did troops arrive at a given area in time to
prevent a disturbance.[42]

Besides being short of men, the officers of the garrisons
in European Russia remained uncertain of the loyalty of
their troops. Revolts had broken out in many units through-

out 1905 and the situation was still tense. On October 26 the sounds of shots from a rebellion on Kronstadt, the island garrison guarding the entrance to St. Petersburg harbor, disturbed the ordinarily quiet sanctuary of the imperial family at Peterhof across the bay. The disorders lasted two days until finally reinforcements from the capital were sent to suppress the mutineers. There were numerous arrests and many of the participants were turnéd over to field courts martial for trial. This action, along with the October 29 declaration of martial law in Poland, where Witte feared protests were leading to separatism, provided the occasion which the Soviet leaders awaited—they issued a call for a second general strike on November 2. Once more St. Petersburg was in darkness, streetcars were idle, telephone service was irregular, and some districts were without bread. The strike did not spread to all the railroads, however, and military escorts kept some trains in service, by providing protection to the crews from reprisals for violating the strike order.[43] Nor was the strike as widely supported by the public as in October; middle-class professional men and white-collar workers did not come out in significant numbers, and the strike did not have much support out of St. Petersburg. As early as November 4 a Soviet publication noted the lack of enthusiasm for the strike, and on November 7 the Soviet leadership called it off, "to spare the forces of the workers" for a resolute battle with the "bloody monarchy which was approaching its last days."

Meanwhile unemployment became a mounting problem: a reporter, who visited St. Petersburg working class districts after the strike that November, found the streets filled with idle men. They milled about, gathered at the corners, or "sat stewing in the dirty tea rooms, quieting their hunger with drink"; soldiers and Cossacks marched among them. With the end of the Russo-Japanese War, war contracts had stopped and the demand for workers had dropped accordingly. Angered by the second strike on the heels of the great strike, some employers retaliated by closing their doors to returning employees. Mounting unemployment and the decline in revolutionary fervor greatly affected the morale of the Executive Committee of the Soviet, which found itself "reduced to the distribution of relief." It handed out small sums to the workers, who besieged its headquarters in endless files.[44]

Witte claimed in his memoirs that he waited to take action against the St. Petersburg Soviet, until it had "lost all prestige." Nicholas, on the other hand, had been urging him to act, but to the Tsar's chagrin, Witte "always hoped to be able to manage without drastic measures."[45] Finally on November 26 the authorities arrested Khrustalev-Nosar, the chairman of the capital Soviet; a committee of Trotsky and two others replaced him.

Partly in retaliation for this arrest, on December 2 several newspapers published a manifesto, signed by the executive committee of the St. Petersburg Soviet and the leaders of several other leftist organizations. "The government is on the edge of bankruptcy," it began. To ensure its final collapse, the document urged all Nicholas's subjects to refuse to pay taxes including redemption dues, to demand all wages and payments in gold, and to withdraw their savings from state banks, demanding gold. With this declaration of financial war, Durnovo struck. On December 3 the police arrested over two hundred Soviet members at a plenary session; those interred included Trotsky and the young Woytinsky. Durnovo also shut down all of the newspapers which had published the manifesto. Two days later Witte told an assembly of the Tsar's top advisors that the mood of the country was calmer, and that "in his soul everyone rejoiced" at the arrest of the St. Petersburg Soviet.[46]

The attempts of those members of the St. Petersburg Soviet still at large to reconstitute it were marked by failure. It could only meet in secret and had no power, while the government on the other hand was regaining its sense of purpose and reestablishing control. The rump Soviet did, however, support the Moscow Soviet in a third general strike call, this time to protest the mass arrests of the St. Petersburg body. The response was weak throughout the country. The workers were tired of strikes and as Witte rightly observed, the revolutionary mood was on the ebb. S. Kaplan recalled that in his section of Belorussia the strikers received no support, or even sympathy, from the middle class. Only under threats of violence would merchants close their shops, and even then they often left them unlocked and continued to do business. The reports of strike committees were most pessimistic and commented on the futility of the strike movement.[47]

In Moscow, however, the December strike took an unexpected turn, when on December 8 the punitive action of the authorities against two groups of strikers provided the spark, which set off a small scale version of the long threatened armed mass revolt. Openly supported by the Moscow Soviet, revolutionaries, armed with revolvers and fire bombs, fought the local authorities, and tried to seize control of the city. Barricades went up, made from boxes, wire, tram cars, and overturned sledges; shots rang in some sections of the metropolis. While a sizeable proportion of the city population sympathized with the rioters, they received little physical support, and Soviet leaders were disappointed with the extent of the uprising. In the ten days of street fighting, there was, however, significant disruption of the economic life of the city, and damage to life and property. Vladimir Zenzinov, a Socialist Revolutionary member of the Soviet Executive Committee, left his impressions:

> Several streets were a terrible sight . . . all the windows were broken and in some places the shattered glass was covered with blood. . . . There were traces of shrapnel on the walls of the homes. In some areas the bullet-pierced water pipes reminded one of a vegetable grater.[48]

Unsure of their men, the officers confined the bulk of the Moscow garrisons to their barracks, since shortly before the uprising a mutiny had broken out in the Rostov regiment then on duty in Moscow. General F. V. Dubasov, Governor-General of Moscow, sent out a plea for help. The railway

from St. Petersburg was in service and the famous Semenovskii regiment arrived to help restore order. As Zenzinov
put it—one or two thousand comrades, poorly armed and
lacking military skill could do nothing against these pro-
fessionals. Actually the uprising had begun to ebb before
their arrival. By December 17 the troops had removed the
barricades, and surrounded the Presnaia factory district,
located on the hilly ground overlooking the Moscow River
to the west of the city. Here a group of revolutionaries,
whose leaders had largely fled, still held out. Dubasov gave
the order; "Destroy all who show opposition, and arrest no
one." On December 19 it was all over.

In an official report Durnovo described the losses of the
Moscow riots as "very great." The hospitals were filled
with the seriously wounded, he wrote, but, since the revolutionaries cared for many of their own dead and wounded,
an accurate count was impossible.[49] The administration
dealt severely with the arrested rioters; many were shot
after drum head trials or even without trials, while others
received exile sentences.

While events in the two large cities dominated the scene
during the "days of freedom," the whole empire shook with
disorders during that period. The two major city Soviets
became the focal points of the revolution, although they
certainly did not lead it. Some disturbances broke out over
local issues, others merely reflected a general mood and a
breakdown of order. On the other hand, events in the
capitals frequently served as a stimulus in the provinces.
For instance in early January a subordinate reported to the
governor of Stavropol in the Northern Caucasus: "I fully
recognize that the local riots appear as a later echo of the
revolutionary movement in the capitals and central guber-
nilias . . . ," while in the Southern Caucasus a police
official saw an even more direct connection. He wrote
Durnovo that the comparatively calm mood of the revolutionaries in Tiflis changed with the December financial
manifesto of the St. Petersburg Soviet, and the strike call
by the Post-Telegraph Union Central Bureau. At a host of
meetings revolutionaries pressed their audiences to join

the strike, heed the call of the soviet, and begin preparations
for the final uprising. The response of the local authorities
was typical: they proclaimed Tiflis and environs under
emergency legislation and arrests of the strike bureaus
followed. "All these measures notably calmed the mood,"
the report added.[50]

The situation in the Caucasus was but one of many outbursts during the first weeks of Witte's chairmanship. Now
here, now there, a series of disturbances flared up throughout the empire, and Nicholas's letters are punctuated with
references to them—a general strike in Finland, a mutiny
in Sevastopol, unabated agrarian disturbances. The Letts
had "completely lost their heads," chased away the authorities and elected their own representatives. He warned his
mother not to go near Kovno or Vilna on her way back to
the capital from Denmark. Urging her to procure military
escort, he then lamented the lack of soldiers to fill such
missions. "There are not enough troops," he cried. In this
Nicholas saw the key to the whole issue, and indeed, in the
short run he was right. The Tsar's estimate was shared by
Mintslov, who wrote in mid-October about the increasing
number of armed bands being formed. Since these men could
not stand up against regulars, the key issue was on whose
side the latter would be. This was still an open issue, he
thought; a colonel from the hussars, for example, told him
that it was impossible to vouch for his men.[51]

Those men left in the Far East were needed desperately. In
addition, they were an increasing menace in Siberia. Travelling in special trains, often held up for days by the strikes,
they had lost all discipline. They looted en route, wrecked
railroad equipment, and caused general panic among the
local population. At times they acted in conjunction with
employees of the Siberian Railway. On January 6, 1906,
the director of that huge line wired the Minister of Communications about a four-day siege in Krasnoyarsk which
resulted in the shutdown of twenty locomotives, complete
destruction of the workshops' office, the school, theater,
and some equipment. The depot could still function, but the
shops would be out for at least two weeks. Among the 470

arrested were some soldiers, and about 200 of the line's employees, headed by the station chief. About a week later the city was calm, according to a report later read by the Tsar himself. However, the weak, incompetent police had not ferreted out the revolt's leaders, believed to be still hidden in the city. Furthermore, train service was not yet on schedule, supplies arrived in disorder, and workmen were not performing properly.[52]

Nicholas wrote his mother that, at the suggestion of Grand Duke Nicholas, he was sending two special trains, under Generals P. K. Rennenkampf and A. N. Meller-Zakomelskii, out to Siberia to restore order. Rennenkampf's train headed west from Kharbin in early January under orders to proceed until the two trains met. Meller-Zakomelskii left Moscow with a hand-picked punitive detachment. His methods were simple, direct, and effective—in some cases his men surrounded a train of mutinous troops, brought them out in small groups and flogged them. A report of mid-January described their actions against protesting workers at a depot in the Yenisei region, where they arrived late one evening. At the general's command they fired on the assembled workers, killing seventeen and wounding twenty-two, while about eighty were put under arrest and imprisoned. The general and his unit boarded their train the same evening and headed toward Irkutsk. Frequently, news that one of the punitive trains was on its way restored order in a given area before its arrival. The end of the rail strike aided these two generals, as troops began to move west in much larger numbers. By late February the Far East commander could report calm among the men on duty in Transbaikal and Vladivostok.[53]

By mid-winter comparative calm existed throughout the sprawling Russian Empire, although reports by Witte, Durnovo, and D. F. Trepov, Nicholas's trusted palace commandant, revealed that the administration still felt very shaky in its control. Labor strikes continued at a high rate during 1906, though never with the unity and impact of the great strike of the previous fall. Troubles were anticipated in rural areas come spring, but, on the other hand, there was cause for cautious optimism. Nicholas's government had survived the fall riots and appeared to be slowly getting on top of the situation. Observers agreed that the revolutionary mood on the part of the general public had undergone a marked decline.

This decline was in part a response to repressive measures used to quell the widespread revolt. In the final showdown the administration got the troops back from the Far East and the ranks had not sided with the opposition. The promise of those quick economic concessions urgently recommended by Minister of War Rediger—pay raises and increased rations of food and gear to go into effect for the lower ranks as of December 6, 1905—undoubtedly helped to keep them under orders.[54] Partly the revolution of 1905 died its own death. It was an elemental, broadly based, spontaneous revolution with no effective central leadership or overall plan. While the role of intellectuals and revolutionary propagandists in preparing the milieu for the outburst was very important, they did not play a central role in directing events that fall. They did, however, pour out a mounting diatribe of criticisms of the outmoded autocracy; coupled with assorted visions of utopias to replace it, this propaganda struck a responsive note in a discontented population.

And Witte's advice to make concessions that October proved sound. The October Manifesto did split the opposition. While most of the reformists were far from satisfied with the promises made, some hoped to use the Duma to press for further change. In addition, the violence of the peasants and the strikers and the radical demands of the Soviet leaders frightened off many of their supporters. The latter began to share, or at least to sympathize with, Witte's view that order had to be restored before any essential reforms could be carried out.

The split between the revolutionaries and liberals is reflected in an experience of Simon Kaplan, a member of the Marxist Jewish Bund of Belorussia. Kaplan recalled a medical call to his prison cell by a doctor in February of 1906. Only a year before, the doctor had been in sympathy with the revolutionary cause and had provided his spacious home for meetings; frequently Kaplan had talked far into the night with the doctor and his wife. Yet, when he made his call at the jail that winter evening, the doctor did not reveal that he recognized his former friend. Mintslov wrote in early December that large sections of the public had already quailed at the violent actions of strikers and revolutionaries; everywhere he heard attacks on the revolution as "unseemly." He, himself, deplored much of the destruction that had accompanied the disorders, but the official repressions equally discouraged him, and by December 31 he concluded sadly: "Reaction triumphs in all of Russia." It was a great letdown, so soon after the flush of enthusiasm with which he had greeted the October Manifesto.[55]

With the administration in control again, Mintslov and his fellow citizens waited to see how many of the promises of October would actually go into effect. As an "educated man" observed prophetically to M. Baring of the London *Morning Post* in late December: "The government has as yet *given* nothing; everything has been torn from it, and more will have to be torn from it."[56] The public reaction to the October Manifesto and the excesses of the "days of freedom" would hardly have encouraged Nicholas to make the changes his words seemed to imply, much less to go on to a real constitutional parliamentary system, even had he so intended when he reluctantly signed the document Witte presented that evening at Peterhof.

PART II

Administration versus Opposition
The Era of the First Duma

CHAPTER IV

The December Palace Conference
Revises the Bulygin Electoral Law

Throughout the "days of freedom" and the months of comparative calm that followed, Nicholas, Witte, and other Tsarist bureaucrats held a series of long and tedious meetings to determine their course of action. Unpleasant a task as it was, they had before them the complicated matter of translating reforms granted in October into the laws of the empire. Meanwhile, as the administration began to regain its bearings and it became obvious that the revolution was on the ebb, many of these men took a second hard look at those concessions, so hastily conceived and so vaguely worded. It became apparent that careful consideration of the new statutes should enable them to preserve many of the sovereign's prerogatives, as he faced the frightening prospect of governing with the aid of a popular assembly.

First on a crowded agenda were draft projects for the new legislative chamber and the franchise law under which it would be elected. Before final inauguration, each of these drafts passed through several stages of bureaucratic review. The initial project or projects—sometimes alternative versions came up for final review—were the work of second level functionaries, familiar with the technical details of legal statutes. From their desks each draft went to a series of preliminary study sessions, usually attended by the ministers and other top bureaucrats, such as department heads from the State Council, until 1906 the main advisory body in the administration. This group made recommendations and presented its revised projects to the

Tsar, who in turn called a palace conference to advise him about the final versions. During 1905-1906 Nicholas chaired four such high level gatherings—in July and December of 1905, and in February and April of 1906.

These were the four assemblies ultimately responsible for the constitutional reforms of the period. The men at the July meetings had approved the statutes for the stillborn consultative Bulygin Duma, which had been announced in August of 1905. The Bulygin Duma had been superseded by the October promise of a legislative assembly and a broader franchise law; it was the December conference that dealt with the franchise extention. The February and April palace gatherings passed judgment on the statute for the new legislative chamber, and on the necessary changes in the empire's law code, the Fundamental Laws of the Russian Empire.

The meetings would not have been held if it had not been for the popular outbursts against the autocratic system. Nonetheless the public played no significant role in drafting the reforms. The famous historian V. O. Kliuchevskii presented his views during the July meetings, and invited representatives of the moderate opposition spoke in December. In neither instance were their contributions notably influential. The Tsar and his advisors drew up the constitutional reforms as they saw fit, and at the last two conferences they did not even ask men outside court and bureaucratic circles to participate.

All four conferences were held at the palace where the royal family was in residence at the time. Shortly after he issued the October Manifesto, Nicholas had moved his family from their summer estate at Peterhof to winter quarters at Tsarskoe Selo—the Tsar's village, that "magnificent symbol," that "supreme gesture" of the Russian autocracy.[1] Begun originally as a country retreat fifteen miles south of St. Petersburg, much had been added to that isolated, artificial world since Peter the Great started it at the request of his wife, Catherine. Behind its high iron fence, bearded Cossacks in red tunics and black fur caps guarded the extensive grounds. A magnificent combina-

tion of natural and man-made beauty, the grounds contained an artificial lake, large enough for sailboats, which
could be emptied like a bathtub. At one end of the lake was
a pink Turkish bath, and on an artificial hillock nearby
stood a Chinese pagoda. Winding footpaths and a pony trail
curved through groves of splendid trees, and gardens lush
with exotic flowers. Two palaces were the "village's"
crowning glories. One, the smaller Alexander Palace, became the favorite of Nicholas and Alexandra, who made
their home in one of its wings for twenty-two years. Alexandra filled her palace with flowers the year round; they
were brought in from the Crimea by train, after autumn
frosts ended the growing season in the gardens and green-
houses of Tsarskoe Selo. The other palace, the Catherine
Palace, had over two hundred rooms and was much larger
and more ornate. The gem of a later Catherine, Catherine the
Great, who told the architect that she wanted it to outshine
Versailles, this so-called "Large Palace" was the scene of
the last three palace conferences. The first one had been
held at Peterhof in July.

Hopes of the participants of the Peterhof conference that
the promise of a consultative Duma would quell the revolution had soon proved vain. If anything the concession had
enraged the public and two months later came the Tsar's
October 17 promise of a legislative chamber, which would
be elected by a broader slice of the populace than the
Bulygin law provided. To study the necessary changes in
the existent electoral statute, Nicholas summoned his
chief advisors to reassemble at Tsarskoe Selo in December.
Many of the same faces were in attendance, although there
were some notable exceptions.[2] Only one Grand Duke was
present, for example, most likely because of the technical
nature of the matter under consideration. A new ministerial council had been appointed in October, and its members of course replaced their predecessors; their chief,
Sergei Witte, was to dominate the December proceedings,
while in July he had been off in Portsmouth, New Hampshire, negotiating a settlement of the Russo-Japanese War.

The men at the December Tsarskoe Selo conference had

to consider alternative methods of broadening the franchise. On the first day they heard eloquent pleas for universal suffrage, and elimination of the multistaged elections included in the Bulygin law. These pleas, accompanied by warnings of the consequences which might ensue if they were not heeded, came from four invited representatives of the public, all of whom were moderate liberals from the conservative wing of the opposition movement. The extension of an invitation to these "experts" on public opinion, as Acting Minister of Internal Affairs P. N. Durnovo sarcastically referred to them, was an unprecedented feature at a Tsarist conference. After their exit, their audience regularly called them the "public men," revealing the awareness on the part of the Tsar's advisors of the gulf between the administration and the articulate public. The other option was the retention of the principles of the Bulygin electoral law, while loosening the voting requirements so as to greatly broaden the electorate. In fact the debate whether to scrap the Bulygin law and adopt universal suffrage became the main issue at the conference; eventually Nicholas decided to expand the Bulygin law and ignore the voice of the liberals.

In order to understand the franchise statute approved at Tsarskoe Selo in December of 1905, it is necessary to review the principles of the law on which it was based; at the same time it is enlightening to have a look at the attitudes of the men who had passed on the final version of the Bulygin statutes. Actually the Bulygin Duma law had its origin as far back as February, 1905, with a rescript issued in then Minister of Internal Affairs A. F. Bulygin's name, and signed by the Tsar. According to that rescript, Nicholas planned to summon the "better people for preparatory elaboration and judgement of legislative proposals," while at the same time "unfailingly preserving the Fundamental Laws of the Empire." After several preliminary discussions, Bulygin directed Sergei Kryzhanovskii, a functionary in his ministry, to compose a draft project for the assembly statute. The latter had his draft ready by the end of May, when Bulygin delivered it to the characteristically indecisive Nicholas to mull it over. In spite of several reminders, Bulygin heard no more about the draft, until, at the end of June, Nicholas finally ordered that a commission under Count Dimitri M. Solskii make a preliminary review of it.[3]

The preparatory work on the Bulygin Duma and all of the other major reform legislation of 1905-1906 was accomplished under the overall guidance of Count Solskii. These efforts capped a long career in the Tsarist bureaucracy. Entering government service in 1852, Solskii was an important member of the State Council for many years, and at the time of the Bulygin reform he was the President of its Department of Economy. In spite of ill health—he was unable even to walk—Solskii and his commission, which included the ministers, were responsible for an enormous amount of paper work and discussion, frequently under enormous pressure to hurry, during those difficult days. While the commission did not make the final decisions on the projects, it played a very important role in drawing up the measures, and it continued to function right up to the opening of the Duma. In his memoirs Witte marvelled that Solskii accomplished so much in his last year of state service. The records of the palace conferences indeed reveal that Solskii played an active role in them in spite of his poor physical condition. His comments showed common sense and a great knowledge of the technical details, as well as the broad ramifications, of the matter under discussion. At the time of the December conference, Solskii was the President of the State Council, a post from which he finally retired in May of 1906; confined to a wheel chair and able to move only with great difficulty, he saw he could not carry on.[4]

From the Solskii commission, the Bulygin Duma project had gone back to the Tsar, who then summoned some forty of his advisors to the July 1905 conference at Peterhof for final approval of it. N. S. Tagantsev, a member of the State Council, who later wrote a valuable book about these meetings, had received his invitation only two days before the conference was to convene. After hasty preparations he left his estate in Tver, and on July 19 he boarded the special train which took him and his fellows to an opening breakfast at the palace. Tagantsev recalled that the single day he spent in the capital looking over the draft legislation had not given him enough time to prepare adequately for the discussion. In his opinion most of the others who had not participated in the Solskii commission review of the Bulygin proposal were equally unprepared.[5]

After a late breakfast Tagantsev and his associates went to the first of what were to be five very long sessions, held on alternate afternoons. Nicholas acted as chairman throughout. He paid very careful attention to the discussion, and although his contributions to it were generally brief, the Tsar played a decisive role in the proceedings. Nicholas's two main concerns, shared by many in the gathering, were: first, it was essential to define the powers of the Bulygin Duma carefully, so that it could not infringe too much on the traditional position of the emperor. Second, the electoral statute must be devised so as to prevent a significant number of the opponents of the autocracy from sitting in the chamber.

From the start Nicholas minced no words about his intentions. "Their main task," he said, was to draw up a Duma statute which was in harmony with the existent law code of the empire, according to which the Tsar was the unlimited autocrat; there was no provision for any kind of an elected popular assembly. In other words, in July of 1905 the Tsar still entertained hopes of granting minimal grudging reforms in order to calm the populace without making a fundamental change in the powers of the sovereign; the comments of many at the conference reveal that he was not alone in his complacent optimism. Well aware of Nicholas's attitude toward his prerogatives, Kryzhanovskii wrote that he tried to keep his draft as nearly in accord with Russian traditions as possible, so as to avoid the criticism that he had aped West European models.[6]

Many of the assembled dignitaries thought he had failed, and a discussion about upholding the Tsar's traditional role in the Empire dominated the first days of the conference.

Count Solskii told Nicholas frankly that even a consultative Duma would change the realities of power, whether his autocratic powers were limited in the text of the law or not. Furthermore, Solskii said, while the sovereign would retain the right to decide issues discussed in the Duma as he wished, he must do so with caution. Perhaps hoping to soothe his sovereign and to ward off attacks from the right, Solskii's close associate in the State Council, E. V. Frish, claimed, however, that while the Tsar should carefully consider the decisions of the Duma, this should not be identified with a limitation of his powers, since this would be a "mode of action" based on his decision to call the "better people" to advise him. And as they had judged Kryzhanovskii's project in the preliminary meeting, Frish insisted, all had been filled with a "single thought—to carry out the Emperor's will to preserve the firmly rooted principles of the Fundamental Laws."[7]

The arch-conservatives at the meeting did not think that the proponents of the project had succeeded, and in terms of time their objections were to dominate the ensuing discussion, which would last into the third session. Beneath their criticisms of the draft was a pervasive fear, shared by Nicholas, that once a consultative Duma were established, it would be but the initial step towards a parliamentary system, and the elimination of the autocracy. The sponsors of the project argued, on the other hand, that the monarch's powers would be guaranteed, since he would retain the right of ultimate decision on all legislative matters.

Perhaps the most eloquent spokesman for the right faction was Count A. A. Golenishchev-Kutuzov, poet and secretary to the Dowager Empress. To him the project upheld the autocratic principle formally, but it was directly opposed to it in spirit. He considered holding elections an aberration of Russian traditions; they would lead to "dangerous consequences" because hostile relationships between all groups of the populace would come out, and the "very principle of autocracy would be shaken."[8] The former Empress's secretary specifically objected to the article stating that the *majority* opinion of the Duma would be considered conclusive. He and his fellows reiterated that the Tsar must hear all views in the Duma, as had traditionally been the case with the State Council. To decide issues by majority vote was to introduce a West European tradition. The Duma must have a purely consultative role, and the number for or against a measure was not significant, since the Tsar, himself, must judge by the contents of an opinion, and not by the number of votes it had received.

Both Solskii and Frish considered the suggestion preposterous that all opinions expressed in the Duma must reach the Tsar. The issue was not what opinion got to the sovereign, Frish said firmly, but what constituted a Duma decision, and this must be the majority opinion. Even from a practical standpoint, the host of views which came from such a large body could only cause confusion, and would hardly provide a basis for legislation.[9]

At last, early in the third session the Tsar ended the debate and accepted article 47, without heeding the recommendations of the conservatives. In the published version it would read:

> The opinion approved (adopted) by the majority of members of the General Assembly of the Duma is viewed as concluding consideration by the State Duma. This conclusion must indicate clearly the Duma's approval or disapproval of the proposals submitted to it. The changes suggested by the Duma must be indicated in clearly expressed statements.[10]

In a closely related debate, the conservatives did, however, modify article 49 to read as follows:

> Legislative proposals rejected by a two-thirds majority of the General Assemblies of both the State Duma and the State Council are returned to the appropriate Minister or Department Head for further consideration, and, with his Imperial Majesty's permission, for renewed submittal for legislative action.

At first the conservatives had fought for complete elimination of this article, which they judged a gross infringement of the Tsar's prerogatives. Having failed to eliminate it, they persuaded Nicholas to require a *two-thirds* vote in both houses to reject a ministerial project. Not content to let the matter rest there, five conservatives then prevailed upon the Tsar to reconsider the article in the next session: Nicholas's assent to reopen the issue reflected his deep fears that he was abandoning too many of his prerogatives.[11] The five conservatives recommended that after a ministerial project had been rejected by two-thirds of both houses, it be returned to the appropriate minister for further consideration "if a special directive of his majesty did not follow. . . ." In other words the bill could not be rejected if the Tsar gave contradictory instructions, and, as the elder Prince A. D. Obolenskii aptly observed, "the proposed clause would completely nullify" the article. Ultimately the conservatives failed in their second attempt to modify the clause, but the amount of discussion devoted to it revealed the real concern of many in the group about retaining the autocrat's key role in the legislative process.

Once the major clauses defining the relationship between the Bulygin Duma and the sovereign were approved, the Tsar turned the attention of his advisors to the electoral statute. Nicholas hoped to frame an electoral law which would bring a pliant group of deputies to the capital, and most of his audience shared that wish. As Comptroller P. L. Lobko put it, the key issue was "how to bring people to the Duma who agree with you [Nicholas] on the basic question of the autocracy." While it could be said that subjects of all classes shared this idea, nevertheless, Lobko warned, there were those who wanted to overthrow the autocracy, and therefore it was of vital importance how they set up the elections.[12]

Most of Lobko's listeners shared his apprehensions about the complexion of the future Duma. Especially prevalent was a fear that too many members of the liberation movement would sit in it, and throughout the conference there were frequent disparaging references to "*zemstvo* types," journalists, men in the "free professions," and less frequently to revolutionaries. To the conservatives these men represented a vocal troublesome minority, who were alien to the Russian spirit and had no grasp of the demands or needs of the public. There was no need to have them in the Duma at all, since "the most educated and talented, the best orators, would show only a negative influence" in the chamber.[13] It was not only the ultra-conservatives who feared the middle class, although men like Vladimir Kokovtsov believed that, in spite of the risk, the assembly should have a small number from the educated middle class to handle the technical work of a legislature.

Kryzhanovskii's draft electoral statute was set up to keep many of the middle class disfranchised. Based on a complex system of multistaged elections, it gave a disproportionate share of the vote to the propertied elements of the populace, and large numbers of middle-class and poor citizens could not meet the high franchise requirements. Not surprisingly, neither the staged elections nor the discriminatory features of the draft were called into question at the Peterhof conference. These two basic principles received silent approbation. There was no significant concern expressed about securing a bill which was democratic, or which would ensure proportionate representation to the different groups in the population. There was not even much mention of the need to determine what kind of franchise law would placate the public, aside from occasional comments about not irritating public opinion excessively. Rather the main aim of these men was to approve a law which would bring "reliable elements" to the chamber, and in July, it apparently did not occur to them to wonder much about the public reception of their measure.

While the conferees accepted the basic features of the draft, there were certain elements in it which aroused considerable discussion. The first major debate dealt with the nature of the staged elections—should the populace vote at these stages as completely separate estates (*soslovie*) or should the "mixed" or cross-class elections included in the draft be approved? The second argument concerned peasant representation in the Duma—what percent of the Duma should be peasant and how could this percent be assured through the electoral law?

The conservative faction vigorously defended a strict class sytem of voting, but once again Solskii countered with a reasoned defense of Kryzhanovskii's draft, which, he claimed, was very similar to a class system of elections. In the country the peasants, small landowners, and large owners would all vote separately up to the final stage of the elections, while in the city elections it was preposterous to talk about separate class elections. In addition, about seventy percent of the electors (*vyborshchiki*), who would meet at the final or *guberniia* (province) stage to choose the Duma members would be from the two "basic classes" of nobles and peasants. A return to the obsolete class system would make an entirely unfavorable impression; it had not even been used in the *zemstvo* electoral statutes. In an eloquent appeal, V. O. Kliuchevskii defended mixed elections; the nobility made their contribution in the *zemstvo* when they worked for general, not class, interests. To revert to class elections would be "unjust . . . and dangerous," and would be interpreted as an "obscurantist symbol of a class Tsar."[14]

Arguments about the electoral law took up the bulk of the third session, and left Nicholas still undecided as to class or mixed elections when they met again on July 25: "It is very difficult to judge this complicated matter, because of its novelty and the uncertainty of the future," he complained. The debate dragged on, dominated by conservatives' criticisms and warnings, until finally the Tsar's uncle, Grand Duke Vladimir Alexandrovich, asked the former Marshal of the St. Petersburg nobility, A. A. Bobrinskii, in disgust if he considered the Council of Ministers a body of revolutionaries. Noting that it included Bulygin, a large landowner with strong local ties, the Grand Duke asked sarcastically: "If we cannot believe the majority of the Council of Ministers, who can we believe? A noble like Count Bobrinskii?" Undaunted, the right faction pursued their points, but finally the Tsar ended the discussion by accepting Kryzhanovskii's project for cross-class elections.

On the other major issue, namely the matter of peasant representation in the chamber, the conservatives managed to win a partial victory. Reflecting the traditional view that the peasants were the bulwark of the autocracy, the conservative block insisted that the electoral law contain provisions which would ensure a large number of peasant Duma members. This time they enlisted the support of the famous Procurator of the Holy Synod, K. Pobedonotsev, who was attending his last palace conference that July. Pobedonotsev, who had not concurred in the group's defense of strictly class elections, spoke as follows: "Historical tradition holds firmly only in the peasantry"; it was impossible to lean on the other classes since they were so diffuse and lacking in solid aims. One could no longer conjure up a clear mental picture of the nobility, but when one spoke of the peasantry, everyone understood what was meant. The peasants were the "dominant kernel of the population, and as a legislative voice, the most important of all."[15]

Several members of the conference, however, did not share the traditional view of the peasantry as docile and loyal to the Tsar, looking only to him to solve their problems. State Council member A. A. Polovtsov, like Solskii near the end of a long bureaucratic career, expressed grave doubts. The peasants will be favorable material for agitators, he warned, especially on the agrarian issue, while his fellow State Council member, Ivan Golubev, raised questions about the capability of peasants for the daily work of a legislator. One of the most consistently sensible defenders of the Ministers' Project, Finance Minister Vladimir Kokovtsov also rejected the theory that the peasants were a "wall which would guard the Duma from undesirable tendencies." To him they were more like a soft "wax," available to be molded, hence he shared Polovtsov's apprehensions. Kolovtsov predicted that those "undesirable elements, which, somehow or other, would undoubtedly penetrate" into the Duma could influence the peasants, and therefore, he was afraid to let in too many. Bulygin agreed that peasant dominance in the assembly would be undesirable.[16]

The question of what percent of the Duma must be peasant continued to dominate the discussion, until finally acting head of the Department of Land Affairs, Peter Shvanebakh, suggested that in "such a complicated matter, the more prudent course would appear to be a compromise." It was true that the peasant element would provide "ballast for the ship" with their "calm and fruitful activity" against "elemental tendencies and the enthusiasms of public opinion." To insure adequate peasant representation, let the peasant electors at the *guberniia* assembly first choose one or two Duma members from among their midst, and then unite with the rest of the electors to vote for the remainder of the area's allotment. The compromise appealed to Nicholas, who had not been convinced that the draft project would have brought enough peasants to the Duma. He then accepted the suggestion that the Duma allotment be raised to at least two delegates from each area, with the further stipulation that of the two, one must be elected by the peasant electors.[17] The compromise version of article 49 stated:

In every provincial electoral assembly the electors from the assemblies of delegates of townships (*volosts*) elect one member of the State Duma from among their ranks. Then the electoral assembly as a whole elects the remaining members (as per roster in article 2) of the Duma from all the qualified electors. The election is secret by means of voting spheres.

This clause ensured a minimum of one peasant deputy from each of the fifty-one *guberniia* assemblies included in the August 6 legislation. The fifty-one encompassed the central sections of the empire, while the border areas were to be covered by subsequent electoral statutes. Once more the right element at Peterhof had modified the original proposal, although not to its satisfaction. If one only peasant per *guberniia* were assured of election, Senator A. Naryshkin observed glumly, their voices would be lost "among the noisy voice of future progressive orators of the Duma."[18]

The conservative block was even more successful in its attack on the literacy requirement included in the draft statute.[19] State Council member A. S. Stishinskii, who would become a member of the ministerial cabinet the following spring, predicted dire consequences from such a proviso, since the honorable and experienced village elders, who had such a high incidence of illiteracy, would thereby be excluded from Duma membership. To Bulygin's observation that Duma deputies should be able to read draft proposals, Naryshkin waxed eloquent about his deep conviction, based on careful observations as a long time rural dweller, that "illiterate *muzhiks*, be they young or old, possess a more integral world-view than the literate." The latter read journals containing theories which led them from the "true path," and they developed a "negative spirit, a spirit of doubt." Later Senator Naryshkin asserted that he had frequently observed illiterate peasants handle their own affairs better than literate, adding that even the latter would need continuous assistance getting through the mass of printed material handed out to Duma members.

The ministers had given the matter of a literacy requirement careful consideration, Kokovtsov replied. Everyone knew that the village elders "judge by feeling," but this would not be their function in the Duma, where they would be faced with complicated law proposals and budget requests. At this point Nicholas interrupted: "I agree that those peasants with an integrated world-view would bring to the business at hand a more healthy attitude and life experience," and after a few more comments from both sides, the Tsar made his decision: "Perhaps, in this matter it would be better, at least for the first time" to exclude the literacy requirement.

The main issues finally settled, the Tsar urged his advisors to hasten their review of the electoral statute. It was published on August 6, 1905, along with the Bulygin Duma law and an imperial manifesto.[20] The latter began with a familiar reference to the "concord and union prevailing between Tsar and people," a concord which had been the "great moral force which had shaped Russia," and was still a pledge to her present and future progress. The time had come, however, to summon elected representatives to "permanent and active" participation in a consultative legislative assembly, to gather by mid-January 1906. From the tone and contents of the manifesto, it was clear where authority still lay: the Fundamental Laws remained intact, where they "referred to the Autocratic power," and "all worry about further improvements" in the Duma statute would be the affair of the sovereign. Should the times require amendment of the law, the manifesto read, "we shall not fail to issue the appropriate directives in due course."

According to the Duma statute, the Tsar would have considerable power over this consultative assembly. He could dissolve it by decree before the members served their five-year terms, provided the dissolution order set the date for new elections. The Tsar did, however, voluntarily relinquish any right over the future Duma's choice of a president, after it was pointed out that this might put the sovereign in the awkward position of having to confirm the election of a man of whom he did not approve. "For example, Petrunkevich," Nicholas interjected, referring to "the hated name of the Tver liberal."[21] Since such a possibility could only lead to conflict with the Duma, Nicholas decided to avoid it in advance.

The Bulygin Duma would have had no power over the administration, aside from the provision in article 35: "Ministers . . . may be required by the State Duma to provide information and explanations concerning the actions of Ministers, Heads of Departments, or their subordinate officials and institutions, which in the opinion of the Duma violate existing legislation." The inclusion of this article had aroused a great furor among the conservatives at Peterhof. One should not put ministers in the position of having to answer before the people's representatives for all their directives, Pobedonotsev protested indignantly. Stishinskii chimed in that this was a step towards a ministry responsible to the legislature. Once again the Minister of Finance, Kovovtsov, found wording which paid some deference to the conservative's position, without greatly changing the original article. In this case the draft was changed to read *violation* of the law, instead of non-conformity to the law which presumably could be subjected to wider interpretations by the Duma.[22]

Two matters of vital interest to any elective assembly were resolved in accord with the draft proposal. Article 34 gave the Duma the right to initiate law proposals, to amend existing laws, or to approve new bills presented by the ministry, "but these proposals could not touch upon the principles of the organization of the state as set forth in the Fundamental Laws." An effort to limit the initiative of the Duma to those measures not requiring new expenditures failed. Article 33, which listed matters within the competence of the Duma, included its right to review the budget and the Comptroller's account of its implementation. Since the monarch would not be obliged to accept the assembly's recommendations about the budget, this represented no assembly control over the public coffers, Nicholas's advisors assured him.

D. F. Trepov, one of Nicholas's favorite aids, neatly summed up the attitude of most of these men as they sat those five long days at Peterhof amongst external trappings marking the fading glories of the Romanovs: to introduce a Duma, regardless of its nature was "dangerous for the autocracy in my opinion." Therefore, he concluded, their task was to draw up a Duma law and electoral statute which would lessen, as far as possible, the chances for conflict between Tsar and popular representatives.[23] Exactly how to accomplish this goal had led to great uncertainty and debate, but ultimately they had approved a complicated system of multistaged elections, combined with a high property qualification for the franchise.

The property qualification was especially high in the

cities, reflecting the fear of the urban voter so prevalent among the upper bureaucracy. Before he left for the United States, Sergei Witte had proposed extending the franchise to some of the working class, but his suggestion did not get into the Bulygin project.[24] In the cities only the upper economic classes could vote—people who paid a high dwelling tax, or owned a fixed amount of real, commercial, or industrial property.

In the countryside, which also included provincial towns since separate urban elections would occur only in some twenty larger cities, all groups of the population were to vote together as electors at the final stage of the elections. Because of the disparate number of voters in the preliminary stages, the vote of one large landowner was equal to that of many small landowners, and a much larger number of peasants. Communal peasants chose their electors at the third stage, small landowners, and this included many of the Orthodox clergy, at the second stage.

In his memoirs Kryzhanovskii made a reasonable case for Bulygin's directive that the electoral law provide for multi-staged elections. Given the geographic and social conditions of the vast Russian Empire, and its lack of an adequate communications system, Bulygin considered direct elections inadvisable. They would have necessitated very large electoral districts, and a less intelligent selection of candidates was likely to emerge than from smaller districts, where the candidates would presumably be known locally in the preliminary stages of the voting process.[25] The men assembled at Peterhof in July of 1905 gave quiescent approval to Bulygin's recommendation, and the indirect nature of the elections was not called into question at the palace conference.

The role of Nicholas in the proceedings at Peterhof was very influential. He paid careful attention to the discussion, as he did at the subsequent palace conferences held that year, and the comments he interjected were brief and appropriate to the point under consideration. He did not act in autocratic fashion, but gave the floor to advisors of various viewpoints, who could then present their cases without being cut off abruptly. Nor did he accept the advice of the most ardent monarchists in most instances, although they were responsible for a few key changes in the draft. Most significant, he assumed the leadership position throughout the discussion, in that it was clear to all his listeners that no decision could be made which was against his will. His were the final decisions on the crucial issues, and once he had made his choice, the matter rarely received further comment.

These were difficult days for the autocrat of all the Russias. Each evening he simply recorded in his diary that a session had been held and noted its length, but on July 27, 1905 he rejoiced: "Today to my delight was free—without tiresome meetings. I played tennis and read a good deal, although I was busy with state affairs a long while after dinner."[26] The meetings were not only long; this was a most unpleasant business. Nicholas had called his advisors to carry out an almost overwhelming obligation. In February he had publicly promised to summon elected representatives of the public to participation in the legislative process. In early June 1905 he had assured Prince S. N. Trubetskoi, spokesman for a delegation of *zemstvo* and elected city officials who came to plead the cause of reform at Peterhof, of his firm intention to carry out this promise.

The problem lay in the differing interpretation of what constituted genuine public participation in the government. Nicholas's articulate subjects wanted a real voice, not a weak consultative assembly. Yet the debates at Peterhof indicated that the Tsar either did not understand, or refused to believe, that even a consultative assembly, if listened to at all, would have had considerable effect on his powers as an autocrat. Indeed this was one of the main issues in the debates, and almost all of his advisors who spoke reassured Nicholas that his prerogatives would remain intact. The impression that some of the more realistic or intelligent ones did so simply to persuade Nicholas to accept the Kryzhanovskii draft is supported by the latter's observation about the preliminary review conferences: "Everybody understood that the project resulted in an actual limitation of the autocracy, but they pretended not to notice."[27] In many ways the most realistic predictions came from the prophets of doom on the right, who rejected many concessions from fear that they would only lead to more demands, which, if heeded, would ultimately result in a true constitutional monarchy. And indeed this is what most of the liberal reformers actually wanted. In the face of their mounting demands, Nicholas and his top officials had reluctantly met at Peterhof, where they debated, fumbled, hesitated and finally approved what to them were enormous concessions, only to find that the public held them beneath contempt.

Virtually no one from the opposition accepted the Bulygin Duma as adequate. The mounting violent disturbances of the fall of 1905, the most tangible evidence of its reception, were accompanied by verbal onslaughts. As always the Social Democrats were the most vitriolic: the Bulygin manifesto was an attempt to deceive the populace, hence participation in any stages of the elections would be a "true crime against the people." The electoral law was a "mockery," since it would result in a Duma in which the workers and peasants, the vast majority of the population, would have "no place." Only a constituent assembly, elected by universal, direct, equal, and secret ballot deserved support. Eventually the Social Democrats called for a complete boycott of the elections. One of the greatest disagreements among members of the League of Liberation took place over what position to adopt toward the Bulygin Duma, Miliukov recalled. While it had much to be said against it, he had argued, in the Russia of 1905 it was an accomplished fact. The electoral law was unacceptable, but a boycott of the elections was pointless. Rather, he had urged, get into the Bulygin Duma and use it to struggle for more concessions.[28] Neither attitude was very promising for Nicholas, who had so desperately hoped that the Bulygin Duma would pacify his troubled country.

As soon as the Bulygin Duma was promulgated, wrote Kryzhanovskii, the radicals, always numerous in Russia, refused to deal with reality and accept it. Unfortunately the rest of the vocal public "consciously or unconsciously sang along." No one wished to understand that to change from one order to another was "technically and psychologically very complicated, very painful for the bearer of autocratic power," and that the only possible path was compromise and half-measures. Nor were the criticisms confined to those from the left. Many of Nicholas's subjects on the right declared their outright opposition to the new institution, regarding it, "not without basis," as a step towards a true legislative body. "And so everyone berated it," Kryzhanovskii concluded bitterly.[29]

Two months later Nicholas abandoned the stillborn consultative assembly with his October 17 promise that henceforth it would be "an unbreakable rule that no law could become effective without the sanction of the State Duma." In addition, those classes of the populace which were still disfranchised under the Bulygin statutes were to be granted the vote, "as far as it is feasible" in the time before the Duma convened, but without stopping the already scheduled elections. The "further development of the principle of universal suffrage" would be left to the new legislative assembly.

It was to inaugurate necessary changes in the existing electoral laws that Nicholas summoned his advisors to the December palace conference.[30] Under consideration were alternative proposals. The first, the project of the Council of Ministers, was again drawn up by S. Kryzhanovskii, but this time under Witte's overall supervision. In his new statute, the drafter of the Bulygin law kept the principles of that law intact, but he included many more voters by lowering the property requirements for the franchise, and adding a new *curia* of workers. The second project was the work of a group of moderate liberal reformers, who had presented their proposal to a November meeting of the Council' of Ministers, and had subsequently received invitations to defend it at a Tsarskoe Selo session.

Nicholas opened the first session of the December palace conference with a request that his advisors "listen to the view of the Muscovites." His remark applied first to

Dimitri N. Shipov, highly respected leader of the right wing of the *zemstvo* movement and former chairman of the board of the Moscow provincial *zemstvo*. Deeply conscious of his enormous responsibility to his fellow citizens, Shipov felt overwhelmed with great trepidation at his initial presentation before such a high level gathering. Yet his anxiety quickly disappeared when he observed how intently Nicholas listened to what Shipov soon began to regard as an effective plea for universal suffrage.[31] Shipov recommended division of the country into electoral districts based on the existent *uezd* (district) system. Districts of 100,000 to 300,000 would have one Duma delegate, those of over 300,000 population would be divided to send two, while smaller districts would be combined to send one Duma member. The total for the empire would be from 600 to 650 legislators, chosen by two-staged elections throughout. Deploring the "disorders and demoralization which permeated society," Shipov warned his audience that the demand for universal suffrage was widespread, and that the failure to grant it would only provide favorable soil for the revolutionaries. The October promise of civic freedoms should include the franchise, based on a democratic, not a class principle. Shipov claimed that bestowal of universal suffrage would ensure a more conservative Duma; Octobrist candidates would then be elected, while without general suffrage their opponents would win.

Shipov was followed by Alexander Guchkov, the former's close associate in the Octobrist movement and a member of the Moscow city council. Guchkov supported Shipov's argument that calling the masses to participation in the country's political life would help to conciliate them. He begged his sovereign not to fear the masses, but to bestow universal suffrage as "an act of confidence and benevolence." Taking a new tack, he further argued that a general franchise was "inevitable," to be "snatched" in the near future if not granted at once.

A sense of urgency, of the need to do something quickly to prevent a second outburst of revolution like that of the fall, pervaded these three days of meetings. All agreed that the country was far from pacified, but they were not agreed on the best means to relieve the tension. Most of Shipov's and Guchkov's audience remained unconvinced that universal suffrage was the answer, in spite of fervent support for it from the other two "public figures"—St. Petersburg Octobrist Baron P. O. Korf, and an *uezd* Marshal of the Nobility from Tula *guberniia*, Count Vladimir A. Bobrinskii. The latter, previously known as a resolute opponent of general suffrage, completely surprised his listeners. "With tears in his eyes" he stated that he had been wrong on the issue, and when Witte reminded him of his position on the matter as recently as November of 1905, Bobrinskii admitted freely that he had since changed his view. He had been convinced by a trip into the countryside where he talked with many individuals that "nothing besides the most democratic project would satisfy Russia."[32] Baron Korf likewise remarked that he had always regarded universal suffrage "unthinkable" in Russia, adding that he too had changed his mind. Insisting that Shipov and Guchkov had underestimated the seriousness of the situation, he urged haste: "Now it is of the utmost importance to save the realm; to do so it is essential to hold the elections as soon as possible." Furthermore, Korf argued, if the Tsar bestowed universal suffrage before the First Duma convened, it would eliminate the need for that body to raise the suffrage issue.

Korf's contention that a quick summons of the Duma would pacify the country came under sharp attack from P. N. Durnovo, acting head of the Ministry of Internal Affairs. "It is impossible to cure the troubles with any kind of elections. . . . We will fall into a great error if we look at the Duma from an opportunistic point of view," he began. He disagreed with Shipov that general suffrage would bring desirable elements into the Duma. He brought up the matter of the third element, and asserted that landowners would not enter a Duma filled with "medical aids, *zemstvo* statisticians and so forth, individuals who recently had been marshals of predatory gangs, raiding their estates." These individuals were "foreign to all traditions" and incapable of judging government business. After

Durnovo's contribution the Tsar called for a needed recess, during which the invited representatives of the public, having presented their case, left the hall permanently.

Sergei Witte dominated the rest of the sessions in terms of verbiage, but this was not a calm, decisive Witte, presenting an effective defense of a project worked out by the ministers under his leadership. Rather this was a disturbed Witte, an unsure Witte, whose remarks at the meeting were often vague, inconsistent, and even contradictory. At the second session the top minister seemed especially irritated, Tagantsev wrote, recalling how each time that Witte rose to that great height to speak, all the while supporting his remarks with emphatic gestures, the Tsar at his side "bent toward the table, as if dejected by his chief minister." Witte's irresolute character, his vacillation, and "outright fear of assuming responsibility" for the project of his own ministry were evident, Kryzhanovskii noted. ". . . He wearied the Tsar and the conference with statements both for and against it, and by the absence of his own opinion," making in general a very poor impression.[33]

According to Kryzhanovskii, Witte had been undecided about the type of electoral law he preferred, when the two men discussed the need for a new one on the night the October manifesto had appeared. By the time of the December conference, it was clear that the first few weeks in office had taken their toll. Witte was even more uncertain, not only about the law itself, but about the advisability of a quick summons of the Duma. More than once he alluded to the danger, or even impossibility, of holding elections in areas where riots still broke out, or which were under special security measures. His real horror was a renewal of widespread agrarian riots; trouble in the cities could be handled, he thought, but outside of them, in the vast expanses of rural Russia, there simply were not enough troops to control an outburst. Yet in another context he spoke about the "talented Russian *narod*, loyal to their Tsar," unchanging, and much more reliable than the urban populace. These general apprehensions and uncertainties greatly affected his attitude toward the electoral law.[34]

"Who can decide now what kind of project will give us

the better Duma?" he asked at one point, noting that the mood of the country was unstable and unpredictable. Considered abstractly, the Bulygin electoral law was better, and he could even include some conservative modifications. However, it was impractical because it was unacceptable, and had been among the causes of the disorders. During the second session he almost defended universal suffrage: "When I judge with my mind, I lean toward the second project," but, and then he hedged, "when I act according to intuition I fear this project." He accepted the view of the public men that universal suffrage was just and in accord with the mood of the populace; he once referred to Russia as "one of the most democratic countries," formed under conditions different from the feudal system of Western Europe. Viewed from this aspect, the second project presented no "special danger." But, as he considered the "disorganization of the administration" and the "uneasy state of the population," he had to conclude that bestowal of universal suffrage would be "dangerous under present circumstances."[35] In the end Witte chose the project presented by his ministry, but only after he had himself criticized some of its details.

At one point Witte declared that the proposal therein for a a separate *curia* of workers, with an allotted fourteen Duma delegates, was "impossible"; in preliminary sessions he had sought another method of extending the franchise to the laboring class. Several conferees agreed that the clause should be altered, including Guchkov, who had referred to those fourteen worker delegates as an "organized strike committee" at the previous session. Eventually the Tsar stopped debate on the issue, and later the conference approved a new proposal which called for three-stage worker elections. At the first two stages they would vote separately. Then, having chosen worker electors at the second stage, the latter would join the other electors from their area to choose its Duma members. The bulk of the working class remained disfranchised, since these provisions applied only to those employed in larger establishments.

Not only had Witte objected to the separate workers' *curia* originally proposed in the draft project, he had favored extending the vote to other workers besides those employed in larger plants. At the December meetings Witte found that many of his ministers criticized these and his other opinions: furthermore they did not unite and defend the ministerial project. Four of them—V. I. Timiriazev, N. N. Kutler, D. A. Filosofov, and the younger Prince A. D. Obolenskii—gave some support to the liberals with their remarks about universal suffrage. Clearly as of December, the unified ministry demanded by Witte before he accepted the post of chief minister was a vanished dream.

The most vigorous disagreements occurred between Witte and his colleague from the Ministry of Internal Affairs, disagreements aired openly before their sovereign and reflecting basic differences in the two men's attitudes, as well as over specific policies. Described by Tagantsev as the "future enemy of Witte, the clearly rightist P. N. Durnovo," the latter suffered none of the uncertainty and indecisiveness of his chief. His remarks to the conference were concise throughout and he spoke to the issue at hand. A frequent contributor to the discussion, he maintained a consistent conservative outlook. More than once Durnovo warned his associates against expecting a quick summons of the Duma to bring calm to the country. Completely opposed to those who spoke for universal suffrage, he also thought that the minister's project would enfranchise too many citizens, and he argued for more stringent voting requirements.

In contrast to his argumentive ministers, Nicholas injected very few comments into the December conference proceedings, although he did frequently end a debate by taking a stand. The impression gained from reading the records of the meeting, that the Tsar grew increasingly weary and became unduly anxious to press the discussion forward, is supported by Tagantsev's recollection that Nicholas seemed overburdened by the sessions; he kept telling them to proceed, as if the discussion "bored him and he did not expect good judgments" from it. Yet Nicholas realized fully that they were dealing with a vital matter. On December 8, 1905, he wrote his mother that he was busy with a number of "important, but tiring conferences," which frequently lasted at least seven hours—"simply awful!" In the same letter he also pointed out that the whole future of the legislative assembly depended on the proper phrasing of the electoral law.[36]

Nicholas made no comment on the big issue before the conference—universal suffrage versus the ministers' modified statute—until he made a sudden, very characteristic, announcement during the second session:

> Everything has been weighed and discussed. This question was completely incomprehensible to me and even of little interest; it is only since the October Manifesto that I have studied it. I have found a tendency toward complete vacillation in both of these sessions. But since this morning it has been clear to me that the first project is better for Russia . . . my intuition tells me that the second must not be accepted. It is entirely too big a step. Today universal suffrage, and it will not be too long until there is a democratic republic. . . . The first project provides a better guarantee of achieving the October reforms. Proceed to a study of project one.

As usual, Nicholas was more frank with his mother. Some individuals had proposed universal suffrage, he wrote, "but I, acting on my firm convictions, declined to agree to it. God alone knows how far people will go with their fantastic ideas!"[37]

Actually Shipov and Guchkov, for all their "fantastic ideas" about universal suffrage, which had after all been mentioned in the October Manifesto as a matter to be further considered under the new legislative order, were on the right wing of the liberal reform movement. But in that conference of Tsarist bureaucrats they were flaming radicals. While a few of the ministers supported their pleas for universal suffrage, Nicholas and the bulk of his advisers did not. In its stead the Tsar accepted a modification of the Bulygin law of 1905, which retained the multistage *curia* elections, but greatly widened the franchise.[38]

Announced when the Moscow riots were at their peak, the December 11 law was in accord with the October promise, in that it gave vote to the majority of the adult males in the empire. Suffrage was limited to those of twenty-five years or more; students, persons on active military duty, and foreign subjects were denied the franchise. No one who did not know the Russian language could be a *member* of the Duma.

In rural Russia there would no longer be a minimum land ownership requirement, and persons with permanently leased land were enfranchised. In urban areas the vote was extended to anyone who owned commercial, industrial, or real property, paid a professional tax, rented an apartment, or received a state salary or pension. These liberalizations of the Bulygin Duma franchise requirements gave the vote to most of the middle class. However, since factory workers in Nicholas's Russia tended to live in barracks or rooming houses, most still could not meet these requirements. The law did, however, add a separate *curia* of workers in larger plants. These men selected representatives to a district workers' assembly where their electors were chosen. The latter then voted at the appropriate *guberniia* or city assembly to choose the area's Duma members with the rest of the electors.

The December 11 extension of the Bulygin law went a long way towards introducing universal male suffrage, although workers in establishments employing under fifty men, individual laborers such as janitors, as well as hired agricultural workers remained without the vote. The statute, which prevailed in fifty-one *guberniias* of the core Empire, retained the complicated series of voting stages which characterized the Bulygin legislation, in that different *curia* voted separately until the final assembly, where the actual balloting for Duma members took place. The number of preliminary stages ranged from one to three.

There were two basic types of final assembly—provincial (*guberniia*) and urban. The latter were held in some twenty larger cities of the empire, each of which was allotted a specific number of Duma deputies to select. The urban electors from the rest of the nation's towns voted with their rural counterparts in the provincial electoral assemblies. (See page 103 for a chart of a *guberniia* electoral assembly.) Only large landowners voted directly for their electors. Small landowners had first to hold a preliminary assembly, where they chose them; the number of their representatives at the district assembly was allotted on the basis of the collective property of those eligible for the preliminary gathering. Thus, small landowners had three balloting stages—preliminary, district, provincial; for communal peasants and village Cossacks there was an additional fourth stage.

The December electoral statute retained the proviso of the Bulygin law which enabled the electors from the peasant communes and Cossack villages to choose one Duma member from "among their midst" before voting with the rest of the area electors at the provincial assembly. It also resembled its August predecessor in that one elector from the large landowners' assembly represented many less constituents than did those of the small landowners or peasants. Throughout the empire the total number of allotted delegates was 524, elected in 92 districts. This total included delegates from the border areas, which were covered by a series of supplementary statutes issued between February 22, 1906, and April 23, 1906. The laws of late April, which set up special rules for the elections in Eastern Siberia, the Maritime Provinces, and Russian Central Asia, were not published in time to elect deputies before the Duma would open on April 27, 1906.

The supplementary statutes favored the Cossacks and the Russian minority in the border areas. To cite some examples: Cossack villages (*stanitsa*) had separate elections and were allotted a disproportionate number of Duma members. The minority Orthodox population in the Polish Catholic Lublin and Sedlets regions sent their own Duma delegate. In Tashkent, of the two allotted members, one represented the minority Russian population of the city,

COMPOSITION OF A PROVINCIAL ELECTORAL AS-
SEMBLY—the chart demonstrates the complex multistage electoral system of the Bulygin Electoral Law of
August 6, 1905. The same system was retained after the
law was modified in December 1905, although the franchise was substantially increased, and a new *curia* of
voters, factory workers, was added. The latter voted in
three-stage elections, the first stage taking place at their
place of employment.

State Duma

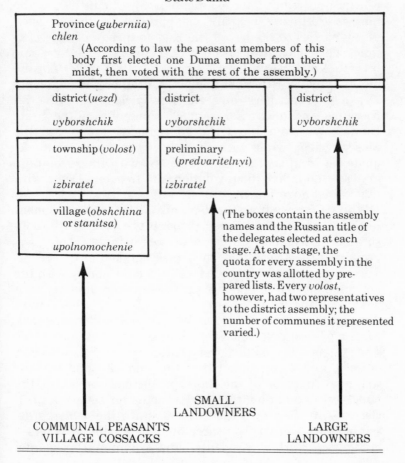

and the other the native majority; the two divisions of society had separate elections.

When compared with its August predecessor, the December 11, 1905, electoral law was very liberal, although it did not meet the demands of the famous four-tailed formula for "secret, equal, direct and universal suffrage," But given the public mood that winter, Miliukov remarked, not even a defective electoral statute could prevent the populace from truly expressing itself in the elections. Furthermore, since the electoral campaign would provide such an excellent opportunity for political groups to influence the masses, Miliukov heartily disapproved of the decision of the parties to the left of the Kadets to boycott the elections. Their boycott decision was accompanied by graphic literature as always. On December 14, 1905, *Izvestiia*, the organ of the St. Petersburg Soviet, contained the following: "Volleys of artillery and election laws! Trampling all freedoms and orders for a quick summons of the State Duma!" With one hand the government suppressed the Moscow riots, while with the other it granted an inadequate electoral law. Reply to that law with the revolutionary cry: "Long live the revolution and freedom. Down with the Tsarist government."[39]

While a far cry from the demands of the reform element in the empire, when viewed through the eyes of its sponsors the December statute was surprisingly liberal, especially if the enormity of their task is taken into account. These monarchists had been faced since the spring with the responsibility of conferring suffrage on the subjects of a vast, multinational empire, a majority of whom were illiterate. They chose in December not to abandon the *curia* system of elections which they had set up in August 1905. The system reflected their very real distrust of the Russian masses, and a conviction that the elections had best be weighted in favor of the more prosperous sectors of the populace. In addition, they had a model for separate *curia* elections in their own institutions, since the *zemstvo* assemblies were elected by three distinct groups of voters—landowners, urban residents, and communal peasants.

Moreover, the *curia* electoral system reflected the traditional class-corporate structure of Muscovite and Imperial Russia's society and political organization. Nicholas's administration was not willing to abandon this type of elections in December, although popular pressure did force it to greatly increase the number of enfranchised.

Some of the arguments they advanced against direct universal suffrage in the Russia of 1905 had validity. In order to provide for a Duma small enough to be a workable chamber, the electoral districts would have been very large. An illiterate population, coupled with a backward transportation and communication system, would have made an intelligent selection of Duma members even less likely in such huge districts. Several of Nicholas's advisors also brought up the point that it was too late to abandon the Bulygin project and to draw up a totally new law, with all the necessary technical changes that would entail, without unduly delaying the Duma opening.

The bulk of an increasingly angry opposition had absolutely no interest in such technical difficulties, however important they were to the men in charge of inaugurating the reforms. So at the same time that many of them were demanding a totally new election law, they also were insisting on a quick summons of the Duma. Then it was not a time for rational deliberation on either side.

CHAPTER V

The Administration Knows
What Will Save Russia

The December election law had capped a series of conciliatory measures announced during the early weeks of Count Witte's ministry, but much remained to be done before all the reforms promised in October were incorporated into the laws of the empire. Witte had urged Nicholas to make these concessions in order to placate the public, split the opposition, and help restore calm in his troubled realm. By the end of 1905 the latter goal was yet to be achieved, although, from the time of the failure of the armed uprising in Moscow, the odds seemed increasingly to favor the government. Still at Tsarskoe Selo the annual holiday preparations lacked their customary glitter, and the Tsar of all the Russias remained despondent and uncertain how to proceed. His mother, having heeded her son's grave warnings to postpone her return from Denmark until travel was safer, would spend Christmas away from him for the second time in their lives. On December 29 Nicholas wrote her that the situation throughout Russia was much quieter, although serious uprisings continued in the Baltic provinces. Nevertheless, there was room for encouragement, since the actions of General Dubasov and his troops in Moscow were having a "calming effect all over Russia." Hence as the New Year dawned Nicholas could be more optimistic, although far from complacent, as he reluctantly waded through the piles of reports which filled his desk each week.

On January 10, 1906, Witte assured his sovereign that fatalities during the riots and numerous arrests had significantly thinned the ranks of the revolutionaries, while steps were already underway to prevent the formation of new illegal societies. The disorders in the cities could be considered under control. Nicholas expressed his relief as he read this prediction with a simple marginal annotation: "Thank God." With the possible exceptions of the Baltic, the Caucasus, and Poland where nationalism and other traditional discontents complicated the issue, he read further, future protests should not be too severe. Yet Witte anticipated that individual acts of terror, so hard to prevent, would remain a serious problem, and there was one large bloc of the populace which the chief minister contemplated with great fear. The agrarian disorders were far from over and unless proper measures were taken, Witte predicted even greater rural violence come spring. Essentially negative measures such as strengthening the village police, more effective use of the regular army, especially its cavalry units, and quicker judicial procedures to bring the guilty into court might help keep temporary calm, but the situation was very tense.[1]

Meanwhile, leaders of the opposition parties grew increasingly restive about the intentions of the administration. In December, 1905, Witte met a delegation from the St. Petersburg branch of the Octobrist Party, which told him that reforms promised in October must be enacted soon. They warned him that the administration's destruction of newly won civil rights, especially freedom of assembly, had only provoked the public and led to a renewed lack of faith in the government. Witte replied that permitting unlimited freedom of assembly would be dangerous, given the mood of the population. He assured the delegation that the Tsar's will to carry out the October Manifesto remained firm, adding that their fears that the Duma would not be summoned were baseless. Work was already underway within the bureaucracy on the necessary legislation, and since he knew what was necessary to save Russia, the administration did not need the confidence of society to proceed adequately.[2]

It was a disillusioning interview for men who had so

recently formed a political organization dedicated to the renovation of their country through achievement of the Tsar's October promises. Political figures to the left of the Octobrists had viewed the concessions as too vague and niggardly from the start, but their skepticism was as much a reaction to the source of the promises as to their contents. On October 19 a member of the St. Petersburg press corps had told Witte bluntly that the press simply did not believe the administration. And indeed there was real basis for this lack of public confidence in the sovereign's willingness to translate promises into policies.

In the first place Tsarist officials continued to use arbitrary methods which frequently were in gross violation of newly announced civil rights. That the regime was fighting for its life and frequently used these techniques in response to citizen violence hardly justified the tactics in the eyes of the opposition. Aside from the administration's arbitrary actions, the Tsar's past performance and his rare public pronouncements would hardly inspire confidence in his readiness to allow effective popular participation in the government. Furthermore, he had signed the concessions reluctantly during the height of a revolt. The promises were not more liberal, or more specific, because Nicholas had conceded more than he approved as it was. The October Manifesto was not a constitution, but only a statement of intent; in fact, the word "constitution" never appeared in connection with the proposed reforms. P. Miliukov had discussed this very point with Witte that fall, and he finally asked the chief minister outright why he refused to use the word constitution. To which Witte replied frankly: "I cannot because the Tsar does not wish it."[3]

Whether he permitted the term constitution or not, Nicholas had no choice but to proceed with the task of drawing up statutes for the new order. The December electoral law was but the first step in what was to prove a very time consuming process, which absorbed much of his and his staff's time during the early months of 1906. They were to complete their labors just before the opening of the First State Duma, by then having approved the regulations for that chamber, and for a reformed State Council. Many of the provisions of those statutes were likewise incorporated into a revised 1906 version of the Fundamental Laws of the Russian Empire, published on April 23 of that year.

These documents provided the legal basis for the post-October system. While a big step toward representative government in comparison with the old autocratic regime, they represented a hedging and a regression, not in spirit with the changes implied in October. Hence the fears of the public that this would occur proved correct. The stages through which the measures passed were almost identical to those which had preceeded promulgation of the Bulygin Duma Statute and the two electoral laws. Twice more Nicholas sent out invitations to secret high level gatherings, and twice more his select advisors assembled in the ornate Catherine Palace at Tsarskoe Selo. Representatives of the public appeared at neither conference. It was simply inconceivable to Nicholas that the public should be called in to discuss his powers as autocrat of all the Russias, or to pass judgement on the law code of the realm.

The men summoned to the first of these winter conferences, held on February 14 and 16, 1906, had to consider three separate projects—an imperial manifesto about the State Duma and a reformed State Council, along with two projects of the Senate, which contained the detailed regulations for these two chambers. All three had been drawn up under the general supervision of the Solskii Commission. Nicholas opened the first session with a request that speakers stick to essentials, since he hoped to conclude the business at hand in one day. While the Tsar allowed that they would be judging a "very serious" matter, still he thought that it was "less difficult" than the electoral law. Contrary to the sovereign's wish the meeting went into a second day, recalled Tagantsev, in spite of his "usual and frequent *dalee* [proceed] to spur us on."[4]

Most of the discussion at the February meeting centered, not on the Duma statute, but on the proposal to reform the State Council into a second legislative house, equal in power to the Duma. Plans to do so were not mentioned in the October Manifesto, although Witte's official report of the same date had specifically called for the addition of elected members to the existing State Council. "That alone would enable the administration to establish normal relations between that institution and the State Duma," the report read. At the December Conference Witte had been frank about his motives: "As a necessary counterweight to moderate the Duma . . . the State Council must stand between the Duma and the Emperor." By February, with the people's representatives soon to descend on the capital, he was clearly worried. Only a reformed State Council could save the situation from "an unbridled lower house," he stressed, since it would act as a check against extreme opinion, as well as a "buffer" to avoid a direct collision between the Duma and the sovereign.[5]

Since its establishment a century earlier by Alexander I, the State Council (*Gosudarstvennyi soviet*) had been a major advisory body to the Tsars.[6] Its members examined the imperial budget and law projects of the ministers, who were members of the State Council *ex officio*. It had no legislative initiative, but could only comment on proposals put before it. The sovereign could accept a majority report, minority report, or ignore State Council decisions entirely, as he saw fit. Nor did all legislation have to go through this body, since the Tsar could also issue decrees which had the force of law. In 1901 an Imperial *ukaz* reorganized the State Council. After that it had four departments: Legislative; Civil and Ecclesiastical Affairs; State Economy; Industry, Science, and Commerce. It still held plenary sessions, but most of the work was done in these four departments, which drew up projects at the recommendation of the ministers.

The chairmen of the four departments were also members of the old Council of Ministers, a body established by Alexander II to deal with policy matters considered beyond the competence of the Committee of Ministers. The latter was made up of the ministers only, and handled more routine business, while the Council of Ministers was summoned by the Tsar and usually he presided over its meetings. When Witte took office in October of 1905, it was as Chairman of a reformed Council of Ministers.

According to Gurko, the chairmen of the four departments of the State Council had a limited, but definite, influence on legislation, primarily as conciliatory agents in ministerial disputes, frequently over fund allocations. Departmental sessions were much more important than plenary sessions, and Gurko could not recall a case when a plenary session revised a departmental project. Since its origin many capable men had served in one or several of these departments; Solskii and Frish, who played such an important and constructive role at the palace conferences of 1905-1906, are but two examples. At times State Council members had stood up to the administration and resisted tendencies toward arbitrary violations of the empire's code of laws. This was unknown to the public, however, who viewed the State Council as a purely conservative force.

The Tsar appointed members of the State Council for life and there was no upper limit to its membership. At the beginning of Nicholas's reign there were less than a hundred members, of whom under forty were active. Such an appointment could be a reward for long service or a dead-end appointment for a shelved official. Its ranks included former ministers, ambassadors, provincial governors, many beyond their peak years. Often the post merely represented a pension at an amount fixed individually for each new appointee.

Witte's opinions of the State Council support Gurko's observations. At a meeting at Count Solskii's on September 21, 1905, Witte stressed that an equal number of elected members should be added to the State Council. Because of the policy of filling it with non-deserving candidates, he argued, the institution had lost the respect of all classes of the population, and even the grand dukes made fun of it. The proposal did not meet with the approval of all his colleagues, however: "This would be a second State Duma with an admixture of old bureaucrats and generals," State Council member Alexander Polovtsov wrote on November

7. "My heart ached at the thought of such a commonplace crowd filling those elegant halls. . . ."[7]

The State Council held its general sessions in a large round hall in the Mariinskii Palace, a superbly decorated room with dark crimson carpet, filled with comfortable arm chairs. Portraits of the five emperors who had reigned since 1800 hung between pillars which supported the balcony. In keeping with the setting, the sessions were very formal, almost solemn. Gurko has left us a vivid picture of this body: ". . . venerable old men, white haired or entirely bald, with wrinkled skin and often quite bent with age, wearing uniforms and adorned with all their decorations—they produced the impression of a living historical tableau." The proposed changes were bound to have some impact on such a staid assembly. Tagantsev put it aptly: the State Council would no longer be mainly "an organ of gracious listeners," but a legislative organ, with a legal obligation to examine bills approved by the Duma, as well as the right to initiate its own measures.[8]

Since many of the men assembled at Tsarskoe Selo that February had served in the State Council for years, or aspired to an appointment to it, the reform of this institution was of immediate interest to them. Consequently, this issue generated significant discussion, and Nicholas failed in his attempt to complete the February conference in a single day. The debate was much less spirited than it had been at the two previous palace conferences, however. Once again Witte and Durnovo were at odds on several issues. For example, they disagreed over the statement in the draft of the manifesto that the number of members appointed to the council should equal the number of elected delegates. Durnovo wanted this restriction left out so that the Tsar could appoint additional State Council members at his discretion. Always more sensitive to public opinion than his Minister of the Interior, Witte argued that to leave the number of appointees without an upper limit would encourage rumors and make a poor impression. Besides he was deeply confident that the conservative element would predominate, among the elected members, since many of them would be chosen by trustworthy elements, such as the nobility, the Orthodox clergy, and business groups. Ultimately Durnovo failed to persuade the sovereign to change the draft, and the State Council had an equal number of appointed and elected members in its 196 man total.

Nicholas made virtually no comments during the February conference, aside from making the final decisions on debated points and urging haste. On several issues the Solskii Commission brought in a minority and majority report. In one instance, on the matter of admitting outsiders into the legislative chambers, Witte had supported the minority view. The Duma president, as yet an unknown quantity, should have only limited discretion over admitting representatives of the press and other non-members, Witte believed: "I fear publicity in general," he warned, ". . . the diplomatic corps of course, should always be admitted, but not those who will throw rotten apples."[9] In this case the powerful chief minister had not been able to get his version of the article into the majority report; furthermore, at the palace conference, the Tsar opted for the majority opinion. In fact, throughout the discussion, Nicholas usually accepted the draft project, although some modifications of detail did occur.[10]

The Duma Statute and the accompanying manifesto were both published on February 20, 1906, while the final text of the State Council Statute did not appear in print until April 24, 1906.[11] The February manifesto, however, announced that elected members would be added to a reformed State Council, and summarized the relationship between the two houses, which were to enjoy equal legislative rights. Even a hasty perusal of this manifesto revealed that the long awaited popular assembly would begin its life with greatly restricted powers. To the Octobrists, whose very *raison d'etre* was their confidence, rapidly waning, in the administration's intentions to carry out the October concessions, the manifesto was a great blow. "Unquestionably" the February statutes contradicted the principles of the October Manifesto and would be a serious obstacle to the proper and fruitful work of the Duma. Especially objectionable was the plan to create a "bureaucratic barrier" to the Duma under the guise of a reorganized State Council. Such was the tone of an Octobrist press release of late February.[12]

While the announcement of a reformed State Council should not have been a shock to anyone who had read Witte's October report carefully, the February 20 manifesto contained another more significant limitation on the popular assembly: the Duma and the State Council would both have the right to draw up new laws, or to amend or abrogate existing laws, "with the exception of the Fundamental Laws" which could be revised *only at the initiative of the sovereign*. The reference here was to the so-called Fundamental Laws of the Russian Empire, an amalgam of statutes, some of which dated from the seventeenth century. This code, which provided the legal basis for the Russian autocracy, had to be brought up to date in view of the constitutional changes of the fall and winter. Finally published on April 23, 1906, just four days before the First Duma opened, the new sections contained the essential provisions from the Duma and State Council statutes, as well as the major provisions of a separate measure of March 8, 1906, which defined the budget and financial powers of the Duma. By thus incorporating key articles regulating the legislative chambers into the Fundamental Laws, the administration insured in advance that they could not legally be changed by the popular assembly; any attempt to do so would be a revolutionary action, contrary to the law code of the empire.

The 1906 revision of the Fundamental Laws received final approval at the April Tsarskoe Selo conference. The last of the four palace conferences called to pass judgment on the post-October system, this time the sessions went into a fourth day, and the Tsar was deeply involved in the proceedings throughout the long discussion. He did not open with a plea for haste, nor did the familiar *dalee* ring out as early or as frequently as in previous meetings. Noting that the project at hand was of "vital interest," Nicholas stressed that it was "better to discuss an issue at length, than to decide in haste and expose one's self and the entire country to terrible dangers."[13] At stake were the prerogatives of the office he had inherited from his father, and the fundamental principles upon which Nicholas and his predecessors had ruled their domain.

Until 1906 the Tsar had been the administrative and legislative authority in the Russian Empire, and there was no provision in the Fundamental Laws for a separate legislative branch. Now, with the newly elected representatives of the populace about to pour into the capital from all corners of the empire, it had suddenly become imperative to define the emperor's prerogatives in concise terms. Frish summarized their problem nicely: "Until now everything depended on the Tsar personally," he observed. Ministers and State Council members had merely presented projects for his approval, and the powers of the executive were not precisely defined in the law code. Thus, warned Frish, unless it were clearly stated in advance what matters would be the proper concern of the State Duma, it could become a "throttle for the administration." The Fundamental Laws must clarify and strengthen the monarch's rights and make it illegal for the Duma to touch them on its own initiative. However, Frish added, after the Tsar proposed amendments to the Fundamental Laws, the Duma and State Council should have the legal right to sanction them. The administration must not "snatch back rights" granted in the February 20 manifesto, or there would be new disorders, as there had been after the October concessions.[14] Frish's opinions were reflected in the details of the draft project under consideration at the April conference.

In addition to defining the prerogatives of their sovereign, the men assembled at Tsarskoe Selo faced another important decision—should the revised Fundamental Laws be published before the Duma opened? On this point Witte saw no reason for vacillation: ". . . if you permit a review of these laws by the Duma, it will turn itself into a constituent assembly at once." He still held this view when he wrote his memoirs. If these laws had not been issued in advance, he wrote, the Duma would have engaged in "dangerous and futile controversies" about its rights and its relationship to the supreme authority. By assuming the functions of a constituent assembly, it would have provoked the employment of armed force and led to the administration's destruction of the new order. "Would this have been for the best? Perhaps yes, had a Peter the Great appeared. . . ."; since there had been no Peter in sight, promulgation before the opening session appeared the wiser course.[15]

Nicholas shared the view expressed by many of his advisors that his powers must be defined and announced before the new legislature met, and the remarks he addressed to the question reveal that his attitudes and convictions had not markedly changed since the previous summer. His most amazing speech dealt with the wording of article 4, according to which he was the "supreme autocratic power." This clause was the "key issue of the whole project," he insisted, adding that since he had first seen the draft a month ago he had been bothered continuously by the question: "Have I the right before my ancestors to change the limits of the powers which I received from them? This mental struggle continues within me," he lamented, and as the decision became imminent, it was harder to make than it had seemed a month before. Meanwhile "tens" of petitions from "all ends and corners of the Russian lands and from all layers of society" had arrived daily, begging him not to limit his powers, yet at the same time expressing gratitude for the "rights of October." Perhaps this meant he should go no further, that he should "remain autocrat of all the Russias." The monarch pleaded with his listeners to believe him; "if I were convinced that Russia wanted me to abdicate my autocratic rights, I would do so with pleasure for her well being." He realized, he said, that to retain his old title, as worded in article 1 of the old code, could give an "impression of insincerity," could even provoke charges that he had retreated from the promises of October 17. He added, completely unrealistically, that these reproaches should be directed at him personally, and not at the government. He agreed that if the former article remained unchanged, if the words "unlimited autocrat" appeared in the new code, there would of course be attacks from the "so-called educated element, the proletariat, and the third element."[16] However that may be, Nicholas had not, moreover, let the events of 1905 shake his basic assumption: "I am convinced that eighty percent of the Russian populace will be with me, will show me support, and will thank me" for a decision to retain the old title. Thus, the Tsar leaned heavily toward rejecting the draft proposal, and retaining the word "unlimited" in his title. He concluded characteristically that this was a matter for his conscience, which he alone must decide.

This was a bombshell which was too much even for that body of monarchists. Hardly a group noted for their sympathy or understanding of public opinion, virtually all agreed that Nicholas simply could not retain the title of "unlimited autocrat" after he had conceded his subjects the right to elect a legislative assembly. Grand Duke Nicholas told him outright that the October Manifesto had already obliterated the word unlimited, and the Tsar's uncle, Grand Duke Vladimir Alexandrovich seconded him. Count Solskii, Count Witte, the Minister of Justice, the conservative Durnovo, who was also a very intelligent realist, supported their position: as of October 17 and February 20 the unlimited autocracy ceased to exist, Durnovo said flatly. He urged his sovereign to concentrate on preserving essential prerogatives, but to give up his obsolete title. None of these men claimed to like the new order, but unlike Nicholas, they had some grasp of what it meant. "I am not in sympathy with the October 17 Manifesto," State Secretary K. I. Palen remarked, "but it exists. Before then you had an unlimited right to issue laws, but not since the October Manifesto. . . ."

Of all his advisors Nicholas found only two that day who voiced any sympathy with his position. Ivan L. Goremykin, who would replace Witte as Chairman of the Council of Ministers before the Duma opened, spoke right on the heels of his monarch and in a similar vein. If the powers of the executive are limited, eighty percent of the population will be "confused, and many will be displeased," Goremykin suggested. The changes of October affected only the legislative, not the executive branch of the government; the Tsar's power would be limited in "areas of legislation, but in the area of administration it would be unlimited." It was impossible to predict all the angles of executive power, hence it was preferable to leave the Tsar's title untouched.

Not only was Goremykin's argument characteristically vague and unrealistic—obviously if the Tsar shared his legislative powers, this would put limitations on his executive authority—it was not in accord with the October Manifesto. According to the latter, the Duma would have the right to "active participation in supervising the legality of the actions of authorities" appointed by the Tsar. Goremykin found support only from A. S. Stishinskii, State Council member and future Minister of Land Affairs in Goremykin's cabinet. Stishinskii delivered an even vaguer speech than Goremykin, which ended with the following flourish: "I agree with the need to state that the Fundamental Laws will be issued by you [Nicholas] directly. In the concept of supreme power, as defined by article one of the Fundamental Laws, it is impossible to separate autocracy from unlimited."

Following Stishinskii's contribution, the Tsar announced that he would defer his final decision. Finally, during the closing minutes of the last session, in answer to Solskii's request whether he should exclude the word unlimited from the final draft, Nicholas replied simply: "Yes, exclude it." So Article 4 read:

> The All-Russian Emperor possesses the supreme autocratic power. Not only fear and conscience, but God himself, commands obedience to his authority.[17]

The first section of the code spelled out the extensive powers reserved to the Emperor. He alone would be responsible for Russian foreign policy; as Commander-in-Chief of the military, his alone were the decisions of war or peace. In domestic affairs the Tsar had the right to grant amnesties, as well as to declare martial law or emergency situations in local areas.

One of the issues which understandably worried Nicholas was his future control over regulations for the court and the imperial family and its domains. "Their review and change must belong personally to the Emperor," he stressed. In the final draft the historic articles on the succession and the royal family were retained. Article 25 provided for their amendment "personally in accordance with the procedure" established by the Tsar, as long as the changes did not violate the law or call for new expenditures from the treasury.

In the realm of administration the Tsar's powers would be extensive. His was the right to appoint or dismiss his ministers without Duma approval, thus ruling out any hope for a cabinet responsible to the chamber. Article 66 gave the legislature the right to present interpellations to ministers or department heads on matters of alleged violation of the law by them or their subordinates.

Beyond these considerable powers the sovereign could resort to extraordinary rights reserved for the executive under the famous article 87:[18]

> Should extraordinary circumstances demand, when the State Duma is not in session . . . the Council of Ministers may submit a measure directly to the Sovereign Emperor. . . . The validity of such a measure is terminated if the responsible minister . . . fails to introduce appropriate legislation in the State Duma during the first two months of its next session, or if the State Duma or the State Council should refuse to enact it into a law.

The same article specifically excepted the Fundamental Laws, the electoral laws, and the State Council and Duma statutes from this extraordinary procedure.

Even without resorting to his special powers, the Russian executive was certain of considerable direct influence on the legislature.[19] He would convene its sessions annually and determine their length; he could dissolve the Duma, or call for replacement of the elected members of the State Council, before expiration of their five year terms, provided the dissolution decree called for new elections and announced the date that the next legislature would open. The two houses would enjoy equal legislative rights, but no measure could become a law without the Tsar's signature. A measure he refused to sign could not be resubmitted for legislative consideration during the same session.

The Duma would open with considerably less power over the government coffers than its proponents had hoped for. The time and conditions for contracting state loans would be determined at the highest level of government. Neither house could exclude or reduce the sums set for the payment of state debts or other obligations of the state. Revenue for the imperial household, in amounts up to the 1906 budget allotment, were not subject to review by the legislature. Extraordinary credits for wartime needs would be under the control of the sovereign. Because of these and similar exceptions, the so-called "iron-clad" expenditures which were not subject to examination by the legislature, about one-third of the national expenditures, were excluded.[20] The rest of the imperial budget was to be examined by the legislature, but if the appropriations were not approved by a stated deadline, "the budget that had been duly approved in the preceding year" remained in force. A similar measure weakened the Duma's authority over annual recruits; if the requested number were not released by May 1, the services could draft men up to the limit set the year before.

Thus, the Duma would convene with significantly restricted powers over the empire's budget, and could not rely on that traditional weapon of parliaments—power over the purse—to curb or coerce the executive. Since its financial powers and other rights were incorporated into the Fundamental Laws, and could be amended only upon the initiative of the Tsar, the popular assembly would open with its wings clipped short in advance.

During the Tsarskoe Selo conferences Witte regularly

revealed his fear of the future Duma, and his driving aim throughout was to keep the vital interests of the state outside of its halls. The Tsar's rights over the army had to be guarded, "otherwise the Duma might ruin" it, he warned. On a similar note—to let the Duma "get stirred up" over foreign affairs would endanger Russia's international position. As to government loans, it would be a "great calamity" if they went before the Duma. Furthermore, if the popular assembly got control of loans and the budget, political parties could make the executive dependent on the legislature. When he wrote his memoirs, he still defended the Fundamental Laws and the prerogatives they reserved for the monarch. Unlimited autocracy was no longer possible, but these laws had avoided a constitutional struggle which would have led to the final destruction of the Duma and the concessions of October 17. While he criticized the excessive use of article 87 by his successor, he saw the failure in the misuse of the article and not the provision itself. He had defended the prerogatives of his sovereign that April, he stressed, and he would continue to do so until the grave.[21]

A confused, frightened Nicholas could only heartily agree with Witte's motives and hope he would be successful in his efforts. In a January conversation with Kokovtsov, Nicholas had expressed horror that he might even be "deprived of his own powers in order to secure pacification of the country." While he intended to give the Duma legislative rights "within established limits," that did not mean he would grant everything without protest. Suppose the Duma demanded that he be deprived of his "historical authority"—what then? Witte's rival, P. N. Durnovo, shared the sovereign's apprehensions, and throughout the meetings took a strong stand for the Tsar's retention of even more powers. He was disturbed by the "ease with which the Tsar conceded his rights." How characteristic this was of Nicholas, Durnovo observed, comparing him to a man who would give up his last shirt upon request.[22]

While the major portion of the Fundamental Laws dealt with the Tsar's powers and with state institutions, articles

27 to 40 defined the obligations and rights of the Tsar's subjects, rights which could be suspended in localities under martial law or exceptional status, where special laws would apply. Freedom of religion, of occupation, of association, of assembly, of the press and of speech—the traditional civil liberties—were all in the document, although in each case a modifying clause stated that these rights would only be exercised within limitations to be determined by future legislation. As Nicholas's advisors argued over the final wording of these clauses, their fear of the public, which most of them shared, was evident. One senses a much greater anxiety and none of the assurance of the previous July, when the assembled bureaucrats at Peterhof hoped to arrange the right kind of Duma through careful statutes. By April they had abandoned past hopes about influencing the composition or actions of the lower chamber and virtually all of them looked to its arrival with fear, not at all confident that it would help solve the ills of their country. Hence the general consensus at Tsarskoe Selo that many items of vital state interest must be handled outside of the Duma halls.

Aside from that, there were few clear cut positions in the April meeting. Tagantsev pointed this up in his commentary about the argument over the clause on annual recruits for the services. Witte insisted that the monarch must have the right to set the annual number of recruits, while the Tsar's uncle, Grand Duke Vladimir Alexandrovich, a frank opponent of the Duma, disagreed entirely. "As long as there is a Duma," he declared, this must be among its rights. This matter touched the entire population, he argued, expressing the hope that the elected representatives would show some loyalty to their fatherland. Compare these positions of the "creator of the Duma" and an "open defender of the autocracy," Tagantsev queried, and "who were the liberals?"[23] And indeed, in terms of the demands of even the minority right wing of the reform movement, there were none at Tsarskoe Selo that April, or at any of the three previous palace conferences held during 1905-1906.

The discussions at these gatherings reveal much about decision-making under the last Romanov, and about the mentality of Nicholas and many of his chief advisors. The Tsar's role in these debates was very important. He listened carefully, however wearily, to the opinions expressed and accepted a minority or majority view as he chose. Sometimes he included a provision to which he personally objected, if he were persuaded that it was the better choice under the circumstances. He did not often follow the advice of the extreme conservatives, although they did secure some significant changes in the draft proposals, especially at the July conference. In addition, three of the most vocal defenders of the autocratic tradition, I. L. Goremykin, A. S. Stishinskii, and A. A. Shirinskii-Shikhmatov, were about to receive ministerial posts.

Nicholas played a key role in the final decisions on debated points in the statutes. While he frequently vacillated on policy throughout his reign and was the bane of ministers trying to work under him, these meetings show that he had certain underlying convictions about his powers as Tsar to which he clung as tenaciously as possible. Furthermore, after he made concessions, he often tried to renege on them as circumstances changed, because he felt he should not betray these principles. His was essentially a negative role in that he did not support consistent policies which he expected his ministers to carry out. But he was stubborn about the powers inherited from his father, and he retained the deciding vote on issues he judged important. He did not lead, but no policy could go into effect if he chose to oppose it.

These qualities of the last Russian Tsar greatly affected his attitude toward the Duma, both during the period before it met and afterwards. Either he never understood, or he never faced the fact, that once he had promised his subjects a legislative assembly, no matter how restricted its rights, this meant that he must accept a permanent and real limitation on his former status as autocrat, if there was to be any cooperation between executive and legislature. ". . . The reforms announced by Me in the October 17 Manifesto will invariably be achieved, and the rights which I granted equally to all the population are inalienable," Nicholas told a delegation from the Autocratic-Monarchist Party on February 16, 1906. Then in the next breath he assured them that his "autocracy would remain just as it was in the past."[24] While many of the Tsar's advisors had a much more realistic appraisal of the realities of his powers once he had taken this step, virtually all of them agreed that many basic royal prerogatives must be reserved for the Tsar.

The decisions taken at the April Tsarskoe Selo conference, and its three predecessors, were viewed as totally reactionary by the majority of articulate reformers in Nicholas's realm, while the basic changes demanded by the latter were simply inconceivable to the men in the administration. The executive had made the constitutional changes of the period only reluctantly, under force. Yet to their opponents they were a retreat from the principles of the October Manifesto, which had been inadequate enough in itself. This basic conflict of attitudes made the chance for effective compromise and a successful First Duma very slim in advance, regardless of the outcome of the elections.

The multistage elections, the first national popular elections in modern Russian history, did not occur simultaneously throughout the empire. They began in mid-March, but in some of the border regions they would be held only after the chamber convened; some were never held. One thing emerged clearly from the results—the voters expressed their opposition to the old regime by thoroughly trouncing virtually all of the rightist candidates. Beyond this broad statement, the election results cannot be judged as an accurate reflection of the specific preferences or political views of Nicholas's subjects.

Most of the voters, a large percent of whom were illiterate, were totally unfamiliar with election politics. Yet they were suddenly asked to pick electors, often from a bewildering array of choices. Many of these voters had no grasp of, indeed no interest in, the complex issues heatedly discussed by party campaigners. Added to this political inexperience was the pressure of time: the situation called for careful reflection and a weighing of issues. Yet only four months elapsed between the approval of the December electoral law, which modified the August of 1905 electoral statute for the Bulygin Duma, and the opening of the assembly. In that brief period, several stages of elections had to be scheduled.

Before these elections could be held, however, newly eligible names had to be hastily added to the published registers of voters which had been compiled under the Bulygin Law. Once the lists appeared, party election committees frequently challenged the local authorities about omissions, sometimes successfully. Any voter whose name appeared on a register had to appear before election officials to procure the necessary papers. Failure to obtain these papers prevented him from exercising the franchise.[25] Not surprisingly, millions of eligible voters could not vote because they failed to obtain these papers or because their names never appeared on the voter registers.

Many voters also opted not to vote because the two major socialist parties, the Social Democrats and the Social Revolutionaries, both revolutionary groups demanding the overthrow of the Tsar, boycotted the elections. These two Empire-wide parties were supported in their boycott policy by virtually all of the smaller socialist groups, such as the Polish Socialist Party. However, individuals in these parties sometimes stood for election in spite of party policy. In addition, the Mensheviks entered candidates in some races. These exceptions represented a small minority, however, and the boycott policy left the Constitutional Democrats (Kadets) as the only country-wide oppositionist party. The Kadets thus picked up many votes which would undoubtedly have gone to candidates farther to the left. People frequently voted Kadet to register a protest, not because they approved of the party's positions on major issues. Hence Kadet success in the elections was not a true reflection of the group's actual strength.

Drawing the support of a large percent of the educated and most articulate people in the Russian Empire, the

Kadet Party was, moreover, the most effective and best organized of the empire's parties. Kadet ranks included some of the most talented orators and experienced writers in the country. The party organized first in the cities, and it was in urban Russia that it had its greatest election successes. Kadet candidates won all six St. Petersburg Duma seats. In Moscow they gave up one of the four seats to I. V. Savelev, nominee of the workers' *curia*; Kadets held the other three. In eighteen of twenty cities eligible to hold separate urban elections, the Kadets won a majority of the electoral races. Of twenty-eight deputies elected in these cities, twenty-six were candidates supported by the Kadet Party.[26]

In the countryside, where most of the empire's population resided, the Kadets had less support. Vast distances and a poor communications network made an effective campaign throughout rural Russia an impossibility, especially in the short time available. What success the Kadet Party did have with peasants usually occurred at the *guberniia* elections, that final stage in the electoral process where the Duma members were elected. Many peasant electors, who made up a sizeable percent of the total of the *guberniia* electoral assembly, had no specific party affiliation. Frequently, the outcome of the final elections depended on whether Kadets or rightist candidates were able to make a deal with enough peasant electors.

Partly because of bargains with peasants, the Kadets won more seats—roughly a third of the Duma total—than any other party. Another large bloc of seats, just under a fifth of the assembly, went to deputies who listed themselves as "without party." Made up largely of peasants, this non-party Duma bloc cannot be described as representing any one set of opinions. Besides the amorphous non-party bloc, there was another large group of deputies, the Trudoviks, which formed just on the eve of the Duma: hence its members had not run as Trudoviks in the campaign.

Not only did many candidates run for the Duma without any specific party affiliation, many of them had to wage a

campaign in areas where violent agitation had not sub-
sided. It was hardly an atmosphere conducive to orderly,
rational electioneering. There were frequent instances of
the left parties using disruptive tactics to break up campaign meetings, giving the police an excuse to close them.

Shutting down meetings was just one example of administrative interference with the electoral process.[27] Such
interference occurred often. And, while a circular from the
Ministry of the Interior to the *zemskie nachalniki* (the
officials charged with conducting the first stages of the
rural elections) ordered these men to abstain from interference in the elections, at the same time it recommended
that the populace be clearly warned against anti-govern-
ment parties whose bankrupt programs must be exposed.
The same circular requested that "disquieting" orators be
removed from electoral premises. To insure compliance,
the police were usually in attendance at *volost* electoral
meetings, and frequently they kept "undesirable" peasants
out. On the other hand, sometimes it was the village elders
who determined which peasants could exercise their right
to vote. There were many instances when the *zemskie
nachalniki* reserved the right to final approval of the
peasants' representatives before the latter could proceed
to the next stage of the elections.

Government employees could only join the Kadet or other
opposition parties at the risk of losing their jobs. Moreover, local officials frequently prevented these parties from
holding already scheduled meetings and they devised various hindrances to the electoral process. To cite but one
example: In Rostov-on-Don a party had to submit a list
of the audience to the authorities in advance of a meeting;
admission was by ticket only. Moreover, police were then
present to see that forbidden subjects were not discussed.

Given all these circumstances, the election of the First
Duma members cannot be viewed as an accurate reflection
of public opinion in the Tsarist Empire, except in broad
terms. The public spoke out firmly in support of removing
the abuses perpetrated by the old regime. It demanded
reforms which would improve the low economic status of so

many of the Tsar's subjects. In the Empire's borderlands demands for more local control and an end to Russification policies aimed at minority groups were added to the list.

The elections in the borderlands, where the majority of the minority groups were found, presented a very confusing picture. A host of local parties came into existence. In these areas the nationality of a candidate was frequently more important than his political views.[28] In many regions there were several national groups, and frequently no one party could muster enough votes to get its candidates into the assembly. As a result many of these national parties made election bargains, or formed blocs to support particular candidates. The Kadets benefited more from these blocs than any other group.

Of the empire-wide parties standing for election, only the Kadets had a policy on local control and national autonomy which had much appeal for regional groups. Their January, 1906 platform statement represented an effort to steer a compromise course on the touchy matter of autonomy. Professing to bow "neither before the cult of deadly unity and centralism, nor before the pressure of centrifugal elements," the Kadets would leave the problem of establishing autonomous regions to a future assembly. Then these areas could be set up peacefully, by a body elected through universal suffrage. Warning that the "pretensions of separate nationalities" should not be heeded at the expense of "state-wide renovation of Russia on the basis of right and freedom," the Kadet statement mentioned that the Poles should be given the first autonomous region; at the same time the unity of the state must be preserved. Finland was to have its constitution "completely restored." Other autonomous regions, none named specifically, could be set up later.[29] The Kadet's position on autonomy inspired many attacks from the right that the liberal party favored "dismemberment" of the empire.

Armed with this plank and aided by the socialist boycott of the elections, the Kadets garnered considerable support in border areas. The one exception was in the Congress

Kingdom of Poland, where a national middle class party, the Polish National Democrats, led by that talented politician Ramon Dmowskii, presented a very strong rival. Like the Kadets, Dmowskii's party benefited from the socialist boycott. On the other hand, Poles living outside of the Congress Kingdon and most of the other national groups tended to support the Kadets.

According to a February, 1906, decision, Kadets could form electoral blocs with other parties and groups only if the latter favored a "constitutional state structure," which would be established by an assembly elected through universal suffrage. Many such blocs were formed in the borderlands, as in the Ukraine, where the Ukrainian Radical Democrats had a program similar to the Kadets, except that the former came out more strongly for regional autonomy. Several Kadet leaders were also members of the Ukrainian party. The Kadets also were successful with several parties in the Baltic area, those in Lithuania providing the only exception. Estonia's two liberal parties—the Progressives and the Democrats—rendered support in the elections and cooperated with the Kadets in the First Duma. The same was true of their counterparts in Latvia, the Constitutional Democratic Party and the Democratic Party.

The Kadets also gained the backing of some of the Empire's Moslems. In February of 1906 the Moslem leader Joseph Akchurian, who was briefly a member of the Kadet Central Committee, helped work out a compromise between Moslem demands and the Kadet program. Kadet influence with Islamic groups was also aided by the stance of the All-Russian Congress of Representatives of the Mohammedans, which urged the Empire's Moslems to participate in the elections; the Moslem organization generally favored the Kadets.

Many of the Empire's Jews voted for Kadet candidates. Suffering under the constraints of discriminatory statutes, the Jewish population was largely concentrated in the so-called Pale of Settlement, twenty-five designated provinces in Western and Southern Russia. According to law, a Jew had to apply for permission to settle outside of the Pale.

Only members of certain groups, such as merchants who paid a high commercial tax, the highly educated and students, were eligible for moving permits; the latter were also subject to Jewish quota limits in educational institutions. Many Jews looked to the Duma to remove these and other disabilities.

Jews living in the Pale organized several socialist parties. Most important by far was the Jewish Bund. Officially entitled the General Jewish Workers' League of Lithuania, Russia and Poland, the Bund was an autonomous branch of the Empire's Social Democratic movement. Along with the minor Jewish socialist groups, the Bund boycotted the First Duma elections, once again to the benefit of the Kadets, especially since there were no other Jewish groups which put forth their own candidates. The Union of October 17 and parties to the right of that group, some of them openly, anti-Semitic, had little influence with Jewish voters.[30]

The Kadets often received aid from the local branch of the League for the Attainment of Full Rights for the Jewish People of Russia. Founded in Vilna in April of 1905 by a group of some sixty influential Jews of widely varying political views, the Jewish League for the Attainment was not a political party. Its founders adopted the name "league" so as to attract other groups to its support. The Jewish League accepted liberal demands for a constitutional order and an assembly elected by universal, direct, and equal suffrage. It called for the removal of anti-Jewish discriminatory laws and asked for broad autonomy for Jewish communities. At its February, 1906, convention the Jewish League decided to support the First Duma elections and to cooperate at the local level with progressive parties, both by giving support to individual candidates and through forming blocs. Dubbed the "Zhido-masonskaia" (Jew-Mason) party by many of its rightist opponents, the Kadet Party profited from these blocs with Jewish groups, especially in the urban elections. Moreover, the Jewish League sometimes used these blocs to obtain slots for Jewish individuals, either as candidates for the Duma, or as electors.

One of the twelve Jewish members of the Duma, the well-known lawyer, Max Vinaver, was a founder and leader of the Jewish League. Vinaver was a nonreligious Polish Jew who had been kept out of the St. Petersburg bar by quota restrictions; thus he had personal experience with the restrictions against Jews. Vinaver was also a member of the Kadet Party Central Committee and he would become a leading member of the Kadet leadership of the Duma. He represents just one example of a figure who belonged to the Kadet Party as well as to a minority political organization. Such personal links often helped the Kadets with their negotiations to form blocs with various minority groups.

Like the Kadets, some of the rightist parties banded together in blocs to support candidates. Off to a slow start, the joint rightist party campaign to "capture the Duma" did not get underway until January, 1906. In St. Petersburg the unified list of rightist candidates for electoral slots included the name of Dr. Alexander I. Dubrovin, medical doctor turned politician, who was to be the guiding light of the extremist Union of the Russian People. Founded in "Chairman for Life" Dubrovin's apartment in late October of 1906, the Union of the Russian People was by far the most important of the right wing parties. However, neither Dubrovin nor a single one of his fellow rightist candidates found their way into the First Duma, and they did very poorly in the electoral contests.[31]

The combination of all of these factors resulted in Kadet Party victories in many more races than the party leadership had expected. The electorate of the Tsarist Empire had rejected the rightist candidates, and expressed itself as overwhelmingly in favor of reform. Moreover, victory at the polls made the Kadets overconfident about the Duma's chances of pushing the administration for even more concessions than those already obtained.

CHAPTER VI

A New Ministry to Greet the Duma

Just one day before the publication of the revised Fundamental Laws on April 23, 1906, the official daily gazette carried an announcement of Sergei Witte's resignation as head of the Council of Ministers. A few days before the item had appeared in the press, Vladimir Kokovtsov paid a visit to Witte in his living quarters at the Winter Palace, where he found him sorting papers in a disgruntled mood. "You see before you the happiest of mortals," Witte announced to his visitor. To his relief a merciful Tsar had released him from the "prison" in which he had been "languishing," and he would shortly be going abroad to take the cure. He wanted to hear nothing about future events in Russia, and he would leave it to his imagination as to what ensued. "All Russia is one vast madhouse and the renowned intelligentsia is no better than the rest," Witte observed bitterly. The chief minister's claims to be well rid of his trying post had their counterpart in his sovereign's reaction: "I have definitely parted with Count Witte," Nicholas told Kokovtsov, "and we shall never meet again."[1]

Whether his was a forced resignation, or whether Witte expected the Tsar to accept it once he had submitted it, are moot points. There is, however, no question about the mounting animosity between minister and monarch, and according to the account in Witte's memoirs, his job had simply become "unendurable." Furthermore, he felt justified in requesting a release, since he had achieved the major

132

goals he set for himself when he took over. The administration was in tenuous control again, the rioting had largely
been quelled and the troops were back from the Far East.
A revised project for the Fundamental Laws had been
approved, and in addition the chief minister had arranged
for the financial independence of the administration as it
faced the dire prospect of governing with a legislative
assembly.

Even before Witte had taken office in mid-October, high
level negotiations were underway with Parisian and other
financial circles for a large international loan; under Witte,
V. Kokovtsov was appointed as the Russian agent in the
French capital. The end of the Russo-Japanese War had left
the Russian government with an empty treasury and a
disordered financial situation. To complicate matters there
had been a run on gold in the empire, since many Russian
citizens had taken theirs abroad. A February, 1905, short-
term loan from the German banking house of Mendelssohn
fell due in early 1906. Furthermore, the internal disorders
had greatly cut customary revenues, while costs mounted
as the administration inaugurated measures to quell riots,
and paid off demobilized troops. Witte took office determined to rectify this disastrous financial situation before
the Duma convened, and he achieved his aim. In early
April Kokovtsov signed a contract for a 2,250,000,000 franc
loan at six percent from a consortium of French, British,
Austrian, Dutch, and Russian banks. French sources accounted for the largest proportion of the loan and also assumed ultimate responsibility for the Austrian share;
British banks subscribed over one-fourth of the total. Having arranged for an unprecedented sum in a long history of
Russian government borrowing of foreign capital, Witte
could assure his sovereign that he would not be dependent
on the new assembly for funds.[2]

Witte stoutly defended this loan in his memoirs. It was
clear from the start, he wrote, that the first Duma would be
"unbalanced and to some extent vindictive." Furthermore,
had he left the loan arrangements up to the legislative body,
it could not have been achieved as quickly and the banker's

terms would have hardened. Perhaps more to the point, a government without money would have been "deprived of the freedom of movement generally necessary, but especially essential during such unsettled times." A situation would have ensured where the Duma could have used the financial needs of the administration to press for further concessions.[3]

Deep involvement in a wide range of complex and difficult tasks, of which the foreign loan was only the final achievement, had left the harrassed chief minister in terrible physical condition. Tired when he took office, by spring his hands trembled and he was plagued by insomnia. But even a healthy man would have been reluctant to continue under the circumstances. The once powerful advisor to Alexander III found his new sovereign turning more and more to Witte's hated rivals, palace commandant D. F. Trepov and Minister of the Interior P. N. Durnovo, for advice. Witte's associates could report directly to the Tsar, and sometimes decisions were made behind his back. "The unity of the government was purely external," wrote the Minister of War, while cabinet sessions were marked by sharp disputes between Witte and his colleagues, especially Durnovo. The former's insistence that he preside over a unified ministry had come to naught and he chafed under his increasingly difficult post. In sum, he had the responsibility, he took the criticisms, while others had more influence on the Tsar than he.[4]

Witte's complaints about Trepov's influence are supported by Nicholas's late January confession to his mother that Trepov acted in a kind of "secretarial capacity," reading Witte's bulky memoranda and reporting on them "quickly and concisely. . . . This is of course a secret to everyone but ourselves," he assured her.[5] Witte found Trepov's role in the palace a real hindrance, but the reputation the latter gained as the dictator of Russia, or even of St. Petersburg where he was Governor-General from mid-January to mid-October of 1905, must be discounted as part of the revolutionary myth. True, his subsequent appointment in the spring of 1905 as Assistant Minister of the Interior in charge of the imperial police had given Trepov additional powers. This appointment helped to build up an exaggerated notion of the man's position in the empire, but the fact remains that no one was the dictator of Russia in 1905. The constant outbursts and lack of central direction throughout the year bear witness against any such claims.

As to Witte's other leading rival, Nicholas had been increasingly pleased by the always outwardly calm, intelligent and capable, consistent and tough man Witte had selected to head the important Ministry of the Interior. At first only acting head of the department, in January Nicholas had promoted Durnovo to Minister. The Tsar's estimate of Witte on the other hand dropped lower and lower, as the long time mutual animosity between the weak sovereign and his forceful and tempestuous minister grew under the strains of close association during those difficult months. By mid-January the Tsar was referring to Witte as a "chameleon," in whom no one retained any confidence, "except perhaps the Jews abroad." Durnovo, however, was "doing splendid work," he wrote his mother. The rivalry between the two ministers became intense and Witte came ultimately to consider Durnovo's appointment one of the greatest mistakes of his ministry.[6]

Witte's vacillating remarks at the palace conferences provide just one example of the kind of indecision about which the Tsar complained. Witte was distinctly worried and uncertain, he made contradictory remarks, and could not make up his mind about draft projects approved by his ministerial council. Meanwhile Durnovo revealed no such uncertainty and held to a consistent conservative position at these meetings, as he did in the direction of his ministry. Furthermore, Durnovo was much less concerned than his chief about the arbitrary actions the administration used to suppress rebellions. He regularly urged his subordinates to use stern resolute measures at the least sign of insubordination or revolt, warning them that negotiations with rebels could only be a short term palliative leading to greater problems in the future. For instance, in an April telegram to the Governor-General of Kiev he recommended a show of armed force and the destruction of all rioters "without the least lenience." If they resisted, their homes should be burned. Only thus could the authorities stop the willful destruction which threatened the "ruin of all the realm."[7]

While never very optimistic about concessions announced at the height of a revolt, Witte had come only reluctantly to Durnovo's conclusion, held by the latter from the start, that pacification would necessitate very harsh measures. Witte favored the use of speedy courts-martial in an extremely dangerous situation, but throughout their terms in office he urged moderation on Durnovo. Against the Tsar's wishes, Witte defended the use of ordinary courts for the trials of many accused revolutionaries. For rural rebels he favored a simplified court procedure, since there was a shortage of available trained personnel. He resolutely opposed the use of military trials against agrarian rebels and terrorists.[8]

When it came to outbursts which threatened his regime or the lives of his officials, the Tsar's sympathies lay with Durnovo's position. Horrified by the mass rioting described in considerable detail in Durnovo's and Trepov's frequent reports, Nicholas's attention was also drawn to the rising number of terrorist attempts on the lives of police and officials. He sincerely regretted the bloodshed in his empire, but he was also convinced that extreme measures were necessary to restore order. As he put it on the twenty-ninth of December: "Many seditious bands have been dispersed, their homes and property burnt. Terror must be met by terror. Witte sees that now himself." And on a report of an incident in Vladivostok in which 162 "anarchist instigators" caused the burning of warehouses and officers' quarters, Nicholas wrote: "Is it possible that these 162 anarchists will be given a chance to corrupt the army? It follows that they should all hang." In addition, Nicholas frequently found time to review troops back from pacification expeditions or to receive individuals who had played an active role in them. A January 10 breakfast guest was none other than General G. A. Min, whom Nicholas had just promoted for his leadership of the Semenovskii Guard against the Moscow insurrectionists.[9]

Meanwhile it was not only loss of favor with the sovereign and snipings from within court and bureaucratic circles which made life difficult for the head of the government. "For six months," Witte complained in his letter of resignation, "I have been subjected to abuse from all those members of Russian society who can shout or write." Early in 1906, shortly before being appointed editor of the Union of the Russian People's *Russkoe Znamia* (Russian Banner), Paul F. Bulatsel had cautioned Nicholas against Witte: "Sire, do not trust that one whom the Masons have put forward and who relies only on the aliens." Maurice Baring, that competent English observer of events in Russia, recorded a tremendous shift in public opinion about the chief minister between October and May: "At first faults but hinted . . . then impatient questioning; conflicting criticism . . . very soon unanimous blame and venemous vituperation, hatred, and abuse."[10] The attack came from all sides of the political spectrum, in a wide range of publications. There were sardonic barbs from the right in the cleverly named *Vittova Pliaska* (*St. Vitus Dance*). The influential conservative daily, *Novoe Vremia* (*New Times*), once observed sarcastically that Russia had two governments—Witte's and that of Khrustalov-Nosar, chairman of the St. Petersburg Soviet until his arrest in late November of 1905—adding that the big question was who would arrest whom: this "silly joke" still rankled Witte when he wrote his memoirs several years later. Newspaper hawkers one cold December day sought purchasers for a "new financial-political paper" with the cry: Read all about how "Witte dances while Trepov drums."

The left hammered at the chief minister for hindering the revolution, while to many on the right he was a traitor to the monarchy. Participants at the first Congress of Representatives of the Nobles' Associations, representing twenty-nine *guberniia* organizations, expressed views shared by many staunch monarchists: the Tsar had signed the October concessions because of political pressures, when he was under the bad influence of "such a despotic will as that of Count Witte." Rumors spread that the chief minister intended to shove the sovereign aside and assume the presidency of a Russian republic. Moderate liberals were increasingly disillusioned by the repressive measures of the "Witte-Durnovo regime," as the opposition press tended to dub the administration. By the beginning of 1906 all the members of the Central Committee of the Octobrists had a complete lack of faith in the politics of Count Witte; they opted not to work for the fall of his cabinet only because they saw no chance for a progressive replacement from within the bureaucracy.[11]

Six months of hard work and constant abuse left Witte "shattered in body and very nervous," unable to retain the calm he deemed essential for a high official. He poured much of his pent-up bitterness into his April 14 letter of resignation, which he used as a vehicle to air bitter complaints about his post. The chief minister asked for a discharge before the new Duma opened, since he would be hard put to appear in that chamber and defend administration policies, some of which he could not approve. Furthermore, how could he appear before the legislature with Durnovo, whose harsh policies had become unnecessary as the revolts petered out; earlier he too had supported firm measures, Witte hastened to inform his sovereign.

Nicholas accepted his controversial minister's resignation the day after it was written, but he held up the public announcement for a week. However, at the final meeting of the pre-reformed State Council, held on April 17, 1906, the rumor circulated that Witte was on his way out. There was much curiosity as to his replacement and about the fate of the rest of the cabinet. In the event it was almost a clean sweep, except for the Ministers of War and the Navy. The ambitious Durnovo, who had achieved such a favorable position with the Tsar, was "depressed and sad and made no effort to conceal the fact" when his subordinate, V. I. Gurko, saw him three days after the dismissal. Of course it was a "great blow" he told Gurko frankly. The two men proceeded to discuss some unfinished ministry business, when the resilient Durnovo suddenly found a cheerful note in the situation: "Just think of Witte," he exclaimed with animation. "How furious he must be to be dismissed along with me!"[12] With their joint dismissal in 1906 these two able bureaucrats permanently completed their long and important careers in the top echelons of Nicholas's government, although both were to stay on as vocal members of the State Council until their deaths the same year, 1915.

Witte's April, 1906, retirement ended an association between Tsar and minister which had always been strained, and by then it had developed into a real loathing, at least from Nicholas's standpoint. With characteristic modesty, Witte attributed the Tsar's hostile attitude towards him to the Tsar's inability to endure those he considered his mental or moral superiors. Foreign Minister A. Izvolskii's observation that Nicholas recognized Witte's unusual abilities, but did not trust him and found him repellent, receives corroboration from a statement Nicholas made to the British journalist W. T. Stead in September, 1905. Agreeing with Stead that Witte had done well at the Portsmouth negotiations, Nicholas said that Witte was a "very clever man," adding however that he did not find him appealing or congenial.[13]

Witte's consummate ambition, his commanding nature and presence, and his vehemence when making a point embarrassed and irritated his reserved, shy, and hesitant sovereign. The fact that Nicholas had more than once turned to Witte in a difficult situation served only to increase his resentment of his minister. His mixed emotions towards Witte were similar to those of the Dowager-Empress, although she must be judged more a proponent of Witte than her son. "What a man he is!," she exclaimed to W. T. Stead in August of 1905. "When you hear him talk he simply overwhelms you with a sense of how right he is in whatever he is proposing." Begging Stead not to disclose her comments, she concluded that her son's minister was "so clever, it is almost as if he were a devil. . . ."[14]

In the fall of 1905 Nicholas had sought the advice of

Count Witte for the last time. There followed the October concessions, and a gradual decline of the revolts which had brought them about. As Nicholas had time to reflect upon concessions made in haste and so contrary to his deeply held views, he came increasingly to question their wisdom and to resent the man who first recommended them. By the fall of 1906 he would write of Witte in bitter tones: "*As long as I live*, I will never trust that man again with the smallest thing. I had quite enough of last year's experiment. It is still like a nightmare to me." His was a deep resentment that did not abate with the passage of time, partly because as long as Witte remained at all active in politics, the Tsar saw him as a threat. Finally in February, 1915, Nicholas would write to his wife of the "calm in his soul," due he conjectured, to a talk with Our Friend [Rasputin], to a feeling that something good would somehow come of the war, or to reading the notice of Witte's death in a recent paper.[15]

Like his sovereign, Witte looked back on these six months of 1905-06 as a grueling experience; for Witte they had ended in failure and ostracism as well. In the first place neither he nor the Tsar really favored the constitutional changes they had sponsored. Characteristically, in his memoirs Witte staunchly defended most of his actions as top minister, while he tended to place the blame for his shortcomings on outside causes. Long after his retirement, however, he was assailed by grave doubts about the October Manifesto, and shortly before his death he sardonically suggested that his grave be marked by a "simple black cross or pedestal on which should be engraved: 'Count Witte. October 17, 1905.'" "Do you think," he asked a friend, that "such an inscription would be permitted?"[16]

Given the enormity of the task which he undertook, Witte's efforts to restore the authority of the Tsarist regime and break the revolution should be judged as part failure and part success, while most of the events which occurred during his term in office were of course out of his control. First and foremost from his viewpoint, the Romanov Tsar had survived the crisis of 1905, and order, however

tense and precarious, prevailed in Russia when Witte retired. On the other hand his efforts to conciliate the opposition largely failed. By instinct an autocrat and by
experience a bureaucrat, the capable Witte lacked the
ability to become a popular political leader. Furthermore,
he had no effective pro-government party with which he
could work, since all the influential public political figures
in Russia, from liberal to revolutionary, soon lined up
against his administration. Nor did he know how to build up
an alternative public following, if indeed that were possible
given the antibureaucratic sentiment of his day. He offered
posts in his cabinet to selected liberals, but since he could
only make these offers on his, and ultimately Nicholas's
terms, they all refused to serve in his ministry. His attempts
to cultivate the capital press corps, his appeal for the
cooperation of the St. Petersburg workers, whom he had
addressed as "little brothers" (*bratsy*), were equally un-
successful. Since the Tsar was always very skeptical of
these approaches to the public, they did serve, moreover,
to weaken Witte's standing with the monarch.

It must be remembered that Witte took office during a
mass revolt, when concessions that would have been judged
enormous a few years earlier were greeted with suspicion
and contempt. A proponent of rational reform from the
top, who had long seen the need for changes in a newly
emerging industrial state faced with serious problems, he
suddenly found himself a reformer in the midst of chaos.
He pleaded that order must precede reform, but the revolt
broadened and it soon became painfully clear that only
considerable force could break it. Meanwhile a disillusioned Tsar came increasingly under the influence of Witte's
rivals, men who always thought that the excesses of the public must be stopped with force, regardless of the effects on
popular opinion. Witte found himself in the middle—he was
too conciliatory and hesitant to please the Tsar, but too
repressive to satisfy the opposition.

In sum, at the end of Witte's six-month ministry the Tsar
retained his throne, but public confidence in the administration had not been restored. Moreover, the large foreign

loan and the revised version of the Fundamental Laws had increased public skepticism about the intentions of the executive to carry out reforms announced in October. Made public just before the popular assembly convened, these new actions of the administration further enraged the public, and it mounted its attack in the press. Witte left office a disillusioned man, and a disillusioned public had few regrets when it read the news. *Rech* (*Speech*), The Constitutional Democrats' new daily, warned that the retirement of Witte and Durnovo as a "concession to public opinion," would not produce the "intended results." These two men had grown together like Siamese twins, and it was fruitless to attempt to "weaken the national indignation" by replacing them. Moreover, if the intent were to introduce a more reactionary policy, the *Rech* editorialists saw Witte's retirement as equally unnecessary, in view of his past performance.[17]

As Nicholas thought about a successor to the forceful Witte, he sought a man who, as he put it to Kokovtsov, "will not act behind my back, making concessions and agreements to damage my authority"; he would suffer no more "surprises or *fait accomplis*" such as the December electoral law. When his choice fell upon Ivan L. Goremykin, he had selected a man to fit these specifications. The appointment was a shock to almost all of Goremykin's contemporaries, and to a man they would have seconded Witte's reaction to the appointment: given Russia's chaotic condition he told Kokovtsov, bluntly, Ivan Goremykin "is not the one to calm these unruly seas."[18]

Witte and his successor had been rivals since the 1890s when they frequently supported opposite policies—Witte was then Minister of Finance, while Goremykin had served as Minister of the Interior from 1895 to 1899. The latter's April, 1906, appointment as chairman of the Council of Ministers was the climax in a very long and successful bureaucratic career which dated back to 1860. Already sixty-seven when he took the chairmanship, Goremykin himself realized that he lacked the capabilities for such a trying post, and only devoted loyalty to his sovereign prompted him to accept it. Just eight years hence he was to respond to a similar summons and serve Nicholas as chief minister for two additional years: the second time he would compare himself to an old fur coat removed from moth balls because of unexpected bad weather!

Throughout his fifty-six years in the bureaucracy, Goremykin found his loyalty to Nicholas and his wife well rewarded. He was one of a very tiny number of St. Petersburg officials in whom the royal couple put their trust, and, unlike so many of Nicholas' appointees, the 'old man' as Alexandra affectionately referred to him, did not lose that confidence. One of the reasons why Nicholas did not waver in his support of Goremykin was that the latter spoke the language that the imperial couple wanted to hear. At the April Tsarskoe Selo conference he had been one of two who shared Nicholas's doubts about relinquishing his traditional title as unlimited autocrat, insisting that, if the Tsar did so, eighty percent of the population would be "confused."

The other defender of the autocratic title at the April conference was Alexander S. Stishinskii, a member of the State Council, who had been in the conservative bloc at all four palace meetings that year. He was about to join Goremykin's cabinet as head of the very important Ministry of Agriculture,[19] a post to which he brought some previous experience with the Land Affairs Section of the Ministry of the Interior. As Ober-Procurator of the Holy Synod the Tsar selected another man deeply dedicated to the autocratic principle, Prince Alexis A. Shirinskii-Shikhmatov. These rightist appointments worried and infuriated the liberal opposition. "The Duma and Stishinskii . . . and his cohorts are incompatible," read a *Rech* editorial of April 28. A few days earlier a writer on the same paper observed that, upon hearing names like Stishinskii and Shirinskii-Shikhmatov, "before one's eyes immediately rose the image of Pobedonotsev." The similarity also struck Witte, who later remarked that the new chief of the Holy Synod had all the defects of his famous predecessor and none of his abilities or strengths.[20]

Shirinskii-Shikhmatov, Stishinskii, and Goremykin were the three archconservatives in the new cabinet, but according to V. Gurko, who regularly attended council sessions at the request of the chairman, the group contained "no sincere champion of the constitutional regime" except the new foreign minister, A. Izvolskii. Some of the cabinet members were resigned to the new order and hoped to establish a *modus vivendi* with the popular assembly without making "useless concessions," but no one really wanted to work with it. Izvolskii later recorded his reluctance to join such a "strange collection of functionaries," who had no common program or interest except "an antipathy to the new order of things and to the very principle of representative government."[21]

Nicholas played a more direct role in the selection of the Goremykin cabinet than he had when Witte held the top ministerial post. His choice of Peter A. Stolypin, whom Goremykin did not even know, as Minister of the Interior was a surprise to almost everyone including Stolypin, who informed the Tsar frankly that he was too inexperienced for the post. The new Minister of the Interior was little known in capital bureaucratic circles, although his family had some contacts at the court. As governor of Saratov he had certain formal contacts with the Tsar, but of more importance, his firm leadership in that province during the revolts of 1905 had been brought to the attention of the sovereign. In an August 6, 1905, report, D. Trepov attributed the restoration of order in Saratov *guberniia* largely to the "energy, complete efficiency, and entirely sensible actions" of the governor. Trepov testified to Stolypin's great physical courage and his unusual success in speaking before unruly mobs. Heartily supporting Trepov's evaluation of Stolypin's oratorical gifts and commanding presence, S. Kryzhanovskii later referred to Stolypin as a "new heroic type of leader," a "new phenomenon" in the upper bureaucracy.[22] Tall and handsome as well, the capable Stolypin was soon to emerge as the strongest member of Goremykin's cabinet and his eventual replacement as the head of the government.

From the beginning Goremykin adapted a passive attitude towards his new responsibilities, which was in harmony with what his Minister of Finance, Vladimir Kokovtsov, described as his chief's "peculiar theory" about the
role of a minister. In Goremykin's view, since all authority
centered in the Tsar, it was the obligation of the ministers
simply to await and carry out the sovereign's orders,
regardless of personal conviction. A minister might advise
the Tsar against a measure, but the decision was never his
about carrying it out. Furthermore, "any attempt to alter
the imperial view," he told Kokovtsov, "will be quite useless and only dangerous to you." Physically lazy, unflap-
pable, wily, and above all indifferent—as Minister of the
Interior Goremykin's nickname had been "His High Indifference"—the new chief minister's very demeanor suggested that he believed his theory. "It is a trifle" was his
favorite expression. Cabinet meetings under Goremykin
were completely different than under his predecessor, since
he was unruffled throughout and expressed his decisions
so calmly and politely that it was hard to argue with him.
Whenever possible he procrastinated, hoping that matters
would somehow work themselves out if he simply ignored
them.[23]

An informed contemporary described the new head of
the government as "not stupid, honorable, but without
special merits," but his caustic predecessor was less reserved in his judgement. To Witte Goremykin was a "bureaucratic nonentity," only distinguished from thousands
of similar ilk by huge side whiskers which he liked to
stroke slowly. The Tsar, however, looked forward to working with a devoted, cooperative, and placid first minister
after six months of dealing with the excitable and aggressive Witte. And beneath Goremykin's calm exterior, Nicholas knew that there existed an unswerving loyalty to
Romanov traditions, and a determination neither to compromise those traditions nor make a strong effort to adjust
to the new order.

The contrast between the two chief ministers was reflected in their views about executive policies toward the

new Duma. Witte wanted to enlist the assembly's support for a number of administration sponsored reforms. He saw this as a method of keeping the deputies busy on constructive legislation from the start, hoping thereby to divert the chamber from mounting an attack for new concessions. Also, if the administration and assembly could cooperate in a reform program, this should help to restore public confidence in the regime. In accord with this aim, Witte had established a special commission to draw up legislative proposals for the First Duma, and he regularly urged his ministers to work out draft projects in readiness for the Duma opening.

Between late January and early April, five of Witte's ministries brought in proposals for general cabinet consideration; an April 23 summary program, which included detailed draft projects, was considered by the Tsar the day before the Duma opened, but Nicholas did not indicate any reaction to the contents on the copy which he read. The longest sections dealt with the peasants, a group which should be given equal civil, economic and legal rights with all other citizens. In accord with that recommendation was the proposal of the Ministry of Justice for a reformed judicial system which would be uniform throughout the empire for all classes. That ministry also proposed reforms of the regulations concerning civil and criminal responsibility of officials. Along with the separate judiciary, the special officials and administrative system established for the peasants should be abolished. In addition to changing their legal status, the program recommended a change from communal to private ownership of peasant land allotments. Moreover, land purchases through the Peasants' Land Bank should be expanded, and the administration should sponsor migration to underpopulated areas. Some state lands should be granted to very poor peasants.

Witte's program also included a series of measures dealing with fiscal and economic matters. Some of these were of a technical nature, such as a bill about the flax and hemp trade, but others were broader in scope. For instance, the Ministry of Finance proposed an income tax, a new inheritance tax law, and the review of some indirect taxes. The report also stated that work was underway on measures to improve the status of workers such as bills for accident and illness insurance, and the regulation of working hours.

These plans of Witte's were greeted with suspicion by the Constitutional Democratic leadership, flushed with the party's unexpected success in the elections and ready to do battle when the chamber assembled. On April 11, 1906, Kadet party publicist I. V. Gessen warned his readers that the administration merely sought to keep the Duma busy on specific legislation, "some admittedly important," in order to divert it from more basic issues. That same week a *Rech* editorialist accused the executive of seeking to avoid conflicts over fundamental issues by "taking into its hands a detailed definition of those subjects with which the Duma should be concerned."[24]

The Kadet charge that the administration was eager to keep certain issues out of the Duma debates was well founded, but fears that the ministry would attempt to steer the course of the chamber's activity proved groundless, once Goremykin assumed the helm. The new head of the government did not share his predecessor's hope that the executive might direct the assembly along safe productive channels. "The Duma," Goremykin told Kokovtsov, "will do nothing but fight the government and attempt to seize complete power." As he saw it, the outcome hinged simply on the government's ability to be "strong and skillful enough to retain its authority in the midst of all this incredible nonsense." In the meantime Goremykin chose to "face the aggressive public, not with an active, lively opposition, but with a quiet, stubborn, passive resistance." He decided to ignore the Duma, and to establish no communication with its chairman or membership. Since any attempt to work with the assembly would be fruitless and might be viewed as capitulation, it was better to avoid the damage that the regime's reputation might suffer from such an effort. The Witte commission which was working on draft projects for the Duma ceased its activities, and when the assembly opened there were no administration proposals ready for its consideration.[25]

The ceremonial opening of the First Duma was held just

147

ten days after Nicholas asked Goremykin to fill the vacancy left by Witte's resignation. It was not a choice likely to evoke much optimism among the eager delegates as they trickled in from all ends of the vast Russian empire, filled with thoughts about the serious responsibility now theirs. And while several of Goremykin's colleagues were an unknown quantity even to the informed public, Shirinskii-Shikhmatov, Stishinskii, and the chief minister himself were known for their absolutist convictions. Had the delegates been familiar with some of the more obscure men in the cabinet, there would have been additional cause for pessimism. As the newly appointed Finance Minister, Vladimir Kokovtsov, waited to participate in the formal opening of the First Duma, he held a fleeting conversation with the new Comptroller, Peter Schwanebach. The latter confessed to his confusion about the composition of the Goremykin cabinet, in that several of the appointees were "not too tenderly disposed toward the idea of popular representatives and hardly capable of inspiring great confidence" among them. Viewed thus, Kokovtsov replied, "we all belonged to this category from our chairman down."[26] No sooner had he said this, when members of the imperial family began to gather, ready to join the assembled ministers and other bureaucrats for that historic occasion when the Tsar of all the Russias would greet a popularly elected legislature for the first time.

Nicholas decided to hold a formal reception for the Duma only after considerable pressure from his advisors. His original inclination had been to avoid the assembly's opening entirely. Would it not be adequate, he had speculated, merely to invite the legislators to his residence at a later date? Ultimately he opted not to go to the chambers; rather the Duma delegates and the members of the reformed State Council received invitations to attend a ceremony at the Winter Palace before the two houses convened in their respective halls. It was a magnificently staged affair, held in the same decorous room where, eleven years before, Nicholas had warned *zemstvo* members to "forget their vain dreams" about popular participation in the affairs of his administration. On one side of the large hall were the Tsar's relatives, and high military and court personnel in glittering uniforms, their jewel laden ladies in *grande toilette* standing nearby. The imperial regalia had been brought from Moscow for the monarch and his wife. Two velvet ropes formed a long wide corridor, down which the Tsar and his suite would proceed to the ermine draped throne. On the other side of this corridor, opposite the be-medaled display of Romanov splendor, were the members of the new Duma, simply dressed in a wide variety of civilian attire. To Gurko the deputies seemed a "gray, almost rustic group," dressed in "deliberately careless fashion."

As this heterogeneous assemblage stood at mute attention awaiting the entry of the Tsar, the emotional impact was enormous, especially for those close to Nicholas. The great contrast in the appearance of the people ranged on either side of the hall seemed but a reflection of a more basic split: "A heavy silence prevailed," Kryzhanovskii wrote later. "It was evident at once that between the old and the new Russia a bridge could hardly be built." The comments of a leading lady of the court revealed another reaction, shared by many in her class. Tears welled up in her eyes due to a "feeling that something great was crashing—as if all Russian tradition had been annihilated by a single blow." The Tsar's young cousin was struck by the solemn, almost funeral-like atmosphere, which dominated the great throne room; even Nicholas, "ordinarily able to hide his feelings, was sad and nervous." The Empress looked very depressed, and Nicholas's mother's eyes glistened with tears as she listened to her son's brief address. Looking directly ahead, the Tsar began in a voice which wavered at first. He soon had it under control as he got into his talk, tactfully presented and conciliatory in tone, but replete with platitudes. He asked the deputies to "justify the confidence of Tsar and people in worthy fashion," assuring them of his firm resolve to preserve the institutions he had granted. He expressed his certainty that the Duma would help him advance the welfare of the people,

especially the peasants, but he put forth no specific proposals. Thus, none of the measures included in the Witte
program were mentioned. Nicholas stressed the need for
order based on justice, pointing out that freedom alone was
inadequate for the well being of a state. He concluded the
brief address with a prayer that God would help him and
the legislators in their work, so that he would be able to
turn "a strong, prosperous, and enlightened realm" over to
his heir.[27]

The deputies responded to these words with "restrained
applause," while "uniformed old Russia applauded vocifer-
ously," according to Samuel Harper, an American scholar,
who was present in the visitors' gallery that afternoon. The
aloof response still infuriated Nicholas's devoted mother
later that spring: "Those dreadful deputies!," she exclaimed
to a friend. "They closed their mouths while everyone else
shouted 'hurrah.' I saw that full well." Typical of Nicholas
in much of its phraseology, her son's speech contained
neither specific recommendations nor a broad legislative
guide. A *Rech* writer observed that the sovereign had
skillfully avoided all touchy subjects, thus arousing neither
fears or hopes. More regrettable, he had not made a single
effort to meet public opinion, on a day when "even the
smallest step" would have returned "tenfold influence and
sympathy." In short, the speech was in keeping with the
regime's well-known ability to miss opportune moments.[28]

The reception at the Winter Palace was to be the Tsar's
only direct contact with the First State Duma, aside from a
few audiences he would grant to its president. Immediately
after the welcoming ceremony Nicholas and his entourage
left for Peterhof by boat, where they resumed their customary isolated existence. The royal family had refrained
even from attending the opera during the Russo-Japanese
War, and after 1903 the court's annual winter social season
had been cancelled. Subsequently, Nicholas and his wife
turned ever more inward to the tiny palace circle, their attention focused on the Tsarevich's health. Their terrible
grief, once it was certain that the long-awaited heir had inherited the dread hemophilia, combined with their horror at

the events shaking the country, brought the devoted couple much closer together. At Trepov's orders they remained virtually confined to the grounds of carefully guarded palaces in the suburbs of the capital. The Tsar did not travel freely among his subjects after the assassination of his Uncle Sergei in February of 1905, and even a trip to the Winter Palace was a rare event. Nicholas chafed under the restrictions placed upon him by the devoted Trepov: "You see this year I have not been able to go about much and there is nothing I like better. I like travelling," he confided sadly to W. T. Stead in September of 1905.[29]

There was no change in this life style under the new system. Nicholas's ministers and other advisors, virtually to a man from the old bureaucracy and many of them the same individuals, still came regularly to meet with him in his residence. Reading through their long and tedious reports still occupied a good part of each working day. As to the new Duma's leadership, it did not take its place within this governing circle. Nicholas and his new chief minister, Ivan L. Goremykin, chose instead to ignore the Duma, and they made no attempt even to become acquainted with influential Duma figures, much less to work with them. In fact, ten years were to pass between the reception for the First State Duma at the Winter Palace on April 27, 1906, and the Tsar's first and only visit to the lower chamber on February 16, 1916.

CHAPTER VII

There Were Few Government
Supporters in the Duma

Upon leaving the Winter Palace the deputies could either travel by carriage or take a steamboat up the Neva River to the Tauride Palace, the building assigned to the Duma for its sessions. A stately neoclassic structure erected by Catherine the Great for her favorite, Gregory Potemkin, "Prince of the Tauride," the palace had stood almost totally abandoned for half a century. Along both routes between the two palaces, the new legislators were to pass excited throngs, which had come out into the bright spring sunshine to view them. People lined the bridges, streets, and river banks, while at two points along the Neva, prison inmates waved white handkerchiefs from cell windows and called to the deputies sailing past below. The street crowds took up their cry and the demand for an amnesty filled the air. Thus, the people's elect entered the assembly chambers with this din still in their ears and the white flags of the incarcerated still waving before their eyes. The electric atmosphere generated by the crowds "penetrated into the hearts of the deputies," and once inside the Tauride Palace, "usually calm people ran about and gestured" dramatically. "We could not but feel," wrote one deputy, that those who had "paid with their freedom in the cause of freedom" must be pardoned soon.[1]

While Duma strategists could not have predicted the heady street scene which continued to the very doors of the Tauride Palace, the best method of handling the emotion-charged amnesty issue had been among their major considerations at pre-Duma conferences.[2] The partial amnesty of November, 1905, had satisfied few critics of the regime, and the large number of arrests since then had refilled the empire's prisons to record highs. The matter of emptying these jails of their political prisoners was bound to come up early in the First Duma sessions, and, regardless of the anticipated virtual unanimity of the deputies on the issue, a very touchy situation between assembly and executive was likely to follow. According to the Fundamental Laws, amnesty was the prerogative of the monarch, and any remote hopes that Nicholas might select the occasion of the Duma opening to announce an amnesty had disappeared that afternoon. Since Duma strategists had not considered such a gesture likely, they had made advance plans to include an amnesty appeal in the Duma reply to the Tsar's speech. Framing this reply, which was to be a summary of the Duma program demands, would be the major item on the lower chamber's agenda as soon as it organized for business.

Meanwhile, this delayed action could not satisfy the demands of the emotional deputies gathered together for the opening meeting of their popular assembly. Worried party leaders, hoping to avert a direct clash with the executive right at the start, thereupon sought an expedient which would play to the pressing crowds without infringing upon the monarch's prerogatives or violating rules already set up for the lower chamber. For instance, an *ukaz* of September 18, 1905, had provided that the only general action to be taken by the Duma at its initial session was the election of a president. Thus, it could not legally deal with the amnesty issue that day, even after his election.

In accord with the *ukaz*, the Duma's first official act was the choice, by virtually unanimous ballot, of Sergei A. Muromtsev to preside over its meetings. The aloof and dignified Muromtsev was a well-known Moscow lawyer, who had long taken an active part in public affairs, both as chairman of the Moscow Society of Jurisprudence and in the *zemstvo* movement. An authority on Roman law, he had been deprived of his professorship at the University of

Moscow in the 1880s because of his open opposition to government encroachments on university autonomy. He had been a member of the Central Committee of the Constitutional Democratic Party since its origin, but he was not one of the party's leading policy makers.

In accord with a hastily conceived plan, before Muromtsev delivered his acceptance speech, he gave the floor to Ivan I. Petrunkevich of Tver *guberniia*. This dedicated *zemstvo* worker and veteran of the liberation movement was the oldest member of the Duma, and he had long held the deep respect of all who sought liberal constitutional reform in Russia. In a brief and moving address, which was interrupted twice by loud applause, Petrunkevich called it appropriate that the Duma's "first free words be dedicated unanimously to those who had sacrificed their freedom" to reform their beloved country. There must be no more such sacrifices, nor could the Duma forget the "thousands of hands stretched out with hopes and prayers" from prison cells. But—and he urged patience upon his fellow deputies—the opening session was not the time for the entire assembly even to discuss the amnesty issue, much less put the house to a vote on it. Rather, the matter should come up during the debate over the reply to Nicholas's speech. In the meantime, however, unable to restrain the "cry of his heart," Petrunkevich had decided to speak to the issue as an individual: "free Russia demands the freedom of all the suffering" and he could not let their cause go unmentioned that day. His audience gave vent to their feelings with heavy applause, but they deferred to his advice and the Duma did not go on record in favor of an amnesty demand. Their emotions had been satisfied, and legality preserved. As the applause died down after Petrunkevich's speech, Muromtsev rose and gave an equally short acceptance speech, after which the chamber adjourned until two days hence.

The drama at the opening meeting of the First State Duma was an augury for much of what was to occur during the short life of that tumultous body. In addition, the decision to let Petrunkevich speak about amnesty as an individual,

and so avoid house action that would give the administration a valid excuse for dissolution, reflected what was
to be the strategy of the Kadet Duma leaders, as long as
they were able to manage the unruly chamber. It would,
however, prove a never ending struggle to stay within the
legal limits imposed upon the Duma, and at the same time
to satisfy the demands of overconfident deputies, who
hoped to inaugurate instant reforms in order to satisfy
the needs of an angry populace. The bulk of these fledgling legislators, not to speak of their constituents, understood nothing of the intricacies of parliamentary procedure,
or of the options actually available to the chamber as it
confronted the administration.

Who were these eager and overoptimistic delegates who
had assembled at the Tauride Palace on April 27, 1906?
To some western observers they presented a fascinating
and colorful microcosm of the diversified Russian empire.
Maurice Baring was struck by the very visual impact of the
lower chamber each time he reentered the Duma hall. Before his eyes was a handsome white room filled with
milling deputies in almost every conceivable type of
headdress and clothing, except uniforms—peasants in high
boots and baggy, rumpled pants, full-bearded Orthodox
priests in clerical garb, frock-coated city gentlemen, Poles
in brilliant costume including a purple-robed bishop, and
long haired young men in informal attire. If many of the
deputies felt out of place in these unfamiliar and magnificent surroundings, "haunted by so many memories of other
days," their western observers did not notice. The room
in which the lower house held its general sessions had
once enclosed a huge indoor garden, and it adjoined a lobby, itself the size of a gigantic ballroom. Making allow-
ances for his buoyant enthusiasm, a description by B.
Pares conveys much of the Duma atmosphere:

> The beautiful hall soon came to be regarded, even by
> the peasant members, as a kind of home. The long side
> lobbies were furnished with great tables covered with
> green baize at which peasants and Intelligents sat down

indiscriminately to write letters to their families. A constant stream of members was always passing through these rooms; and all congregated from time to time in the great noisy corridor. Here the chief leaders walked up and down arm in arm; and isolated peasants, Russian, Cossack, or Polish, sat about on the different benches and were quite ready to converse with any stranger. Members and correspondents gathered without distinction at the buffet and in the restaurant, and little groups of acquaintances wandered through the pleasant gardens outside. The building contained its own postal and telegraph office. If the Duma did nothing else, it brought together for the first time representatives of every class and of every interest in Russia. It was of course far more Imperial than any other European Parliament. It would be difficult to imagine a more picturesque gathering.

Pares' enthusiasm was not shared by S. Kryzhanovskii, who had frequent occasion to pass through the Tauride corridors and gardens that spring. Nicholas's loyal bureaucrat found it repellent just to be among that "motley crowd of deputies"—many of them unshaven and "even unwashed" —who purported to represent the Tsar's subjects. If they were truly a representative sample, Russia's only hope lay in enlightened absolutism. Why, they were a "gathering of savages!," he exclaimed in his memoirs; it was as if the Russian lands had sent everyone to St. Petersburg who was "uncivilized and full of hatred and spite."[3]

Any analysis of the political composition of this polyglot assembly must be approximate, since party tallies shifted constantly throughout the sessions.[4] Furthermore, owing to the nonsimultaneous scheduling of the elections, some of which were yet to be held when the Duma opened, the total continued to rise as delegates trickled in from the border regions. Among the last were those from the Caucasus and Central Asia who arrived only in mid-June. The 436 nominating ballots cast for Duma president at the opening meeting were almost one hundred short of the allotted total of 524 deputies. Actually the First Duma never reached that figure: a few deputies simply never showed up in the capital, while nine peasant deputies from Tambov *guberniia* had their elections declared irregular. As of the twentieth of June an official tally listed 476 members, and there were just under 500 at the time of dismissal. Even at that late date, some twenty of the deputies allotted to the Caucasus, Siberia, or Central Asia had not yet been elected.

Not only do party rosters vary with the date of the estimate, the figures also differ from one source to another. However, every student of the Duma has assigned the highest number of deputies, although never an absolute majority, to the Constitutional Democrats, commonly known as Kadets from their party's Russian initials. The party had run candidates in the 1906 elections under a new name, *Partiia Narodnoi Svobody* (Party of National Freedom), but it never caught on. Membership in the party's Duma faction was in a state of constant flux between an estimated 140 in late April and 175 at the time the sessions ended.

The Kadets wanted to change the Russian autocracy into a constitutional parliamentary monarchy something like the British model. They believed that the administration must be responsible to an elected legislature, which would also have effective power over the national budget and expenditures. The assembly should be elected by universal, direct, and secret ballot. The Constitutional Democrats stood for the traditional civil rights, guarded by an independent court system. All would be equal before the law and all legal restrictions based on nationality, class, or religion must be removed. There should be no creed enjoying special state protection. The arbitrary actions of the Tsarist regime and its frequent violations of the judicial rights of its citizens must cease. There were to be no extraordinary courts and the death penalty should be unconditionally abolished. Such were the basic beliefs of this largest parliamentary faction.

The Kadets were much less opposed to government intervention in the economy than their liberal counterparts in the west. Their platform stressed the importance of government measures to improve the stagnant rural economy including, where necessary, the increase of the acreage under peasant control through confiscation of private, imperial family, and government-owned lands. Private owners would be paid a just compensation, and all expropriated acreage should be transferred to a state land fund for future distribution. The party favored progressive income and inheritance taxes, and the gradual lowering of indirect taxes. Workers should have the right to organize, assemble, and strike; the eight-hour day was to be the eventual norm for all enterprises, and where feasible it should be introduced immediately.

Kadet success in the 1906 elections was partly the result of more effective party organization and leadership than that of their rivals, qualities which would also enable the party to assume the leadership of the Duma. In addition, their candidates were the most vocal proponents of radical reforms since their socialist competitors, the agrarian oriented Social Revolutionaries and the Marxist Social Democrats, had both adopted official positions against participation in any stage of the elections. A few of their members got into the Duma, however, since local party units did not always adhere to the boycott decision. Then, at the April, 1906, Stockholm conference, to the dismay of many Bolsheviks, the Menshevik majority had rejected the Social Democrats' previous decision to boycott the First Duma elections. The policy reversal took place before all the elections had been held in the borderlands, and Social Democratic candidates were especially successful in the Caucasus.

These late arrivals to the First Duma soon formed the nucleus of a Social Democratic Duma fraction. Formed in mid-June by the Georgian deputies, the new fraction was joined by a few other leftists, including part of a fifteen member "workers' group" which then dispersed. Once it was organized, the eighteen-man Social Democratic fraction made it increasingly difficult for the Kadet leadership to control the lower house. These leftists viewed the Duma purely as a tribune from which to further the socialist revolution, and they hoped to use the conflicts between administration and assembly to broaden and deepen the revolutionary mood in the country. In favor of a republic, they rejected the Kadet position that effective change could be accomplished under a constitutional monarchy. The fraction provided the Kadets with the only well-organized leftist opposition in the First Duma.

In its short life, the Social Democratic fraction failed, however, to enlist most of the left members of the First Duma into its ranks. A few days before the Duma had convened, several intellectuals of peasant origin had formed about 125 deputies, mostly peasants, into a loosely organized group called the Trudoviks. To the left of the Kadet majority, the Trudoviks remained the second largest group in the chamber throughout the sessions, although they could never be certain of their membership total. The Trudoviks had no party discipline or consistent ideology. They had only a project of a platform and were not a true political party; they had no organization beyond their Duma group. Their ranks included a few members of leftist parties, but mostly it was made up of peasants who had no commitment to any particular party.

The Trudoviks should be considered to the left of the Kadets, not so much because they supported more radical positions, but because of their attitude towards their functions as Duma deputies. They were to resort to very extreme language and tactics in their attacks on the administration, and they were much less concerned than the Kadets about parliamentary procedure or overstepping the legal rights of the chamber. As the second largest group in the Duma, the Trudovik votes were important to the Kadets as they attempted to steer their programs through the house.

Thus, about three-fifths of the Duma belonged to the Kadet majority or to the two main groups to their left—the Trudoviks and the Social Democrats. Many deputies never joined any fraction at all, while only a very small percent of the chamber sat to the right of the Kadets. The extreme right parties had won no seats in the elections. Of about forty or fifty right deputies, the largest number, about twenty, belonged to the Union of October 17, while about twelve were members of small splinter groups such as the Party of Democratic Reform. The Octobrist Party had been formed after Nicholas issued the October Manifesto, and its members were dedicated to supporting the concessions in that document as the basis for a reformed autocracy. The party Duma fraction lacked discipline and organization. Made up as it was of persons strongly devoted to the freedom of the individual, some of whom were highly respected members of the liberation movement, in the First Duma they were united, not by program goals, but by a desire to restrain the excesses heard from the tribune. Many a heated session was marked by an eloquent speech from one of the moderate right deputies, urging his fellows to remain within the legal limits set on their chamber. In spite of the enormous personal respect several of them commanded, they never mustered much support for their recommendations. Izvolskii recalled their aptly being referred to as a "general staff without any troops."[5] With very few exceptions, even these right members of the First Duma favored broad reform programs and objected to the arbitrary abuses of justice perpetrated by the administration. However, they were frequently at odds with the Duma majority over tactics chosen to discredit the regime.

In addition to these major fractions, each loosely organized on the basis of a program or tactics, there were several Duma groups which united on nationality lines. Proponents of more local autonomy for non-Russian areas of the empire, some of the deputies in these groups also banded together into a larger organization called the Union of Autonomists.[6] Formed shortly after the Duma convened, the Union of Autonomists's only membership requirement was that a deputy favor regional autonomy and equality for all nationalities in the empire. The Autonomists's program of May 11, 1906, stressed the indivisibility of the empire, but called for a change to a decentralized state, administered on democratic principles, which gave broad autonomy to individual regions. A system of democratic local self-government, to be decided upon by the populations involved, should be established in each of these regions. Recognizing that many areas of the Russian Empire had a mixed ethnic composition, the Autonomists stated that the rights of minorities must be guaranteed in each autonomous unit. This should include the right to use native local languages in schools, the press, and all public and government institutions. There must, moreover, be an immediate guarantee of the right to cultural and national self-determination for all citizens. Special privileges given to any religion or nationality must be eliminated.

Thus, the program of the Autonomists would remove the legalized discriminations levied upon citizens of the Tsarist Empire who were not Russian or who professed a faith other than Russian Orthodoxy. These discriminations were among the major causes of the revolution of 1905, and revolts in the borderlands, where the national minorities were largely concentrated, were especially intense. Not surprisingly, many of the deputies from these areas came to the First Duma determined to abolish these discriminations, an aim they shared with many of the Russians in the chamber. Tired of abuses from non-native officials, they wanted to be governed by people of their own nationalities in local autonomous units. Some of these deputies joined the Union of Autonomists to help them achieve these aims, although there were many Duma deputies belonging to an ethnic minority who joined neither a nationality group or the Autonomists.

A deputy who belonged to the Union of Autonomists could simultaneously be a member both of a minority Duma group and of an empire wide party's Duma fraction. The affiliations of the Union's officers reflected its joint party membership and its ethnic variety, as well as its close ties with the Kadets. Chairman Alexander R. Lednitskii, lawyer, Polish patriot, and a deputy from Minsk *guberniia*, was an important figure in the Kadet Duma fraction. The fact that Lednitskii, a Pole, won his seat in a Belorussian *guberniia* is evidence of the mixed ethnic groupings common to the northwestern regions of the empire. The Union had two vice-chairmen, Ilia L. Shrag of Chernigov and Ali M. Topchibashi, both of whom belonged to the Kadets. In addition they each led a minority group in the Duma. Shrag was the chairman of the Ukrainians' organization, frequently listed on Duma rosters as part of a larger unit, the Groups from the Western Regions; the latter included deputies of Polish, Ukrainian, or Belorussian origin. Ali M. Topchibashi, nobleman, lawyer, and a Baku oil industrialist, headed the twenty-eight-member Moslem group, the second largest of the minority organizations in the First Duma. Made up of Moslems from such widely separated geographic areas as Kazakhstan and the Caucasus, these men wanted full autonomy for Moslems in religious affairs and in communal administration; like the Ukrainians, they wanted the right to use their native languages in schools and other public organizations. However, only a few of Topchibashi's fellow Moslem deputies joined the Autonomists. In addition to the Moslem from Baku, the Caucasus had another representative in the leadership of the Autonomists: the secretary, Prince V. I. Gelovani, was a Georgian, and like the other Union officers, a member of the Kadet Party.

In addition to the Moslems, the First Duma had several members of another non-Christian faith who hoped to use the chamber to end their inferior legal position in the empire. The twelve Jewish deputies, all of whom were either doctors or lawyers, did not constitute a formal fraction, but they met together to discuss tactics. They were widely divided on the matter of Jewish nationalism, from the influential Kadet, Max Vinaver, who opposed all manifestations of it, to five Zionists who wanted to fight for civil rights for Jews, as well as their recognition as a distinct nationality. As a compromise between these extremes, the Jewish deputies agreed not to deliver speeches on the Jewish issue without first clearing them with the Central Bureau of the Jewish League, of which Vinaver was chairman and all twelve were members. Nine of the Jewish deputies joined the Kadets and three belonged to the Trudoviks.

The largest concentration of Jews in the Russian Empire lived in the so-called Congress Kingdom of Poland, a region referred to in the 1906 Fundamental Laws as the Vistula Region (Privislianskii krai). However, not a single Jew won a deputy election in that area, in part because of the effective campaign and organization of the Polish National Democrats. That party sent thirty-three deputies to the First Duma where they united into the most influential of the national organizations in the Autonomists, the tightly knit and disciplined Polish Kolo (circle). Its members objected to the recent change in their homeland's historic title, as well as to the centralized administrative system and the Russification policies of the Tsarist government. The Kolo favored autonomy for Congress Poland, but not for areas of former Polish territory, such as Lithuania or the Ukraine. There was considerable friction between deputies from the western borderlands and the members of the Kolo, and the Poles representing those areas remained out of that organization.

The deputies from the western borderlands also frequently disagreed over the complex issue of deciding on the boundaries of autonomous units. Many of the Belorussians demanded autonomy for a "Northwestern Region," but since the territory they hoped to unite contained some Lithuanian areas, their plan clashed with demands of the Lithuanian deputies for their own separate region.

The conflict of interest among many of its members was just one of the factors that weakened the effectiveness and unity of the Union of Autonomists. Many Autonomists divided their loyalty between their own national groups, the empire wide parties, and the Union. Furthermore, a sizeable number of deputies of minority background did not belong to the Autonomists, or give them support. For instance, some peasants of Ukrainian and Belorussian origin joined the Trudoviks, where they could concentrate their energy on peasant grievances. The Trudoviks worked hard to enlist peasants of minority origin into their ranks, urging them not to join bourgeois national parties and thus sell out their class interests. There were, however, cases of peasants, especially Ukrainians, who joined the Trudoviks and a minority group simultaneously.

More than 210—less than half of the total—of the delegates to the First Duma were of non-Russian origin, according to figures found in Michael Voskobiynyk's recent study. Yet non-Russians made up more than fifty-five percent of the population of the Empire. Elected largely in the borderlands, these non-Russian deputies also included a sprinkling who were elected in Russian *guberniias*. Virtually all of them belonged to the opposition and gave their support to Kadet efforts to use the Duma to push the administration for more concessions. However, the minority deputies also had their own unique demands and they formed the Union of Autonomists to strengthen their bargaining position.

Due to the short life of the First Duma, the Autonomists did not get a draft bill proposing regional autonomy onto the Duma agenda; however, the matter was slated to come up for fraction discussion on the day before the Tsar dissolved the chamber. Meanwhile, throughout the sessions the minority deputies had used discussions on the assembly floor to air their special complaints about the administration of the empire, sometimes to the dismay of the Duma leadership. It seemed to the First Duma's secretary, Prince D. I. Shakhovskoi, that, besides matters of empire wide interest and "even dominating over them," came the concerns of the nationalities, concerns which frequently took "possession of men's minds."[7] Nor did urgings from the Kadets that the Duma concentrate on reforms of empire wide interest, which would equally benefit the minorities, deter the latter from also pursuing their own separate goals.

When the First Duma convened on the twenty-seventh of April, 1906, a large share of its members were not yet committed to any of these groups, and a sizeable percent of the total membership remained outside of them until the end. About a hundred deputies, mainly peasants, even referred to themselves as *bezpartii* (without party), and an estimate of the *bezpartii* total appears on the lists of all Duma analysts. Efforts to enlist the support of these non-committed deputies, either to a group, or for specific measures as they came before the house, occupied much of the time of the fraction leaders. The peasants remained especially elusive, and, even if one did consent to join a fraction, his allegiance was far from certain. There were some two hundred peasants in all, about half of whom joined the Trudoviks. Many of them proved to be very articulate, if windy, spokesmen for rural Russia. They came to the capital determined to put forth the demands of their constituents for more land, and for a chance to lift themselves and their children out of poverty and ignorance. They arrived with high expectations and little comprehension of the complicated task before them, with only vague notions about the nature, or the powers, of the body to which they had been elected: B. Pares observed, for example, that many peasants fully expected that the Tsar himself would be a member of the popular assembly![8]

It was the job of the Kadets to try to unify this diverse and unexperienced assembly in support of their program. By virtue of numbers, but even more of ability, the Kadets were the strongest group in the First Duma. Their ranks included many landowners with considerable experience in the *zemstvo* movement, as well as a large percent of the empire's professional and technical people; since some of these professional men were also landowners with *zemstvo* ties, the two groups were not mutually exclusive.[9] After the Duma opened, the Kadets picked up perhaps forty non-committed deputies, some of whom were peasants, but the party never won the allegiance of many businessmen or workers.

With only a little over a third of the Duma total, the Kadets soon had a near monopoly of the responsible positions in the chamber, a dominance achieved mainly through bargains with the leaders of the second largest group, the Trudoviks. The two groups had formed a coalition at a joint party caucus held a few days before the Duma opening. It was the aim of this so-called "united opposition" to cooperate in the assembly in order to force more concessions from the monarch. On paper the coalition was certain of a majority in the chamber, but the outcome of any vote was always in question, given the dubious loyalty of so many of the coalition's adherents.

Furthermore, the coalition itself was far from solid. If accord on Duma policy was difficult among the Kadets, Miliukov reminisced, it was "simply impossible" in the First Duma.[10] It became a constant struggle to maintain the support of the Trudovik leaders. They had to be consulted regularly lest they bolt at the time of a vote, and frequently it took enormous persuasion to prevent their sponsoring a rash measure, likely to provide a perfect reason for dissolution. In spite of these many built-in handicaps, the Kadets managed to keep the coalition functioning for much of the life of the First Duma. In part a result of the Kadets' skill on and off of the floor, their success in crucial votes was also a reflection of the broad underlying unity of the chamber in its desire for basic change and in its opposition to the administration.

It was the leaders of the Kadet-Trudovik coalition who had decided on the candidacy of S. Muromtsev for assembly president. Two days later they had met again and chosen candidates for the two vice-presidential posts. The nominees, both Kadets, won with substantial majorities in the house, while the post of Duma secretary also went to a Kadet. It was only at the rank of assistant secretary that members of other groups held office. Of five assistant secretaries, there were two Kadets, two Trudoviks, and one deputy from the Polish Kolo.

In terms of their percent of the Duma membership, the Kadets were also overrepresented on all the important committees, especially the standing committees. They played a major role in all phases of Duma activity and the five most powerful men in the Duma—Feodor Kokoshkin, Vladimir Nabokov, Ivan Petrunkevich, Feodor Rodichev, and Max Vinaver—were all Kadets. These five were active on all of the key committees, and they played a significant role in drafting Kadet proposals and piloting them on the floor. Frequently one of the five made that all-important speech ending a deadlock or avoiding a precipitous action by the chamber.

There was another man whose name would have headed the list of influential Kadet deputies, had he not been under litigation for a press offense—permitting a Kadet paper to publish the revolutionary December 2 manifesto calling for a financial boycott of the administration—and hence ineligible to sit in the Duma. As a member of the Kadet Central Committee, Paul Miliukov was, however, able to take an active part in the work of the party Duma fraction from the Duma corridors. He was a familiar sight as he sat entrenched at a table in the Tauride Palace buffet holding conferences, making on-the-spot decisions, and buttoning-up potential voters. He could observe events on the floor either from the visitors' gallery or from the press box just to the left of the speaker's platform. From the latter spot Miliukov was able to make direct contact with the deputies on the floor.[11]

Both Izvolskii and Kryzhanovskii remarked that the powerful Kadet was more dangerous and troublesome from the lobby than he could have been, had he occupied a deputy's seat. Actually, from the standpoint of the Tsar and his advisors, Miliukov was but one of many troublemakers, and from the start to finish most of the administration viewed the First Duma as one huge disaster. Even Izvolskii, perhaps the least opposed to parliamentary government of Goremykin's cabinet, described the composition of the lower house as "disconcerting," dominated as it was by the "compact and strongly organized" Kadets with their "pronounced radical tendencies."[12]

Nicholas had been worried about the composition of the First Duma even before he learned the outcome of the elections. In early January he told Kokovtsov that the December liberalization of the Bulygin electoral law caused him the "gravest apprehensions," and by mid-April, as the returns began to come in, he was clearly upset. As he explored the reasons for the disturbing election results in a letter to Witte, Nicholas found one major cause in the "excessive liberalization" of the franchise. That electoral law, combined with the inertness of the "conservative mass" of the populace, and the dismal failure of the government to intervene effectively in the elections, accounted for the success of the opposition at the polls. As Witte pointed out in his memoirs, the latter complaint was hardly just, since a circular of late September, 1905, had committed the bureaucracy to a policy of permitting free elections.[13]

Actually, neither Nicholas or his chief minister had any notion how to sway the public successfully in an election campaign, and the only kind of influence within their capabilities was essentially negative, such as the harrassment of the opposition. There had been many violations of the policy of noninterference in the elections, and, all professions in his memoirs to the contrary, Witte had himself engaged in some of that activity. To cite but one instance; in February of 1906 Miliukov headed a Kadet delegation which complained to St. Petersburg prefect V. von der Launitz about the endless difficulties faced by the Kadets during the campaign. The prefect replied that Witte had instructed officials to make life difficult for the Kadets, because they "engage in too much self-advertising," and it was hard to tell when the Kadets left off and revolution began.[14] These efforts to hamper the campaign of the opposition failed in their ultimate aim, and in spite of, or perhaps partly because of, considerable harrassment, critics of the regime won virtually all of the seats in the First Duma.

The outcome of the elections and the antiadministration tone which dominated the assembly proceedings from the first day only served to reinforce many of Nicholas's convictions about public opinion and constitutional government. These ideas made it very difficult for the Tsar to adjust to his new role of governing with an elected assembly, and they left him very uncertain as to the best method for dealing with this strange new phenomenon in his realm. There was nothing in his background or experiences to assist him. Steeped from childhood in the traditions of the Russian autocracy, and convinced that any tampering with that system was undesirable for the welfare of his country, Nicholas was not mentally prepared to become a constitutional monarch. He had no personal acquaintance with the trappings of elections or with campaign propaganda. The very thought of becoming involved in such activities, or in mounting some kind of campaign to win over the public was incomprehensible, even abhorrent, to the Tsar. In the past, when Witte had made references to public opinion in the Tsar's presence, Nicholas had often angrily asked what concern it was of his.[15] To the Tsar public opinion represented merely the views of the intelligentsia, which were unworthy of serious consideration, since the bulk of the populace was loyal to the regime and unaffected by such ideas. After he had promised his subjects an elected assembly, there was no marked change in his stance toward the public. Nicholas never made a concerted effort to build up a following from among the populace, and even the manifestos from the throne continued to come out in their familiar archaic phraseology.

On the other hand Nicholas did not assume the pose of a mediator, who chose to remain above the political arena. Rather he remained a very important factor in decision-making in his administration. As of 1906, he and his advisors could no longer govern Russia without paying some heed to the new legislative assembly which had been granted so reluctantly. However, the Tsar never accepted the kind of political activity and organizations which were an essential aspect of successful representative government. Nicholas despised the radical parties, but he was almost equally suspicious of the Octobrists, in spite of the fact that their entire appeal rested on the renovation of the monarchy in accord with his October Manifesto.[16] He was simply unable to approve the kind of renovations which they deemed necessary.

Nicholas's attitude toward Russia's political parties was reflected in the curious and tenuous legal position under which they had to function. A Senate *ukaz* of March 4, 1906, required all associations to register their statutes with the authorities, who then had the option of granting or refusing the organization the privilege of legal, or, as it was termed, "registered" status. The registration of an organization which later deviated from its statutes, or appeared to be a threat to the social order or the safety of the regime, could be revoked.[17] The administration used this *ukaz* to deny legal status to all the mass opposition parties in the nation; only the Union of October 17, the small Party of Peaceful Renovation, and the extreme right Union of the Russian People were "registered" at the time of the First Duma. As to the other parties represented in the chamber, only their Duma fractions were registered, since they were composed of duly elected deputies.

Actually the March 6 statute was available to the authorities if they wished to hinder a political organization, but the existence of opposition parties was implicitly accepted by the administration, even if they were not sanctioned by law. Still one cannot but sympathize with the London *Times* reporter who later pondered how the Tsar's ministers could work with an assembly in which the chief party, the Kadets, was not legalized! Moreover, the law frequently forced political organizations, as well as the authorities, into false stances. Numerous rules were developed to get around the edict, the enforcement of which depended on local officials and varied from place to place. For instance, a Jewish Bund paper which might be sold openly in Vilna might be proscribed in Odessa. Party meetings might be announced in advance as "nonparty," a legal fiction at times openly recognized by the police. For instance, a late March, 1906, report to Police Director E. Vuich referred to a "nonparty pre-election meeting (really Kadet)."[18]

The need to announce partisan meetings under nonparty labels was but one of many obstacles under which the nonregistered parties had to operate. The March *ukaz* on associations also contained stringent regulations about meetings; advance notice, accompanied by a statement elaborating on the purpose of the gathering, was required. Police representatives, permitted to attend as observers, could close an assemblage if it "departed from the subject of its business," or if opinions were expressed which might cause friction between different groups of the population. The provisos of the *ukaz* were subject to very wide interpretation, recalled the influential Kadet Ivan Petrunkevich, and while many successful opposition meetings were held, there was always the threat of closure hanging over them. Furthermore, with open air meetings completely forbidden, and such likely spots as schools, inns, and restaurants legally unavailable for public assemblies, it was a constant problem finding suitable meeting sites.[19]

The Kadet party remained without registered status until the end of Nicholas's reign; in fact, the Union of the Russian People was the sole mass party which ever achieved that status, and it was the only sizeable political group receiving any endorsement from the Tsar. Even then, Nicholas never gave the Union all out support and his attitude towards it remained equivocal and inconsistent. There was much about the Union of the Russian People, its banners enscribed with the traditional "Orthodoxy, Autocracy, and Nationality" which appealed to Nicholas. He liked their strident publicity calling for restoral of the autocracy and the reestablishment of law and order. Yet, there was also much that was somehow disquieting about the new organization, especially its efforts to attract the discontented of all classes. The Tsar looked in vain for familiar names from old established families as he scanned the lists of Union members. The Union was a new and unknown group which had sprung up from outside his administration and the implication that it was trying to save the latter from its own weaknesses made the sovereign resentful. Nor could he approve some of the Union's vicious attacks on his ministers and other bureaucrats.[20] Perhaps the most basic, Nicholas observed the actions of the Union of the Russian People from the same standpoint as he viewed any popular organization. He was always suspicious of any efforts on the part of the public to influence his policies or his officials, no matter how loyal their professed motives.

In its statement of 1905, the Union urged all "honest" Russians, regardless of occupation or class, who were loyal to "Tsar, Fatherland, and traditional Russian principles," to unite in legal struggle against the "repulsive manifestations of the recently granted freedoms." Openly anti-Semitic, the rightist group barred Jews from membership in its ranks, and in spite of its professions about waging a legal struggle, many members of the Union published propaganda designed to incite pogroms, or participated in them. In its publicity the Union played on the superstitions and fears of the discontented, especially those whose financial status had suffered because of the revolts of 1905. The blame for their plight was placed on intellectuals, radicals, revolutionaries, and especially the Jews. Because of the "disruptive anti-state activity of the united Jewish masses," no more than three Jews should sit in the Duma, declared the party statement of 1905.

Since the Duma had been granted by the Tsar, the Union accepted its existence, hoping, however, to change it into an advisory consultative body. Through such an assembly a "firm monarch" could establish direct union with his subjects; only thus could the old unity between the people and a sovereign, whose "pure soul" had been separated from his subjects by the "ministerial bureaucratic system," be restored. In the future there must be firmer control by the judiciary over the actions of the ministry and the bureaucracy. Generally speaking, however, the old autocratic system ought to be reinstated, and the new Duma should act as the "bulwark" of the autocrat, without pressing for additional limitations of his powers.

During the 1906 election campaign the Union of the Russian People had received virtually no support, verbal or financial, from Nicholas's government, aside from what advantages it had from being the only legal mass party. In addition, on December 23, 1905, the Tsar had accepted medals for himself and his heir from a deputation of the Union, after which Nicholas expressed his confidence that their organization would help him to overcome the enemies of Russia.[21] The Union's total defeat at the polls in the First Duma elections and the victory of the opposition were a great shock to the Tsar, and would lead to a reappraisal of the 1906 policy towards the elections.

The attitude of the Tsar towards political campaigns can also be seen in the official policy of the Holy Synod that year. Priests were told to warn their flocks not to be led astray by materialistic nonbelievers, nor to be snared by "hopes of much freedom in civil affairs." Only those who proceeded along the "path of peace, love, and order," and stood for the true faith, the Tsar and an indivisible fatherland, were deserving of support at the polls. The Orthodox clergy were told to vote and permitted to be Duma members, but they were forbidden to join political parties. In spite of Holy Synod policy, of six Orthodox priests elected to the First Duma, only two could be classed as moderate conservatives. The other four proved to be outspoken critics of the regime and supported programs which the administration viewed as impossibly radical.[22]

With even Orthodox priests among the First Duma opposition, it soon became appallingly obvious to Nicholas that his preelection qualms about the Duma composition had real basis. The electoral law had not brought supporters of the monarchy to the capital, and the wager that a large percentage of peasant deputies would provide a bloc loyal to the Tsar soon proved to be another illusion. In an effort to influence the peasant legislators and to preserve them from leftist approaches, P. Durnovo tried out an idea proposed by Colonel M. M. Erogin, rightist Duma deputy and Marshall of the Nobility from Grodno *guberniia*. Erogin suggested that the Ministry of the Interior sponsor a low-cost dormitory to house the peasant members of the assembly. Here they would come under the beneficial influence of Erogin and a few other conservative members of the chamber. Located in a corner of St. Petersburg at a convenient distance from the Tauride Palace, at one time the dormitory housed over seventy residents. A country priest, who was a fellow deputy, acted as a kind of house father, and "every attempt was made to discipline" his wards. For instance, according to B. Pares, the residents were sometimes asked to sign minority resolutions which were contrary to stands that they had taken in the chamber. Ultimately Erogin's rather naive plan backfired. Persuasive Trudovik leaders made their way to the dormitory where the government had obligingly housed a large number of potential Trudoviks under one roof. Many of the residents joined the Trudoviks or Kadets, some remained nonparty, but there were few conversions to the regime.[23]

Not only did the peasants fail to rally to the support of the administration in the Duma, they provided a number of perplexing problems to city officials. Many of them had pledged to send a large share of their ten-ruble daily remuneration back to the village, and it was soon evident that the remainder was not enough to sustain a man in the big city. Some took jobs as porters, domestics, and so forth, while the more enterprising among them set themselves up as petty traders including one who was a vendor of fowl! There were incidents of rowdiness and inebriation, which were difficult to handle without violating the deputies' parliamentary immunity. In at least one case, however, a local bar keeper took the law into her own hands. To the careful explanation of one unruly customer that as a Duma member he was inviolable, she retorted sharply: "For me you . . . are fully violable." Whereupon she proved her point by punching him in the face and throwing him from the premises.[24]

Aside from a few individuals like Erogin, there were no conservatives in the First Duma, and it opened its proceedings eager to press for further concessions, much to the horror of the administration. The very first words delivered from its tribune had been the amnesty appeal of Petrunkevich, "one of the most malicious enemies of the government and the existing order," to quote Gurko.[25] Apart from the man's irritating audacity, the regime saw such a request as preposterous, given the revolutionary situation throughout the realm. Yet Petrunkevich's words had been received with heady enthusiasm by virtually his entire audience.

Petrunkevich's remarks about the amnesty issue went unmentioned when Nicholas received the president-elect of the First Duma at Peterhof the next day. But, since Nicholas's continued silence on the subject was not unexpected, Duma strategists had taken that possibility under serious consideration as they hastily prepared for the meeting of April 29, 1906, at which time the chamber would reopen its doors for business.

CHAPTER VIII

The Administration Rejects the Duma Program

On the morning of the twenty-ninth of April President Muromtsev rose at his place under a huge, "rather shiny study in blue and white" of the Tsar. Mounted in its portentous frame capped with the Imperial crest, the solemn and erect figure of the monarch in full dress uniform dwarfed the dignified Muromtsev as he called the second meeting of the First Duma to order. By then the word had spread among the deputies that there still had been no announcement of an amnesty from the emperor, and many of them had rushed into the chambers in a frustrated angry mood, convinced that the time had come to take a stand. However, fearing that open debate on the explosive issue might well lead to a direct conflict with the administration, the Kadets were ready with another delaying technique.

This time they had picked Feodor I. Rodichev, soon to become one of the assembly's most popular extemporaneous orators, as their spokesman. Trained in the law, Rodichev had, however, devoted most of his energies to his rural estate and to active work with the local *zemstvo*. He had been a major instigator of the famous 1894 petition to the Tsar from the Tver *zemstvo*, which contained the bold request for more popular participation in the affairs of Nicholas' administration. Rodichev's role in the 1894 incident had resulted in the loss of his voting rights, but he had continued his active participation in the movement for constitutional reform.

Rodichev proposed that the First Duma promptly elect a

thirty-three man commission and instruct it to compose a reply to Nicholas' welcoming address. When they had a draft ready, they would bring it onto the floor for discussion by the full house. While the contents of such a document ought not to be completely decided in advance, Rodichev continued, the commission should be specifically directed to inform the sovereign of "the unconditional need to announce a full amnesty for all religious, agrarian, and political prisoners." A positive response to that petition on the part of the Tsar would be "an act of the highest political wisdom," Rodichev exclaimed, warning, however, that popular feeling would not be satisfied by a "niggardly partial amnesty." Keeping the prerogatives of the monarch carefully in mind, Rodichev further advised the assembly to put its amnesty statement in the form of a request, and not a demand. Rodichev stressed that haste was imperative in drawing up this request, and then he wound up his heady address with a dramatic plea for unanimity: "The people's hopes, the people's feelings must be satisfied. . . . Sacrifice your doubts in the name of country, in the name of love." And so the Duma had its first exposure to one of its three most "striking orators," to use the appellation of Maurice Baring; and while the English observer was not himself especially attracted to Rodichev's "rather theatrical eloquence," he admitted that he was in a minority.[1]

First to respond to Rodichev's suggestions was the popular Trudovik, Stepan Anikin, a village schoolteacher of peasant background, who had been elected to the Duma in Saratov *guberniia*. Another fluent orator who was to be a frequent contributor to the chamber's proceedings, Anikin's brief remarks containing no specific recommendations about the Rodichev proposal, were interrupted twice by enthusiastic applause. Amnesty was not a question of mercy, but of justice, Anikin insisted, given a situation when "thousands, maybe tens of thousands" of their peasant brothers still sat in prison. Most of them were not guilty, and if some had acted badly, they should not be judged for "being seized by the wave of the freedom movement." Anikin had no sooner completed his remarks when his fellow Trudovik, Aleksei Aladin, deputy from Simbursk *guberniia*, took the floor. "A violent and talented speaker" distinguished by "an uncompromising directness of speech and powerful driving force," Baring included Aladin as one of his choices for the three top speakers in the First Duma, although with one reservation; in times of real excitement Aladin's voice became so high pitched that it worked to his disadvantage. In the Englishman's opinion the flamboyant Trudovik would have been "twenty times as effective as an orator" if he had curbed his passions. In spite of, or perhaps because of, this tendency, Aladin's impact cannot be denied, and even Izvolskii, who hardly approved either his tactics or ideas, called him a "brilliant speaker." Miliukov, whose lot it was to deal with the impetuous Trudoviks in numerous heated strategy sessions, was less complimentary. The Kadet leader referred to Aladin as the "least restrained speaker in the First Duma," and he heartily disapproved of the Trudovik's fluent, but "crude, arrogant, and provocative" style.[2]

Of peasant background, Aladin had attended the University of Kazan where he had been arrested for circulating socialist propaganda. Sentenced to exile in northern Russia, he escaped and then spent several years in France, Belgium, and England. He made contact with Russian revolutionary circles while abroad, and like so many of his fellow emigres, he returned to his homeland only in 1905. Thus, a broader background, as well as the "red flower which he seldom forgot to wear in his buttonhole," distinguished him from the "gray mass of peasants" which predominated in the Trudovik group.[3]

Aladin's maiden speech in the First Duma was brief, but characteristic. As he put it, his remarks on the amnesty issue were not aimed at his fellow deputies, but at those authorities who still had time "to understand with whom they were dealing. . . ." "Behind us is all the country," he warned, while "our brothers in prison, in exile, or at hard labor" are confident that we will bring them back. And if not—and there followed a "forceful gesture," then a shout of "enough" from the floor. But Aladin had yet to

177

complete his remarks with what he described as "simple, clear words" for the administration: "Spare our country! Take the matter into your hands and do not compel us to take it into our own."

These two fiery Trudoviks set the tone for many of the ensuing speeches, while worried Kadets and moderate rightists kept pointing out the constitutional limits faced by the assembly and the dangers of presenting an ultimatum to the administration. They managed to head off suggestions that an amnesty petition be presented to the sovereign at once, either by the Duma president personally, or by telegram. The issue had occupied most of two long sessions when a deputy from Perm said flatly that since everyone agreed on the desirability of Rodichev's proposals, it was time to stop talking about them. At that point the well-known Kharkhov law professor, Nicholas Gredeskul, who had only been able to assume his deputy's seat after a directive from the Minister of the Interior secured his release from exile in Archangel, made a plea for a unanimous vote. Gredeskul recommended that the amnesty statement appear as a request, not a demand, if that were the only way to achieve unanimity. His advice prevailed, and amongst shouts and noisy applause, Rodichev's measure passed as originally introduced, with one modification which had been proposed earlier by a Ukrainian Trudovik, Ivan Zabolotnyi of Podolia *guberniia*. In accord with the latter's suggestion, the Duma voted to direct its thirty-three-man commission to include an appeal for an immediate stay of all death sentences, whether from regular or military courts, along with the amnesty appeal. The stay would remain in effect until the Duma was able to complete a law abolishing the death sentence.[4]

The subsequent vote for the membership of the thirty-three-man commission put most of the influential Kadet deputies on that body. Included also were the colorful Trudoviks, Aladin and Anikin, who had already given their fellows a sample of their oratory. These two and many of their associates were often the bane of the Kadets as the latter attempted to direct the Duma proceedings, but their speeches gained them much sympathy among the public. Miliukov attributed the Duma's popularity in the country to the Trudovik group, adding that a few of them were popular heroes. Their speeches were quoted widely in the press and certain Trudovik's names were known "in the most remote corners of Russia," Petrunkevich wrote; their words inspired love and hope, and they reflected the mood of many voters. As coalition allies, however, they left much to be desired. The ways of constitutional struggle, with its inevitable compromise and delay, were alien to the mood of the Trudovik group, or its supporters. The masses wanted real change in their situation and they expected their elected representatives to do something quickly. The Trudoviks responded to the impatient mood of the public, both on the house floor and in house committee and strategy sessions.[5]

Difficult allies as they were, the Kadets had no alternative other than constant cultivation of the Trudoviks in order to keep their votes. Very often it was Paul Miliukov whom the Kadets sent over to Trudovik headquarters to sound out their position on a given measure. Miliukov found his mission a little more difficult each time. On the whole we had very cordial relations with the Trudoviks at first, he reminisced, but that initial "stage of friendly contact passed quickly." As the intellectuals in their group gained in influence, "systematic attacks on the Kadets" became common fare at Trudovik meetings.[6]

The Kadet's success at mustering Trudovik support lasted throughout the period when the reply to Nicholas' speech was to dominate the Duma proceedings. Actually the decision to frame such a reply had been adopted in principle even before Nicholas gave his talk at the Winter Palace reception. On the eve of that event a pre-Duma fraction meeting had been held, and it was at that gathering that the Kadets sold the others on the idea. A nine-man commission, to be composed of three Kadets, three Trudoviks, and three Autonomists, was charged with the task of preparing an initial draft. Ultimately, the Kadets played the major role on the commission, since the Trudoviks largely deferred to their recommendations, and the nationality groups never could get together on three men to fill their allotted slots.[7]

The Kadet's inspiration to prepare such a document had come, not from anything said by the Tsar, but from procedures in the British parliament. The document's very title, "The Duma's Address-in-Response to the Speech from the Throne," had a British ring. The Kadets opted to reply to Nicholas's brief and formal remarks of welcome, as if they were a parallel to the speech read by the British monarch, or his representative, after the swearing in a majority of the House of Commons. But the parallel was a false one. The Tsar's address was not the program of his ministry, while the King's speech to Commons contains the program of the British cabinet. Once read, the Throne Speech is open for discussion in the House of Commons, which then formulates its "Address-in-Answer." In keeping with the British model, the First Duma used its Address to the Throne to put forth its program demands and aspirations, but it can in no way be viewed as a response to specific proposals from Nicholas or his ministers.

"Clearly at a loss what to do" with the chamber it had summoned, the government had not prepared any legislative projects or alternative means of occupying the deputies, wrote Kryzhanovskii.[8] The Duma leaders, however, ignored the silence from the administration and went ahead with previously made plans to compose an Address to the Throne. The draft worked out by the small Kadet-Trudovik commission became the basis of the version finally brought before the full house by the thirty-three-man commission on May 2, 1906. Then began the memorable fourth session of the First Duma, which was to last, without formal adjournment, from May 2 until May 5, 1906.

During those days the entire Address was read through three times; after the second reading, the deputies discussed it sentence by sentence. Many of the points raised were irrelevant and the debates were very diffuse and lacked focus. As many a deputy mounted the podium his real interest lay in the reception his words would receive back home, and not in the contribution he was making to the draft project. "We listened to whole dissertations about Bashkir and Kirgiz lands, about the situation of the Don Cossacks, about the land relationships between Baltic pastors and their parishoners. . . ."[9] So wrote Vladimir Nabokov, deputy to the First Duma from St. Petersburg.

Nabokov was the scion of a distinguished and properous noble family, whose father had been Minister of Justice under Alexander II and his successor. A highly educated and cultured man, the younger Nabokov had been lecturer in criminal law at the prestigious Imperial School of Jurisprudence from 1896 to 1904. Much to the disapproval of most of his relatives, during that period Nabokov had adopted an increasingly liberal and antiadministration tone in his writings, which cost him his minor court title in 1905. He severed all connections with the Tsarist government, and eventually became one of the founders of the Kadet Party, and a major financial contributor to that organization.

Foreign Minister Izvolskii rated Nabokov one of the Kadets' three best orators in the First Duma. A highly skilled parliamentarian and debator as well, he was his party's choice to pilot the all important Address to the Throne through the assembly. B. Pares found his performance impressive: "In a voice under whose soft inflection lay the suggestion of a great reserve of strength, he over and over again gave matter-of-fact and convincing answers to the objections of individual members." When he was not speaking, continued Pares, Nabokov could be seen casually moving about the hall, a slip of paper in his hand. Following a word with a Trudovik leader he might jot down some brief notes, after which he would proceed to the benches on the right to seek out a respected Octobrist. "It was often more interesting to watch him than to follow the debates," in Pares' opinion.[10]

Nabokov prefaced his initial reading of the Address proposal with an allusion to Nicholas as a "constitutional monarch," being approached for the first time by the elected representatives of his subjects. The remark, which brought forth a burst of applause, was certain to horrify the Tsar; yet from that monarch's viewpoint it was but an apt introduction to the string of excessive requests that followed. While clothed in language which was correct and even embued with loyalty towards the person of the sovereign, in the judgment of Izvolskii, the Address was simply an attempt by the First Duma to assume the rights of a constituent assembly and to revise the Fundamental Laws in an "ultra radical sense." The result was "great consternation" in administration circles, and Izvolskii's colleague from the Ministry of Finance could still convey the widespread feeling of indignation years later. The First Duma "convened only to attack the government," Kokovtsov almost seemed to sputter, and there was "general agreement" that the assembly mounted its attack during the debate on the Address to the Throne.[11]

Yet as the skillful Nabokov attempted to guide the heated debates provoked by the Address proposal, he and his Kadet colleagues were always cognizant of the constitutional limits set upon the new chamber. Miliukov, one of the authors of the draft, claimed that they had maintained a "strict division" between the rights of the Duma and the prerogatives of the monarch, in that "intentions," that is, announcement of actions planned by the chamber, made up one section of the project, while those reforms "desired" from the monarch made up another.[12] In point of fact the division was not all that distinct, and the proposal Nabokov read can be better divided into three broad categories, which frequently overlapped each other throughout the document: (1) criticisms of the arbitrary actions of the administration and requests for basic changes in its mode of operation, (2) statements of constitutional reforms deemed necessary to "renovate Russia . . . on the firm foundations of civil freedom," and (3) declarations of Duma legislative goals, to be put into specific bills later.

The members of the Duma saw the Address simply as a broad statement of essential reforms, while to the executive it was a list of preposterous proposals. Hence the diametrically opposite judgments of Miliukov and Izvolskii, made years after the event. And so it had been in the spring of 1906, when regardless of loyal language, regardless of the care taken not to violate the Tsar's prerogatives, the implications were clear from the moment that Nabokov put the Address proposal before the house. It was rife with recommendations that the Tsar would not grant. For example, the document concluded with a request from the monarch for a "full political amnesty, as the first pledge of mutual understanding and cooperation between Tsar and people." Along similar lines: "The nation awaits the immediate suspension, by your sovereign authority, of the execution of all death sentences" until the First Duma can enact a law abolishing capital punishment forever.

The fact that these statements were phrased as petitions, and not demands, was irrelevant from the Tsar's point of view. His regime had just survived a very severe threat, and while his throne was apparently still intact, he was far from sanguine about the future. Nicholas and the bulk of his advisors sincerely believed that it would be against the best interest of themselves and the state to empty the jails in May of 1906. Furthermore, they considered the death penalty an essential weapon in the continuing struggle against revolution and dissent.

To Nicholas these were only two of many unacceptable sections of the Address. Equally irritating were the hard-hitting criticisms of his bureaucracy which permeated the text. At one point it referred to the "independence of officials, who separated the Tsar from the people, as the major ulcer" in Russia. Since the independence of these officials was worse when they operated "under the cloak" of the extraordinary laws, the Address concluded that it was "necessary to liberate" the people from those laws. Yet it was these special emergency measures that permitted the suspension of the civil rights of citizens and gave extra powers to local officials in areas where they were invoked which had been a major weapon of the administration in its pacification of the country. Men like Durnovo and Witte, who had questioned the efficacy of the extraordinary laws early in 1905, had judged their application essential to cope with the mounting revolts later the same year.[13] Given the tense situation which prevailed in the spring of 1906, the administration had no intention of abrogating these measures.

The Address was silent on the touchy matter of regional autonomy, stating only that it would be among the "urgent tasks" of the Duma to solve the question of the "long-due demands of the separate nationalities." There was no mention, however, of specific measures such as the right to use local languages in schools and other public institutions. The document simply noted that the "spiritual union" of the diverse tribes and nationalities in the empire would be possible, only if the "need of each to maintain and develop its uniqueness" were satisfied; it would be the concern of the Duma to satisfy this need. Another of the chamber's legislative tasks would be a "radical transformation of local administration" in order to establish "self-administration . . . on the basis of a universal suffrage law." Hence the document remained deliberately vague on the matter of a decentralized or a centralized administrative system.

The Address called, however, for several other basic constitutional reforms which would have required considerable reworking of the recently issued Fundamental Laws of 1906. Most important was the section dealing with the ministry. According to the Fundamental Laws these men were responsible to the Tsar. According to the Duma Address, "only a ministry which enjoys the confidence of the majority of the Duma can strengthen faith in the government." Such faith was essential to the "peaceful and proper work" of the assembly, and it would be achieved when the ministers were "responsible before the peoples' representatives," and no longer permitted to "commit violence while hiding behind the name of your Imperial majesty." The Address also reflected the deputies' discontent with the limitations on the competence of the assembly, which had been so carefully inserted into the Fundamental Laws. "There cannot exist that sphere of legislation which will be forever closed to the free examination of the representatives of the people in union with the Monarch." They chafed under the prospect of attempting to achieve the proper cooperation between assembly and sovereign while a "State Council composed of nominated dignitaries and people elected from the upper classes" stood in the way.

Here then were several statements stressing the need for constitutional changes which Nicholas could not approve; as he saw it, he had already made too many concessions. The clauses of the Address which dealt with legislative goals of the First Duma contained some equally objectionable measures from the executive's standpoint. Among "urgently necessary" legislation would be "precise laws" on personal immunity, freedom of conscience, association, speech and the press. Bills would pass the chamber which guaranteed the rights of labor to organize and strike, while other legislation would establish equality before the law for all citizens, and abrogate all existing legal restrictions based on religion, nationality, sex, or class. The "yoke of arbitrary tutelage" should be removed from the peasantry, and it should have the same rights as other classes. As to the matter of land reform to benefit these oppressed citizens, the Address took a clear position: "The most pressing task of the Duma" was the satisfaction of the peasants' acute need for land, and it must draw on treasury, monastic, and imperial lands, and also engage in "the compulsory confiscation of private estates" to alleviate that need.

In other words every section of the Address was replete with proposals that the administration was highly unlikely to accept. However, the text passed virtually as introduced by Nabokov except for two minor changes. One had added church lands to the categories to be available for reallocation to the peasants, while the second resulted in the insertion of a clause about "strengthening the principles of justice and law in the army and fleet" into the final version. In spite of the fact that the document survived almost intact, the final vote had come only after a long, unusually rambling and sometimes spirited, debate. At last, late on the night of May 4, it was time for the last reading. Lev

Petrazhitskii, a Kadet deputy from St. Petersburg, made a fervent plea for unity—"the more unanimous, the more convincing" was the essence of his message. The highly respected Octobrist, Count P. A. Geiden, took the floor and announced that, while he and his associates could support most of the Address, they still had a few reservations. Agreeing with Petrazhitskii about the importance of unity, Geiden and about ten others thereupon retired from the hall. At 3:00 A.M. the rest of the house voted in favor of the document and promptly commissioned a delegation of Duma officers to deliver it personally to the sovereign.[14]

Considering the wide diversity of opinion in the First Duma, the virtually unanimous acceptance of the Address to the Throne was an impressive achievement for Nabokov and his fellow Kadets. Their success can be explained partly by their wise decision not to take a definite stand on certain issues where opposition was likely. Hence the ultimate question of a unicameral or bicameral legislature was left open in those clauses which criticized the existent State Council. In the statement promising passage of a law establishing universal suffrage there was no mention of the famous, but controversial, four-tailed formula, which called for general, equal, direct, and secret elections.

Omission of a statement calling for Polish autonomy caused some friction between the Polish Kolo and the Kadet leadership of the Duma. Nevertheless, the Kadets, who were opposed to the general decentralization of the empire along national lines, opted to avoid mention of regional autonomy in the Address, since any specific position on that complex issue was bound to rouse the ire of some group in the assembly. Alexander Lednitskii, leader of the Union of Autonomists, argued in the debates that if the First Duma concentrated on the "nationwide matter of liberation," then the needs of the nationalities could be granted afterward, and ultimately the bulk of the non-Russian deputies supported the Address as presented.[15]

The huge vote in favor of the Address was a reflection of the consensus among the deputies about the need for fundamental reforms. Overlooking certain omissions in the document, they united readily in their criticisms of arbitrary officials and in their demands for broadening the powers of the new legislature. Who among them would deny that the Russian populace sorely needed legal guarantees for long sought civil freedoms?

Thus, early on the morning of the fifth of May the First State Duma jubilantly approved a document which verbalized many of the pent-up frustrations of their constituents. It was the popular assembly's first chance to take a stand and there was no inclination to mince words. Yet in the midst of all the celebration, the American scholar Samuel Harper thought that he detected an undercurrent of fear; he himself felt very apprehensive. That night he had listened to some "very radical" speeches; "I am not prophesying," he concluded, "but I don't see how the Answer can fail to make trouble. I believe there will be excitement soon."[16] Events of the weekend soon bore out this observation.

The next morning the focus of activity switched from the Tauride Palace to Peterhof where an angry monarch and his staff were appalled at the boldness of the Duma statement. Nicholas's response to Muromtsev's note requesting an audience for the Duma officers was short and blunt! "I will not receive the deputation. Send the Address to me."[17] News of the Tsar's refusal reached the Duma president through official channels, and he had no opportunity to speak with Nicholas personally. The rest of the Kadets heard about Nicholas's decision at a Sunday morning meeting of the party's Duma fraction. The group reached a consensus that they should not push for personal delivery of the document, and Miliukov went to seek Trudovik approval of their decision. His argument that the time was still premature for a decisive break with the administration prevailed and the Trudoviks supported the Kadets in the Tauride Palace the next day.

On Monday, May 8, Muromtsev read a curt note from Ivan Goremykin, the new chairman of the ministerial council, to the assembled deputies: "The Tsar directs me to inform you of his desire to have the Answer to the

Throne speech sent as a written report to his Majesty."
There followed a proposal by Kadet Paul Novgorodtsev
of Ekaterinoslav that the chamber abide by the monarch's
wish, since the impact of such a "great historic act" as the
Address could not be diminished by any form of presentation. Novgorodtsev then urged approval of a "formula
of passage" to that effect, stressing that it was not the time
to stand on formality, since the "significance of the Address
lay in its contents and not in the method of presenting it."
Thus, the First Duma had its initial introduction to a procedure which it would use frequently. Through a "formula
of passage," the house summarized its position on a matter
which had been under discussion, and voted to go on to the
next order of business.

Before Novgorodtsev's formula came to a vote, the fiery
Aladin gave vent to the general frustration and anger
evoked by the snub from the palace. "When it came to a
petty matter of etiquette on the one hand and an expression
of the needs of the people on the other," Aladin knew where
he stood. The Duma had a moral obligation to get the
people's needs heard at once, regardless of the rules of
etiquette. He expressed dismay and sorrow that "in the first
step of our activity we have not met the deserved response
from the administration," and he predicted that each subsequent step of the chamber would meet similar obstacles.
Aladin spoke forcefully, but he proposed no alternative
course to Novgorodtsev's motion. His words had no effect
on the outcome of the vote, which was unanimous.

Nicholas's refusal to grant an audience to the Duma
deputation had, however, made a deep impression on the
lower house. " 'The government is defying us' was the general expression" that Monday morning, Baring noted. Considering the "intense bitterness" which prevailed, the
English journalist could only marvel at the moderate stance
taken by the assembly. Years later Izvolskii voiced a similar view: Nicholas's decision was greatly resented, wrote
the Foreign Minister, but "thanks to the good sense" of
some of the Kadet leaders, the chamber did not press the
issue. Coupled with this deep resentment was a real un-

certainty just how to proceed, along with great concern about the next reactions from the administration. The refusal to receive the elected delegation, in itself an insignificant act, was perceived by the Duma "as a bad omen, as a dangerous warning" in the opinion of I. V. Gessen, Miliukov's close collaborator on *Rech*.[18]

The deputies were to wait until the end of the week for the official response to their Address. Meanwhile the lights burned late in Goremykin's roomy residence on the Fontanka, where the chief minister had been holding almost nightly cabinet sessions since late April. In keeping with his policy of ignoring the Duma, however, neither Goremykin nor his associates had yet put in an appearance in the ministers' box at the Tauride Palace. Nor had there been any serious effort on the part of the administration to learn about the composition, mood, or inclinations of the people's representatives, complained Petrunkevich. In sum, the ministry had treated the new chamber like an "unfriendly camp," thus revealing that it had no intention of participating in parliamentary affairs.[19]

The bold contents of the First Duma's Address suddenly forced a hasty reconsideration of the chief minister's policy. "Unwilling as Goremykin was to have anything to do with the Duma," wrote V. Gurko, "the government was obliged to break its silence and make some sort of answer." The preparation of this reply led to "extreme wrangling" in the Council of Ministers, with Goremykin still "inclined entirely to disregard the Duma's Address." Several of his colleagues protested that such a course would only further embarrass the government in the long run and their counsel ultimately prevailed. Once the decision to make a reply was definite, the question of the proper method of presenting it came under protracted discussion. Nicholas toyed with the idea of making a personal appearance in the Tauride Palace, but he finally deferred to those who recommended that he let Goremykin speak for the executive before the deputies. As to the contents of the response, there was no debate over its general tone: "We were all agreed," recalled Kokovtsov, that since the Duma's Address was "utterly unacceptable," it must be staunchly opposed. The Tsar heartily concurred with their inclinations, and upon reading a draft of the reply, he told Kokovtsov that "he would have preferred it to be even stronger and more decisive. . . ." Nicholas did not insist on changing it, however, in the hope that "there would be no occasion to say afterward that the government had not been moderate in dealing with the representatives of the people. . . ." Yet in spite of all his efforts, Nicholas added ruefully, he "was sure that the matter would not stop there!"[20]

After the Tsar gave his approval to the text of the government statement, which in broad outline was very similar to Witte's program of April 23, copies were printed up for distribution to each of the deputies at the time of Goremykin's appearance.[21] That event took place on Friday, May 13, 1906, at which time the chief minister, accompanied by his entire cabinet, "betook himself with great pomp and ceremony" into the Duma chambers. After the proper introduction the aged minister proceeded to read the administration's declaration—B. Pares compared his manner of delivery to that of a "school master reading a lesson"— in a "voice that was hardly audible and which betrayed no emotion, even though his hands were shaking with agitation." Goremykin only raised his voice once, reminisced Gurko, namely when he came to the passage which dealt with the question of land reforms: any measures which involved the "compulsory expropriation of the land of private owners, including that of peasant proprietors who have redeemed their land by purchase . . . is absolutely inadmissible." To emphasize his point the normally phlegmatic bureaucrat "even lifted his finger as a threat." He then went on to elaborate on the government position. The inviolability of private property, that "cornerstone of public well being" must be upheld, since without it the existence of the state was "unthinkable." It was the administration's conviction that the admittedly serious agrarian problem must be dealt with through alternative measures. Those he mentioned included government sponsored efforts to raise agricultural productivity, the transfer of more land to the peasants through the Peasant Land Bank, the opening up of unoccupied crown lands for settlement, the encouragement of internal migration, along with measures to improve the conditions of land tenure. In addition, peasants must have the same civil and political rights as other groups of the population.

Goremykin's blunt announcement that the Duma's land reform clause was "inadmissible" was as irritating to the deputies as any remark in the entire declaration. Furthermore, the measures he mentioned in the area of land policy sounded like mere extensions of programs which had already been tried, without making an appreciable dent in the vast problems of rural Russia. The administration's position on land confiscation was moreover, but one of many categorical rejections of the Duma program put forth by Goremykin on the thirteenth of May.

The chief minister castigated the assembly for proposing "radical amendments to the Fundamental Laws," since these statutes "were not subject to revision on the initiative of the State Duma." Cited specifically were sections requesting a responsible ministry, the repeal of all limitations on the competence of the legislature, and the abolition of the State Council. On the matter of an amnesty the reply was also negative: while the liberation of some individuals jailed by administrative procedures, "whose release did not threaten public security," was already under review, "it would not be in accord with the general welfare during the present troubled times to pardon criminals who had participated in murders, robberies, and other acts of violence." Because of the serious threats to public order which still were prevalent, the existent exceptional laws must be retained and used, in spite of their admitted defects. Improved laws to replace them were already at the drafting stage in the appropriate bureaucratic departments.

Goremykin was silent on the matter of abrogating legislation which discriminated against persons of a minority nationality or creed. As to the matter of regional autonomy, the chief minister remarked only that the administration would pay "special attention" to the organization of local administration and self-government, while taking into consideration "the peculiarities of the outlying regions."

Goremykin's statement did not confine itself to rejecting or ignoring points raised in the Duma Address. It also vouched for the executive's "readiness to give the fullest cooperation in the settlement of questions . . . which do not exceed the legal limitations on the Duma's legislative initiative." Since cooperation must be a two-way street, the executive branch was preparing bills on such matters as local court reform, tax reform, and universal primary education which would be sent to the assembly. While several of these projected bills might have met a favorable response under different circumstances, they went virtually unnoticed that day.

Goremykin's listeners waited out his rather lengthy presentation in stunned and painful silence, their anger increased by the minister's "haughty and disdainful tone." "No sooner had he finished than V. D. Nabokov leaped to the tribune" from where he began "clearly and calmly without rhetoric or emphasis, to express the universal feeling of bitter disappointment." Adopting the approach that the ministry had inserted itself between Duma and sovereign, he directed his attack at the former:[22]

> We do not have the beginnings of a constitutional ministry, we have the same old bureaucratic watchwords. . . . The Chairman of the Council of Ministers invites the Duma to constructive work, but at the same time . . . categorically refuses to support the most lawful demands of the people.

Under these conditions, Nabokov queried, how could the regeneration of the country, promised by the chief minister, possibly occur? To the Kadet orator there remained but one way out of the situation: when they "invite us to a conflict, when they tell us that the government is not there to carry out the demands of the people's representatives . . . we can only say, 'let the executive authority submit to the legislative authority.'"

"Deafening applause" greeted Nabokov's dramatic oration, recalled Kokovtsov grimly. Then followed a series of speeches, "each more stinging than the other, full of violent attacks upon the government. . . . Every word was followed by ever more passionate applause, which fanned still higher the flaming ardor of the speakers." During this torrent of abuse, Goremykin "sat silently, smoothing his whiskers." Finally, taking advantage of an intermission, the elderly minister and his cabinet left the chambers. The only one to return, Minister of Justice Ivan Shcheglovitov, later made a feeble attempt to reply to the onslaught. Shcheglovitov insisted that the ministerial statement was based on the law, and denied all allegations to the contrary. He claimed further that the main foundation for all actions of the executive was the law code of the empire. Admittedly there could be difficulties for some time, since it was essential to operate under imperfect old laws, until new ones replaced them. Still he was optimistic: the necessary changes in the laws would be better achieved, given the clash of opinions between Duma and administration, and he was puzzled at the Duma's intense concern about these differences of viewpoint.[23]

The Minister of Justice's vague and somewhat curious speech had no visible effect on the mood of his enraged listeners, and as soon as he finished they resumed the attack, only to add his name as a specific target. While some of these men delivered extemporaneous orations, advance rumors about the contents of the government statement had prompted the Kadets to line up seven men to prepare rejoinders. Hence Nabokov was ready when Goremykin's performance confirmed the rumors. His famous demand that the executive submit to the legislature was topped by the ebullient finale of R. Rodichev—"Ministers! Your consciences should tell you what you should do; retire and relinquish your places to others." Their colleague F. Kokoshkin put it right on the line; "I think that the country suffered such a blow today, not only to its calm, but to its dignity, that there is but one way to rectify it—the present ministry must go into retirement."

Representatives of the other Duma fractions largely followed the Kadet lead, including moderates like Count P. Geiden. Normally the Count concentrated his efforts on trying to curb the excesses of the Duma, but on the thirteenth of May he was unable to conceal his anger. His hopes for peaceful and beneficial work as a legislator, who could work in cooperation with the administration, had been misplaced, he said sadly. Goremykin's declaration demonstrated that the government was "completely bankrupt, incompetent"; it had worked out no new measures, and had even announced its willingness to "adhere to the same methods," in spite of their admitted failure to calm the populace. Then to add insult to injury, the ministers had not even sat through the replies to the speech of their chief. By leaving the hall they had demonstrated their true relationship to the assembly, and Geiden was left with one conclusion; since "further work with the present government was unthinkable," the cabinet "should give way to another which has the confidence of the Duma." Yet—and here Geiden admitted that his was a minority view—he still did not believe that the Duma should *demand* that the ministry retire, since to do so would be stepping beyond the legal rights of the chamber.

Thus, however strong his condemnation of the administration, Geiden could not go along with the swelling trend begun by the Kadet speakers.[24] His cautions were ignored at a hastily called corridor session, chaired by P. Miliukov, during which the Trudoviks and Kadets agreed to support a resolution of no confidence in the government. They then accepted the draft version proffered by Ivan Zhilkin of Saratov *guberniia*. And so the third of the triumvirate of Trudovik leaders was about to make his mark upon the assembly proceedings. Like Aladin and Anikin, Zhilkin was of peasant origin, and he too represented a Volga *guberniia*. Before his resolution went out onto the floor, Zhiklin and three Kadets made some hurried editorial changes. Beneath flowery prose, its message was clear. Since the government refused to acquiesce in the Duma's demands, thus revealing its "open scorn for the vital interest of the nation," it was the "sacred duty" of the assembly to express its complete lack of confidence in it. The ministry must retire at once, in order to be replaced by a successor which enjoyed the confidence of the lower house.

Zhilkin's motion passed with only eleven nays, one of which was Count Geiden's. Of these eleven, ten signed a declaration on May 15 which stated that, although they did not support Zhilkin's statement because it seemed to go beyond the rights of the chamber, neither did they approve the ministry's position. Henceforth Goremykin could not even expect support from the moderate wing of the First Duma.

Once the First Duma had voted its noisy and almost un-animous approval of Zhilkin's resolution of no-confidence, a situation emerged about which witnesses of very unlike views could for once agree, both at the time and as they looked back on the May 13 session. Maurice Baring's on the spot prognosis—"matters have come to a complete deadlock"—concurs with the recollection in Miliukov's memoirs that May 13 had marked the "beginning of open struggle." Both Kokovtsov and Izvolskii viewed the session much like the prominent Kadet: The Duma stance of May 13 "only served to widen the now open breach with the government," and from that date forward the relations between the two branches of government "grew more im-possible every day."

In its reporting of the May 13, 1906, session, the Kadet *Rech* took a most enthusiastic line: "Yesterday we lived through a historic day . . . two worlds met and measured their strength." The old world still had physical force on its side, but the assembly represented moral force, since it embodied the "will and thought of the people." The paper boldly suggested that Goremykin's declaration, with its belated announcement of the executive's inadequate pro-gram, was a "risky experiment." If his intent were to show the lower chamber its place, he was too late, because the First Duma had already shown the cabinet its proper place. There was, however, one less confident and encouraging comment on the same page of that newspaper: "An informed source" disclosed that the retirement of the chief minister and his cabinet was unlikely.

The informed source proved to be accurate, much to the dismay of the opposition. The Goremykin cabinet did indeed remain in office, albeit somewhat shaken and apprehensive about the outcome of the May 13 session. In his diary entry for May 14 A. Polovtsov alluded to the military forces being held in readiness to deal with expected disorders. Two days later the elderly chief minister called a meeting in order to sound out his cabinet on the situation and then report back to the Tsar. After hearing their varied opinions, Goremykin adjourned the session before any consensus about their next course emerged. It was agreed only to observe the Duma carefully and be ready for any emergency. And as his colleagues left their chief's home on the Fontanka his parting comments were characteristic. First he urged them to keep their views to themselves, and then he observed wearily:[26]

It is our common duty to bear up patiently under our intolerable situation until we should clearly see that there was nothing more to hope for.

CHAPTER IX

Impasse

The Goremykin cabinet was to remain in office for almost two months after the bitter confrontation of May 13, 1906. An impasse ensued, with the administration continuing to disregard the deputies' requests, while the latter worked busily on legislative projects, most of them along lines categorically rejected in the chief minister's speech.[1] As the weeks passed the executive branch was likewise to come under increasingly severe criticisms from the floor of the Tauride Palace. Meanwhile the administration mounted its own campaign to discredit the assembly with the public. Starting on May 5, the very day that the deputies had approved their Address to the Throne, telegrams disparaging the new order began to appear regularly on the pages of *Pravitelstvennyi Vestnik*, the official gazette. Usually signed by officers or members of ultramonarchist organizations from widespread corners of the Empire, the telegrams were frequently addressed to Nicholas himself.[2]

Of eleven such missives printed together on the third page of the May 5 issue of the daily, some cited the Duma specifically, while all were against the demands aired in its debates:

It is evident from its Reply to the Throne Speech that the Duma demands the destruction of the State Council, made up as it is of your true servitors. . . . The people's elect seek sole power . . . We beg you not to listen . . . to the demands of the State Duma. Rather point out with what matters it should occupy itself, and then, if it continues to act in a revolutionary spirit, we beg you . . . to disperse it. . . .

The President of a local branch of the Union of Russian Folk also referred directly to the assembly in his wire: "Seeing how the first steps of the State Duma sharply depart from centuries of Russian tradition, and knowing how harmful" the demands expressed there would be to the country, the telegram urged Nicholas to resist the pressures of the new legislature.

There was some variance as to detail, but all the telegrams printed on May 5 warned the Tsar against granting an amnesty, and most of them urged him to preserve the death sentence as a necessary weapon in the struggle against revolution. Their senders saw themselves as staunch defenders of law, order, and tradition against dangerous new ideas, but their gibes at the popular assembly cannot be regarded as the spontaneous pleas of concerned citizens. Rather the telegrams were the fruit of a deliberate campaign, which was "well-organized, supported in the highest circles," and aided by officials in local areas, according to V. A. Maklakov, Kadet lawyer and member of the last three Dumas. A frequent critic of his party's tactics, Maklakov's testimony in this instance deserves a hearing, since he had connections in high political circles. Even more significant, in his book on the First Duma Maklakov adopted a highly legalistic approach to the issues at stake between monarch and sovereign, and he tended to argue the case for the administration whenever possible. In the matter of the derogatory telegrams, however, he made a clear indictment of the administration. The appeals were "tactless in themselves" and their appearance in an official organ was "quite improper," he thought, since executive solidarity with their contents and authors was thus implied.[3]

Not only was the telegram campaign a reflection of the poor judgment of the administration, it was likewise an excellent example of the lack of political aplomb of the last Tsar's government. These testimonials from Nichollas's "good, loyal Russians"—representing that eighty percent of the population he was certain remained dedicated to him— may have given comfort to a shaken sovereign, but as devices to influence public opinion, they were incredibly blatant and naive. As he read the telegrams in the spring of 1906, their very phraseology and tone suggested to Maurice Baring that they could not represent widely held views, nor did he regard them as likely to enlist many supporters in the cause of restoring the autocracy. On the other hand, if the intent were to arouse the ire of the deputies, the telegrams must be viewed as a true success. To the Duma members they were but another example of the attitude they could expect from the Goremykin ministry, and "exasperated by the government's disdain"—the phrase was Foreign Minister Izvolskii's—the assembly made the telegrams the subject of one of its many interpellations (*zaprosy*).[4]

According to the Duma statutes, a *zapros* could be sent to any minister or department head to inquire about illegal actions allegedly perpetrated by himself or his subordinates. It took the signatures of thirty deputies to introduce a *zapros* for assembly consideration. Once on the floor it could be amended, rejected, or approved by the full house; if it won majority approval, it went to the appropriate minister, who then had one month to reply, or to give the Duma reasons why he could not answer. For example, a minister might refuse to release information on matters not subject to public airing, such as state secrets, divulgence of which would be detrimental to the national interest.[5]

Even Maklakov, who thoroughly disapproved of the First Duma's overuse of its right of interpellation, called the telegrams "splendid grounds for an interpellation." His fellow Kadets shared his opinion and on May 16, 1906, just eleven days after the telegram campaign got under way, the Kadet party sponsored such a *zapros*.[6] In view of the appearance in *Pravitelstvennyi Vestnik* of "testimonials which contain audacious disrespect for a higher legislative institution, and which rouse one part of the population against another," the sponsors of the *zapros* proposed that the Duma direct some searching questions to the chairman of the ministerial council. Goremykin was to explain how and by whom these wires were selected for publication. If the choice were made with his knowledge and consent, the Duma requested the elderly bureaucrat to reveal "with what aims" they were printed.

In his response Goremykin chose to regard the inquiry as coming under article 40 of the Duma statute, rather than under those clauses which dealt with the right of interpellation. Article 40 stated that the Duma could ask the ministers for explanations pertinent to matters then directly under Duma consideration. A *zapros* on the other hand, was to deal with allegedly illegal *actions*, and not the policies, of the executive branch. In this case the interpellation came as an inquiry about the *policy* of selecting derogatory telegrams, hence Goremykin had an opening for the application of article 40. Since he was unable to discern what matters currently being examined in the Duma were related to the telegram issue, Goremykin informed the chamber, he felt no obligation to reply to their queries.

Duma president Muromtsev received the chief minister's sardonic refusal on the twenty-third of May and three days later he read it aloud to the assembled lower house, after which he gained the chamber's approval for a letter from himself to Goremykin. In that letter the Duma president unwittingly affirmed the minister's position that the matter really came under article 40, when he insisted that the telegrams were indeed a matter of concern to the Duma.

> I consider it my duty to announce that anxiety about the defense of the dignity of the highest state institutions . . . from criminal attacks in official organs is a matter of constant concern and interest to state institutions:

On June 2 a disappointed house heard Goremykin's second refusal to budge from his stance in an even more sarcastic note. In response the deputies resorted to a second *zapros*, asking this time if those guilty of making the choice of the telegrams had been punished. The second inquiry proved equally ineffectual, but the chamber let the matter drop there, after condemning the ministry's third refusal to reply in a June 30 "formula of passage" to the next item on the agenda.

The tortuous course of this *zapros* revealed much about the impasse between the First Duma and the executive. In this case the chief minister "openly ridiculed" the new assembly, to quote V. Maklakov, and while his resort to article 40 had legal basis, Goremykin's attitude was very telling, if one looked beyond the letter of the law. The Goremykin cabinet openly objected to the proceedings in the Tauride Palace and it saw no hope for compromise with the First Duma. In this instance it took advantage of a poorly worded *zapros* to avoid making a reply, but there is no evidence to indicate that a well-phrased query would have evoked a cooperative response. The administration never made any explanation of the selection of the telegrams, and what is more significant, it did not stop printing them.

The numerous refusals of the ministers to give satisfactory replies to interpellations did not deter the deputies from resorting to the device with rising frequency. Introduced almost daily after mid-May, by the fifth of June, 132 interpellations had been read, discussed, and approved. Of a total 391 brought before the First Duma, some 300 were sent to the appropriate ministry, while the remainder went to committee for further consideration. Broadly speaking, these hundreds of interpellations probed into actions of the administration which seemed to be: (1) beyond the bounds of legality, (2) unduly capricious, even if within the limits of the laws, or (3) an affront to the dignity of the Duma. While some, like the matter of the telegrams in the official press, came under the realm of large issues in the conflict between two branches of the government, very many cited individual cases of injustice which had been brought to the attention of the deputies.

Imprisonment without charge, searches without a warrant, administrative exile, dismissals from employment—"all the defenselessness of the citizen in the face of state authority flowed like a torrent through the Duma," recalled Maklakov. Most of the *zaprosy* regarding the abuses of the civil rights of individuals went to Minister of Interior Peter Stolypin. On one occasion a representative of his ministry replied to thirty-three such interpellations at once, justifying almost all of the cases on the need for state security. Another common defense of the actions of officials was the existence of their special powers in areas declared under emergency legislation. As weeks passed, however, the ministry tended more and more simply to refuse to make any reply.[7]

As a device to change the arbitrary methods of the administration, the First Duma could claim little success for its interpellations. The assembly had no means of compelling an official to answer a query, much less to resign; of course it could not put aside his orders. As a means for the public airing of the irregular acts of Tsarist officials, however, the *zaprosy* had some importance. For the first time in history the Tsarist administration could be legally subjected to public criticisms on a large scale, and it had no effective way to restrain the many Duma orators who jumped at the chance to do so.

However, as the number of interpellations rose sharply, their shock value began to wane. Kadet Paul Novgorodtsev recalled listening to "endless accounts day in and day out" about unjust detentions, arrests, and exiles. Many deputies began to flee the chambers during the boring discussions of *zaprosy*; witness Muromtsev's June 5 warning that if one more man left, the house would lack a quorum, that is the required one-third of the membership total. It was soon apparent to Kadet leaders that the long debates about interpellations were using up precious time to no immediate purpose. Early in the sessions the Kadets had originated some of the *zaprosy*, particularly those which dealt with larger issues, but as the sessions wore on they came almost exclusively from the Trudoviks. These interpellations decrying the arbitrary regime resounded from the Duma chambers throughout the nation, and herein lay a major reason for the Trudoviks' widespread popularity, wrote Petrunkevich. Yet they also revealed one of the fraction's weaknesses, since, in spite of mounting evidence that the interpellations brought no tangible results, the Trudoviks firmly resisted Kadet efforts to restrict the number of *zaprosy*, or to designate specific times for discussing them. Even after an agreement that only "urgent" interpellations should get to the floor, there was still a flood of them.[8]

The frequency of pogroms in the empire, and the matter of administrative complicity in these outrages was one matter which no one in the opposition could label as "non-urgent." The issue was especially important since the incidence and intensity of the pogroms had risen sharply during the fall and winter before the chamber opened. Many deputies shared the view that the Jews' lack of legal rights added to their vulnerability to these excesses. Hence the interpellations aimed at the pogroms were also related to the issue of abrogating anti-Jewish laws.[9]

On May 8 the Duma accepted an interpellation about the participation of the police department in the printing of inflamatory material which led to "mass murder of peaceful citizens," by arousing one group of the population against another. Furthermore, an investigation by the administration into accusations that this material came from a press established by the police department had led to reward, not punishment, of the guilty. Aimed at Minister of the Interior, P. Stolypin, the *zapros* asked if he knew the facts in the case and what he intended to do to prevent such illegal actions in the future.

According to the Duma statutes, a minister had a month in which to reply to a *zapros*: actually since the events in question took place before the Duma met, Stolypin was not under legal obligation to reply to this one. During the month interim another terrible pogrom erupted on June 1 in Grodno province in the city of Belostok. The news reached the Duma on June 2 and two Jewish deputies urged Stolypin to stop the pogrom at once. The minister promised to act immediately, but the pogrom continued into the third day. Meanwhile some of the Jewish deputies sponsored a second *zapros* about the pogrom issue. Their June 2 interpellation asked Stolypin whether necessary measures were being taken to protect the Jews in Belostok and if he intended to stave off similar excesses in other areas. After an emotion-packed discussion, led off by V. Nabokov's assertion that the administration frequently assisted the perpetrators of pogroms, either through direct aid or a hands off stance by the police, the Duma unanimously accepted the interpellation.

In a new departure, on that same evening, the assembly elected a thirty-three-man investigation committee, which promptly chose three persons—two Kadets and one Trudovik, who was also a member of the Jewish Duma contingent—to go to Belostok on a fact finding mission. The decision to send deputies to investigate the conduct of Tsarist officials, at the same time when the executive branch would presumably be making its own investigation in response to the June 2 interpellation, was a direct slap at the administration. This decision would be among the causes for dissolution of the First Duma. However, at the time of its appointment, the committee met with the approval of a large bloc of the public, angered as it was to learn that a pogrom had gone on for three days after a supposed change to a new order in the empire. The Duma received numerous statements from aroused citizens protesting the events in Belostok. Collections were taken up and supplies sent to help those who had been wounded or left homeless in that troubled city.

Only six days were to elapse between the June 2 decision to send a deputation to Belostok and the deadline for Stolypin's reply to the first *zaprosy* dealing with the pogrom issue. Finally, on June 8 the handsome minister made a personal appearance in the chamber to present his case. Stolypin admitted that individual gendarme officers, acting independently, had been involved in illegal political agitation, but he claimed that they had received orders to stop in good time; nor had the police set up a "criminal printing press." Such deplorable practices would, moreover, not be tolerated while he remained in office. On the other hand, Stolypin denied that local officials had regularly participated in pogroms. An unfortunate incident in Tsaritsin had, however, given cause for censure of the police.

There ensued a violent expression of doubt and displeasure at Stolypin's remarks, followed by the famous speech of Prince S. D. Urusov, a member of the Kadet Party, who had been an Assistant Minister of the Interior, as well as a recent governor of Bessarabia. Since that province had a large Jewish settlement, Urusov was personally familiar with their plight. Insisting that he did not doubt Stolypin's sincerity, Urusov likewise insisted that, as long as those conducting pogroms could act with impunity, "massacres and civil strife" would continue, independent of any minister's policy. Urusov noted further that, in areas where the police carried out their duties conscientiously, these abuses of justice did not occur. Urusov then alluded to the matter of a printing press which had operated somewhere in the Ministry of the Interior for a brief time until Witte, driven to a fit of "nervous asthma" when he heard about it, had called for an investigation. The press had suddenly disappeared, after Witte questioned the man who did the printing, and neither Stolypin, or any one else would ever learn the truth about that affair. Further abuses would also occur as long as "unknown persons . . . are able to seize parts of the state machinery with their dirty hands." Under these circumstances, Urusov had to judge Stolypin's declaration "unconvincing," since no minister would have the power to act against these "dark forces."

Urusov ended his speech midst shouts of "pogrom makers," aimed at the ministry. He was followed by other deputies whose accusations against the administration would last into the next day. Meanwhile Stolypin's attempts to reply met only with hostility. His claims that he had responded to the best of his ability, that the pogroms were being investigated, and that the guilty would be punished met only boos and catcalls. He came to a stop and left.

On June 9 the chamber adopted a "formula of passage" to the next item of business. In it they denounced the pogroms and condemned the administration for its activity in connection with them. Beyond taking this verbal stand, the First Duma had no method of affecting the executive, however frustrating and unsatisfactory the deputies had found the reply to their interpellation.

Having quickly perceived the futility of constant hammering of the administration through *zaprosy*, the Kadet leaders turned their main efforts toward legislative projects. It had become evident that the First Duma dealt not with isolated instances of injustice, but with a regime which must be changed at the root, wrote Novgorodtsev; the *zaprosy* had pointed up the extent of the evil, but change could come about only through legislating basic reforms.

In at least one case a Kadet law project came directly out of the administration response to an interpellation. The *zapros* in question dealt with death sentences handed down by a courts-martial in Riga to eight workers, who had been convicted for involvement in the deaths of three policemen. The May 6, 1906, sentences had been duly confirmed by the Governor-General of the Baltic provinces, who had also denied the culprits any right of appeal. News of the sentences soon reached some Trudoviks, who immediately spread the word to their fellow deputies. The lower house was up in arms.[10]

The application of the death sentence was to inspire the "most impassioned" interpellation debates in the First Duma, wrote Maklakov. The workers sentenced in Riga instantly became the subject of the first of several similar interpellations, all of which requested the executive to stay particular death sentences until the First Duma could pass a law outlawing capital punishment. The May 12 *zapros* regarding the Riga workers passed unanimously, as did most of the interpellations introduced into the First Duma. It contained no accusation of illegality on the part of the officials who had imposed the sentence, since the trial had been held in an area under emergency legislation, where civilians were subject to military justice. Instead the deputies asked Goremykin whether the death sentences had been halted through "telegraph communication" to the Governor-General of the Baltic, in view of the fact that the Duma's Address of May 5 had "stressed the necessity of halting execution of death sentences."

The chamber did not have to wait long for a reply from the ministry. On May 16 Goremykin sent word that the *zapros* in question had been referred to the Minister of War. Then that very night the news reached the Tauride Palace that the sentences had been carried out. That was the response from the executive branch, M. Vinaver observed tersely, adding that a great blow had been dealt to any lingering hopes that it could be significantly moved by appeals. To add to the impact, previous allusions on the Tauride floor to the Riga workers, some of whom were mere youth, had led some of the deputies into an emotional involvement in their destiny.[11] Certain Trudoviks began talking about a direct appeal to the people, a tactic the Duma leadership was determined to avoid. At a meeting on the seventeenth of May, the Kadets decided to answer the executive, as well as try to calm the mood of the lower house, through quick sponsorship of a bill abrogating the death sentence.

Composed hastily the same night, the bill was ready for introduction onto the floor the next day. Once again the Kadets chose their able parliamentarian, V. Nabokov, as spokesman. At his suggestion, and over considerable objection from the left, the bill was referred to a special fifteen-man committee, and not passed at once. Immediate passage would have been in violation of the Duma statutes.[12] According to that law the signatures of thirty deputies were necessary to introduce a legislative project into the assembly. Such a project could call for the enactment of a new law, or the amendment, or appeal of an existing law. If the proposal received majority approval in the Duma, the appropriate minister was then sent a copy. He had one month to prepare the necessary legislation, and only if he failed to do so could the Duma write and pass its own measure. Hence, it would have been illegal for the

Duma to pass a law abrogating the death sentence on the same day as Nabokov brought in the proposal.

In the case of Nabokov's proposal, the chamber did, however, resort to a device which it employed regularly in order to avoid the month's wait for a reply from the minister before the matter could legally come before the full house. Once the Duma had given its approval to the general outlines of a measure, it could form a special committee to draw up a specific bill. The assembly would then hold a floor discussion of the measure, supposedly to formulate "directions," or provide "material," which the small committee could use as guidelines in its preparation of the project. In reality these discussions often became open debate on the bill itself, although they could not culminate in a house vote on the final bill.

Among the guidelines provided for the special committee chosen to work out the bill abrogating capital punishment, was a recommendation that the group report back in a week. Hoping to avoid the month delay provided by law, the Duma also urged the executive branch to judge the proposal as soon as possible. The request was of no avail, and identical responses from the Ministers of Justice, War, and Navy explained that the full month was essential for the proper consideration of such a complex measure. The ministers' refusal to hurry infuriated many of the deputies, and there was extreme pressure on the Duma leaders to ignore constitutional forms and to submit the measure to a final vote on May 26, the date scheduled for the committee report. Once again those counseling adherence to legal restrictions prevailed, however, and the final house discussion of the law abrogating capital punishment was not held until June 19, 1906, exactly a month after Nabokov had submitted the original proposal.

The June 19 session was distinguished by the most violent confrontation between the deputies and representatives of the executive which was to occur in the First Duma.[13] First to speak for the administration was Minister of Justice Ivan Shcheglovitov, who denied that it was an opportune moment to abolish the death sentence for political offenders.

Interrupted once, noisy shouts of "Resign! Retire!" echoed in his ears as he left the tribune. Next on the docket, the Chief Naval Prosecutor pointed out, quite accurately, that according to the Fundamental Laws, the military codes, which alone provided for the death sentence in Russia except in the instance of crimes against the person of the sovereign, were beyond the competence of the assembly. These two men had put the administration viewpoint in forthright terms and it was in direct opposition to that of the Duma. Hence tensions were already high when President Muromtsev announced that the Chief Military Prosecutor, General Vladimir P. Pavlov was about to speak for the Minister of War. The response from the floor was instantaneous. To their generation, wrote Maklakov, the hated Pavlov was the personification of the death sentence; Pavlov was famous for removing lenient judges and he did all he could to prevent the condemned from escaping the gallows. After Muromtsev's introduction, the general could not utter a word because the chambers so resounded with whistles, desk pounding, and disorderly howls. A white-haired old gentleman jumped up, shook his fist and shouted at the top of his voice: "Get out murderer, executioner! Out!' The outburst, which was not limited to any fraction of the house, completely prevented Pavlov from making his statement. Muromtsev hastily called for an hour intermission, after which the representatives of the executive reappeared, aside from Pavlov. The house heard out the presentation of Assistant Minister of Internal Affairs A. A. Makarov in silence, although the familiar cry of "Retire" followed his remarks.

Before proceeding to the final vote on the bill outlawing capital punishment, several Duma orators expressed sharp reactions towards the representatives of the executive who had appeared that day. Their hatred for Pavlov—"all his life a bloodletter and executioner" exclaimed Anikin at one point—dominated the discussion. Appalled by the tone of his fellow legislators, Count Geiden spoke briefly for those who believed that no one's freedom of speech, including a man like Pavlov, should be violated in the Duma's chambers. Vinaver retorted that he too revered the principle of freedom of speech, adding however, that even that principle had its limits. While he would agree that the Minister of War had a right to present his case, Vinaver considered the choice of Pavlov to represent him an unnecessary "provocation" of the Duma. As a result Vinaver "wholeheartedly shared the indignation of all" who had noisily prevented Pavlov from speaking.

Thus, on June 19, Max Vinaver, one of the most influential Kadets in the First Duma, openly sympathized with what Petrunkevich later called the Trudovik tactic of "shouting the ministers from the hall." To their leader, Aleksei Aladin, the issue was clear cut and simple. The Duma should let anyone speak who had a minimum of integrity and honor, who "could look an honorable man straight in the eye." Since Aladin did not believe that the "executioner" Pavlov met those requirements, in the "name of the Trudovik group" he was ready to inform the Minister of War that "Pavlov would not be permitted to say another word from the tribune."

The climax of the passionate June 19 session was the triumphant passage, in spite of the administration's outright disapproval, of a measure totally abrogating capital punishment. Until a complete review of the criminal codes could be completed, the Duma law provided for automatic replacement of the death sentence by the next most severe punishment on the books for the offense in question. The measure applied to military as well as civilian courts, and would even have abolished capital punishment by the military in wartime, had it become the law of the land. A simple statute of two short articles, the law ending capital punishment was the only piece of legislation which the First Duma initiated and carried through to final approval. It was probably unconstitutional since military codes were beyond Duma competence. The measure remained a dead letter since it was never passed by the upper house; it was sent to that body on the day after passage, but it never emerged from a State Council special commission.

Like so many of the law proposals introduced into the

First Duma, the statute outlawing capital punishment was a ringing declaration of principle, announced largely for public consumption, rather than a serious piece of legislation. Before it could become a law it had to be approved by the State Council and signed by the Tsar. His administration's position on the issue was a matter of public record, and the Duma leaders knew full well that the likelihood of obtaining his signature was very remote.

A mere listing of some of the other major legislative proposals introduced into the First Duma gives witness to the kind of broad sweeping measures which came before it: May 15, civil equality; May 8, inviolability of person; May 30, freedom of assembly; May 12, freedom of conscience; June 1, freedom of association; July 4, freedom of the press. There they all were on legislative parade—the cherished civil rights which had been the goal of the Russian liberation movement. Heady with the victories already achieved through pressure on an unsure autocrat, the deputies worked to provide legislation which would guarantee civic freedoms, some of which had already been promised in the October Manifesto.

In his speech to the Duma on May 13, Goremykin had noted that existent "temporary regulations" establishing civic freedoms should be replaced by permanent statutes. At the same time, he warned, it was "essential to arm the administrative authorities with effective means . . . to prevent abuses of the liberties which had been granted and to combat . . . threats to the public and the state." There was no reference to civil equality in Goremykin's speech, other than the comment that peasants should have "equal civil and political rights with the other classes." Second-class status for peasants was, however, but one of many legalized discriminations which the First Duma hoped to eliminate. Of particular concern to the deputies were the irksome discriminatory laws against Jews. Goremykin's silence on the issue of anti-Jewish restrictions reflected the view of his sovereign that these statutes should remain unchanged.[14]

The project about civil equality provides an excellent

illustration of the broad and vague nature of First Duma legislative measures. First mentioned on May 15, 1906, the measure came up for discussion before the full house on June 5.[15] Piloting the debates this time was Kadet Feodor F. Kokoshkin, a professor of constitutional law at Moscow University and the party's leading expert on constitutional questions. Kokoshkin was ill much of the time while the First Duma was in session, but he still played a major role in determining Kadet strategy in the chamber. Kokoshkin proposed that the assembly elect a thirty-three-man committee to work on the civil equality project. Stressing the complexity of drawing up such a measure, he noted that the final project must abolish discriminatory laws, like the restrictions on Jews, as well as replace existing laws with positive legislation. Hence, he proposed that legislative work be divided into four categories. One category of legislation would remove all special privileges granted to the gentry, while the other three would remove all discriminations levied on the basis of: (1) class (especially those against the peasants), (2) nationality or religion, and (3) sex.

In other words the proposed measure should provide for no less than the abolition of all legalized discriminations then in effect in the Russian Empire. Meanwhile the debates about the proposal provided an opportunity for many a deputy to express his opinions against, or give examples of, these discriminations. Not surprisingly, deputies from the minority groups were especially anxious to air their special grievances against the Russian administration.

One of the main spokesmen for removal of the anti-Jewish laws was S. I. Rosenbaum, a Zionist lawyer from Minsk *guberniia* in Belorussia where there was a large concentration of the empire's Jewish population. Rosenbaum's plea—that it was a matter of having no means of subsistence for many Jews crowded into cities in the Pale, subjected to unfair discrimination—found support from deputies of other minorities. I. K. Zabolotnyi, a Ukrainian, had no time for administration supporters who blamed the misery of "both of the oppressed nationalities" in his region, namely the Jews and the Ukrainians, on the tendencies of members of each group to "stick together." To Zabolotnyi, it was like telling two men who were manacled together that their misery came, not from their oppressors, but from their being "manacled together on a single chain." Zabolotnyi urged that the oppressed unite against the administration and support the proposed civil equality measure.

Count Geiden pointed out the difficulties of ending a long entrenched system of legalized inequality in one fell swoop, but as usual his fellow deputies paid no heed to his cautions. The chamber proceeded to elect the thirty-three man commission to put the broad principles it had elaborated into specific bills, after having ignored Geiden's suggestion that it was unrealistic to expect a single committee to draw up projects on such basically different and complicated issues as Jewish equality and the legal status of the peasantry. The committee took up its complicated task, but it had only begun to function when the First Duma came to the end of its existence.

Nor did any of the other measures designed to guarantee civil rights to Nicholas's subjects get beyond the initial stages in the First Duma legislative process. At the time of dissolution, the first three on the above list were in special committees, while the remainder had not even been taken up in plenary session after their initial introduction. In addition to these projects there were several bills dealing with the institution of the Duma. A June 1 project to strengthen the inviolability of Duma members was in committee, as was a proposal to amend those sections of the Duma statutes which crippled the assembly's legislative initiative. Significant preliminary work on a new electoral law for the Duma elections, and on a measure for local government reform had brought these projects near readiness for consideration by the house.[16]

The bulk of the work done on First Duma legislative measures must be attributed to the Kadets. They had put in many hours even before the chamber convened, while in the special committees chosen to draw up final bills, the

Kadets again took the lead. It was a hectic time for the members of these legislative commissions, and First Duma memoirists chafe at the charge that their assembly accomplished virtually nothing during its short life. Given the large number of uneducated deputies in the assembly, the technical aspects of its business fell on the shoulders of a fraction of the total membership, and many of the most capable deputies served on more than one legislative commission. Committee meetings had to be held mornings or at night after general sessions, which themselves often ran into very late hours. They "worked literally every free hour," recalled P. Novgorodtsev, adding that, even after the decision not to hold plenary sessions on Wednesday or Saturday, there was never enough time to handle the crush of business.[17]

In spite of the heavy work schedule, the difficult task of putting broad principles into specific bills, and getting committee members of diverse views to accept a final version, left most proposals still in committee when the First Duma came to a close. Actually most of the broad proposals still in committee when the First Duma came to a close never made it to committee. They were put on the agenda for future consideration, but the mounting number of interpellations cut deeply into the time available in plenary sessions. The Duma leaders realized that the assembly should devote more of its time to legislative measures, but they had not come upon an adequate means of channeling and limiting the *zaprosy* by the end of the First Duma.

To Kokovtsov, however, the proceedings in the lower house were all of a piece:

> Inquiries on the most varied subjects poured in upon the government from the Duma as if from a horn of plenty. Interspersed with these were disjointed discussions of the most radical projects relating to the agrarian problem, general political amnesty, the abolition of capital punishment and so forth.

Since amnesty was the prerogative of the sovereign, there had been no project of a "general political amnesty" on the Duma agenda, but Kokovtsov was right in an additional claim that the assembly never gave serious consideration to a number of the legislative measures the administration presented to it. With one exception, these proposals were neither discussed or rejected; they merely appeared on the agenda as brief announcements that they had been received. It was only after the establishment of two permanent committees, budget and finance, that any government projects were even sent to committee.[18]

The nature of these administration bills, when contrasted to the sweeping measures introduced by the deputies, revealed as much about the gulf between assembly and executive as the frequent heated clashes between representatives of these two government branches on the Tauride floor. In his May 13 address, Goremykin referred to several specific projects under consideration in the ministries for future presentation to the Duma. Then on May 15 came the first actual proposal from the executive branch. It was an appropriation request from the Minister of Education to rebuild a greenhouse and construct a clinic laundry at Dorpat (Iurev) University! And while none of the government bills which followed dealt with such trivial matters, neither did they provide for any of the broad reforms sought by the Duma.

Yet not all of them deserved to be totally ignored. For example, the projects of the Ministry of Justice, announced to the assembly on June 1, would have led to important improvements in local court procedures, and to the establishment of the principle of criminal responsibility for officials. Under the existing system, officials could not be indicted for civil service offenses without the approval of their chiefs. The Kadet newspaper *Rech* admitted that both of these bills contained desirable reforms, but concluded that partial reforms were pointless, since the whole system needed an overhaul. The First Duma took no action on either measure.[19]

Of sixteen projects which arrived from the ministers—most of those mentioned in Goremykin's speech did not appear—the only one to receive consideration in a plenary session was the June 19, 1906, request for appropriations to assist victims of famine. It was a matter of dire necessity that additional relief be provided to rural areas, and both Duma and executive realized the seriousness of the situation. The harvest of 1905 had been poor in extensive areas and it was clear by early 1906 that heavy expenditures from the treasury were needed for seed and food. By late spring there was considerable evidence that the 1906 harvest would also be disastrous. The ministers were to discuss the grim agricultural situation in mid-July and arrive at the following pessimistic conclusions for their sovereign: of 127 *uezds* in Western Russia and the Volga regions reporting poor yields in the summer of 1906, 88 had seen a similar crop failure the previous season. The result was that these stricken areas would be left with absolutely no reserves of seed or food to tide them over.[20]

Members of the First Duma had also been receiving increasingly disturbing reports of the suffering and hunger in the provinces, especially along the Volga. An interpellation of May 16 questioned the Minister of Internal Affairs about administration plans for dealing with the shortages and asked if he intended to remove irksome bureaucratic obstacles to famine aid from private persons and organizations. In addition, it sought an explanation for a government circular forbidding aid to families of persons arrested for participation in agrarian disorders.[21] On June 22, just four days short of the legal month delay allowed a minister before his reply to a *zapros*, Peter Stolypin made a personal appearance before the lower house. Before Stolypin began, confessed Gurko, the latter had some misgivings about his chief's ability to present the ministry's case successfully. "But I was mistaken," Gurko admitted. Not only did the Minister of Internal Affairs speak "loudly, distinctly, and masterfully," but he had an imposing appearance which proved a great asset. Tall, handsome, and slender, his was a "dignified . . . even Majestic" stature.

Furthermore, his talk was "permeated by an inner conviction and sincerity," and topped off by some "happy phrases and figures of speech."

Stolypin outlined the administration program of famine relief and summarized expenditures already made from the imperial budget for measures such as the distribution of grain, seed, and cattle fodder. While not denying that a policy of refusing aid to families of those arrested for rural disturbances had ever been in effect, he stated that it was no longer a permissible policy. Stolypin also admitted that there had been instances of officials hindering private groups who tried to extend supplementary relief in famine areas. Some of these had been cases of pure misunderstanding, Stolypin explained, and he assured his listeners that henceforth such private efforts would meet only cooperation from centrally appointed officials. As to the Duma itself, it could play its role in this important matter of famine relief by approving an appropriation request for additional funds which would soon be forthcoming from the administration.

Stolypin's June 12, 1906, presentation in the Tauride Palace was a sample of many which were to follow before his assassination in 1911. Prince Peter Dolgorukii, Vice-Chairman of the Duma, agreed with Gurko that it was an impressive performance, due to Stolypin's "calm, self-confident manner" and his ability to present data so that everything sounded "clear and simple." Dolgorukii, a long time *zemstvo* worker with considerable experience with famine aid projects, disagreed with the minister's claims about the administration relief program; yet the vice-chairman had to concede that Stolypin's arguments would give the impression to anyone, with an inadequate knowledge of the facts, that the administration was doing what it could to cope with the problem.[22]

Stolypin's ability to handle himself so ably before the Duma was to serve him well in the near future. Clearly the strongest figure in Goremykin's cabinet, he would soon replace the latter as Chairman of the Council of Ministers, at the same time retaining the important portfolio of

Internal Affairs. Unlike so many of his colleagues in the Goremykin ministry, Stolypin, or the man he sent to represent the Ministry of Internal Affairs, generally made a strong effort to defend administration policy in specific terms before the new assembly. On the other hand, like their colleagues, they made no significant concessions to First Duma demands. It would not have been in accord with administration policy to do so.

First and foremost, Nicholas was unalterably opposed to the reforms sought by the First Duma and no man could have remained in the cabinet who recommended that he give in to assembly demands. Secondly, Stolypin himself considered the Kadet program, as outlined in the Address to the Throne, totally unrealistic and dangerous, and unsuited to the needs of Russia in 1906. Apprehensive about the First Duma before it opened, at first the newly appointed Minister of Internal Affairs had favored a "watch and wait" policy. He even conceded that it was not surprising to hear violent language from men who had so recently acquired freedom of speech. By mid-May, however, the stands taken by the new assembly confirmed his early fears. His attitude toward the fledgling legislature was in part a response to the proceedings on the floor, but it must also be seen as a reflection of his general political outlook.[23]

In Stolypin's opinion Russia was not ready for parliamentary government, and the discussions in the Tauride Palace served only to reinforce this conviction. He considered the empire's electorate too unstable and uneducated; its educational and economic level had to be raised substantially before it could participate adequately in the legislative process. In order to achieve an upgrading of the electorate, the country needed a thorough reorganization of its social, economic, and administrative structure. An outdated system had, moreover, been considerably weakened by the Asian war and the subsequent internal revolution, still far from under control. Order had to be restored, he thought, and it would take a strong, efficient central government to do so. Essential basic reforms could likewise be better achieved from the center, and the dilatory nature of parliamentary government could only be a hindrance at such a crucial time. Not an advocate of a return to the old absolutism on the other hand, Stolypin was in favor of retaining the Duma, but he would tolerate it only in so far as it fit into his scheme for rebuilding Russia. It should remain as an organ to advise the administration and to ratify its measures, without diverting administration plans. These then were the underlying views which guided Stolypin in his dealings with the First Duma, and its successors.

Just seven days after Stolypin's talk on famine relief before the assembled deputies, the Duma took up the appropriation request that he had told them to expect. From Minister of Finance V. N. Kokovtsov, the request sought Duma approval of a 50,000,000 ruble expenditure for victims of poor harvests. Since the executive branch could not meet the emergency from its regular funds, and as it did not anticipate a favorable balance in the year's budget, it asked that the money be granted as "extraordinary credits" to be raised by "special measures," namely a loan.[24]

The Duma referred Kokovtsov's request to both its budget and famine relief committees, where the decision how best to respond to it presented Duma leaders with a real dilemma, Vinaver admitted. Should the Duma give money to a government in which it had expressed "no confidence," hence weakening the assembly's "principle position?" On the other hand, if the Duma denied the administration the funds, it would be acting against starving citizens, an inhumane action which would be badly received by the public.[25] Furthermore, an outright refusal to approve the request might give the executive branch a just cause for a showdown with the legislature.

On June 23, 1906, the chairman of the famine committee reported its recommendations to a plenary session. As a compromise measure the assembly should grant 15,000,000 rubles, less than a third of the sum requested. It should be used for seed and food, and a demand for a strict accounting of the funds should accompany the appropriation bill. Reporting for the budget committee. Kadet M. I. Gertzenstein of Moscow expressed his group's disapproval of resorting to another loan; the money should be found in the current budget. Ultimately the recommendations of these committees were largely incorporated into the measure, in spite of Kokovtsov's efforts to defend the administration's request for the larger sum and for special means to finance the expenditures.

The 15,000,000 ruble appropriation for famine assistance was the sole ministerial project to be discussed in a full session of the First Duma. Furthermore, it was one of two measures from any source which got to the stage of final acceptance by the lower house. Unlike the other bill, the one abrogating capital punishment, the famine relief appropriation received State Council approval as well. In spite of requests from administration representatives that the upper house restore the original 50,000,000 ruble figure, the State Council voted for the First Duma version of the bill, and it became a law when Nicholas signed it on July 3, 1906.

The 1906 search for famine relief funds in an already overstretched imperial budget was a repeat of past crises faced by Nicholas's government in years of poor harvest and the debate about this bill highlighted the broader problem of the dire situation in the Russian countryside. The man who sponsored it knew that it was merely another stopgap measure, and so did those who voted for it in both assembly chambers that June.

CHAPTER X

Private Property Must Remain Inviolable

The peasant question and the land issue! Virtually every-one in Russia, who gave any thought to the problems of his country, knew that the poverty and backwardness of rural Russia was the most pressing issue in the empire. In 1906 some eighty percent of Nicholas's subjects still depended on agriculture for all, or a large share, of an often precarious livelihood. As they tilled their plots, they faced the tremen-dous physical hazards to agriculture ever present in that vast northern land. In addition, most Russian farmers used very primitive methods to cultivate the soil. The situation had been getting worse throughout the late nineteenth century because a rapidly expanding peasant population had put increased pressure on already overworked land, especially in the central agricultural region, once Russia's main granary. In that area, as in most others in a country only in the early stages of industrialization, there were few opportunities for nonagricultural employment to supple-ment meager farm incomes. Of course in years of poor harvests—and 1905 and 1906 fit into that category—chronically bad conditions were much worse.[1]

Even in good years, however, backward techniques and, over extensive areas, an outdated communal system of land use and tenure, resulted in very low yields from most of Russia's arable. A relatively small number of commercial farms, located mostly in the south and west, provided much of the tonnage for the important grain export trade, so vital to obtain foreign exchange: during the first decade of the twentieth century wheat on the average accounted for forty-eight percent of Russian exports.[2] These commercial farms were an exception in a huge expanse of unproductive, often subsistence, extensive peasant agriculture. Scattered throughout were the estates of the gentry, also worked by the peasants, and frequently as inefficiently managed as the villagers' communal lands. To supplement their own tiny plots it was common for the peasants to rent a share of the estate lands in return for labor or, less often, for a rental fee. These arrangements were frequently made on a short-term basis, giving the peasant no incentive to try to improve his methods of tillage for future advantage. In addition, land rental costs had been rising steeply.

Some of the estates were owned by absentee landlords, interested only in exploiting their property to keep up an increasingly costly urban life style. Complaints of falling income and rising costs were a commonplace among urban folk who strove to live off landed property, as well as among estate owners still on the family estates. Frequently the estates were mortgaged to the hilt. In addition, the total acreage in the hands of the gentry had been declining at an accelerating rate for a generation. Low world grain prices during the last fifteen years of the nineteenth century had added to already pressing economic problems, forcing many a noble to sell off sections of the family property, piece by piece. Much of this land had gone to the peasants, either through direct sale or through the Peasant Land Bank, a state institution which bought up land for resale to peasants at a low cost.

In 1905 the peasantry was already in possession of the larger share of the total arable in European Russia, where the majority of the population lived; comparatively speaking, the gentry and a small number of capitalist farmers did not control vast acreage.[3] Yet to the peasants the landlords' estates were the cause of all their own land hunger. Unaware of the often precarious condition of the bank book at the local manor house, all that the peasants could observe was an apparently grand living style compared with their own miserable existence in crowded dirty huts.

They harbored deep grievances against these local squires, whose lands they had to till for such small recompense. Furthermore, those peasants who managed to purchase sections of the gentry lands found the prices rising sharply in recent years.

To many of the peasants suffering from very serious economic problems, finding it harder every year to pay burdensome dues and taxes, the best solution seemed to be to divide up the large estates to supplement the acreage under peasant control. In part this desire was the reflection of long held village traditions. "Our backs are yours, but the land is ours" had been a peasant saying during the days of serfdom. Then came the Emancipation of 1861, under the terms of which considerable land tilled by the peasants had gone to the landlords. The former especially resented the "cut-offs," lands which had been used in common before their assignment to the landlords by the emancipation act. The peasants thus felt cheated and the conviction lasted through ensuing generations that they had a historic right to some, if not all, of the squires' acreage. Eventually the rallying cry throughout the expanses of rural Russia became "land reform." Land should go to land-poor peasants at the expense of all nonpeasant proprietors—the state, the church, and the imperial family, as well as the private landlords. More land was necessary if the peasantry were to survive, and it was only fair that the land should belong to those who tilled it.

The villagers' conviction that land reform was necessary was shared by many members of the liberation movement, including a surprising number of landlords who expressed willingness to give up part, or all, of their own property. Far from a large percent of the gentry, some of these men were moved by humanitarian motives, while others viewed the sacrifice as the only way to avoid a peasant *jacquerie*. Another consideration influenced many of the liberationists. If they were to enlist the peasants in the cause of overthrowing the autocratic system, it was essential to have an agrarian program which appealed to the villagers.

A few economists and agricultural experts, including some

from within the bureaucracy itself, insisted that the small addition to each plot possible even after total land redistribution could not bring about basic changes in the overall peasant economy. They stressed that the situation in rural Russia would change significantly, only through the employment of improved techniques of cultivation, which would greatly raise the low yields then prevalent. While proponents of land reform heartily agreed that land productivity also had to be raised, few were swayed by their opponents' arguments against land confiscation. Kadet A. A. Kaufman, frequently called in as an outside expert to advise Duma leaders on agricultural matters, admitted frankly that many points about land reform were subject to valid argument. A reasonable case could be made for preserving some large farms for instance. But, he wrote, to object in principle to the alienation of private property was a rejection of the sole available means of responding to peasant needs.[4]

Kaufman's position reflected that of the majority of the members of the Russian reform movement, and by the spring of 1906 all of the major opposition parties had a land reform plank in their party statements. It had been a relatively simple matter to adopt a broad position in favor of land reform, but as party leaders met to draft even the basic outlines for such a vast undertaking, they opted to leave many points vague and open for future settlement. In the first place they faced a dearth of accurate statistics on the amount of arable that would be available for distribution to the peasants. Then a host of practical questions immediately loomed: Should there be compensation to those whose lands were expropriated, and how should it be funded? Should the expropriation of private estates be partial or total? Would the destruction of all the large farms in the empire be detrimental to the national economy, dependent as it was on agricultural exports? Should land owned by a peasant be subject to confiscation if it exceeded a set norm? The problems connected with determining an equitable norm were staggering. In addition to the practical matter of regional differences, there was the question of the

theoretical basis for making the allotments. The two criteria most often advanced were a just "consumption norm,"
namely enough land to sustain a family at a decent level,
or a "labor norm," which would entitle each household to
as much land as it could cultivate. Perhaps most basic was
the problem of how, and by what governmental unit, should
land reform be administered? And once the allotments were
made, should the plots be held under terms of peasant
ownership or long-term lease? What about a procedure for
reallotments as family units changed in size?

To the socialists it was a matter of primary importance
that the land reform not create a class of small peasant
owners, and that the administration and ultimate title to the
lands remain under some governmental unit. The Social
Revolutionaries claimed to have the solution to this dilemma with their demand for "socialization of the land." The
land would belong to no one and an individual would have
only the right to work it. Land would become public property, "the possession of the entire nation," without compensation to former owners. Private property, whether belonging to an individual or a group, would be abolished, and all
land put under the control of central, regional, and local
units of popular government. The latter would consist of
"democratically organized, classless, rural and municipal
communes."[5]

After their 1903 party congress, the Social Democrats, the
major socialist rivals to the SRs, sought the return to the
peasants of the "cutoffs," that is those lands lost by the
peasants to the landlords at the time of the emancipation.
Coming almost half a century after the settlement of 1861,
the implementation of such a proposition would have caused
enormous practical difficulties. Perhaps more significant,
the hard-hitting jeers it evoked from political enemies had
many a receptive listener in a predominantly peasant country. Partly in an effort to compete with the Social Revolutionaries' call to give the land to those who tilled it, in April
of 1906, after bitter debate, the Social Democrats accepted a
platform advocating the "municipalization of the land."
After confiscation from private owners, the land would be

parcelled out and administered by regional organs of local self-government, organized on democratic principles.

Owing to the decision of the central committees of these two socialist parties to boycott the elections, few of their members sat in the First Duma. However, their ideas on the land issue were reflected in the agrarian bills presented by the Trudovik group. Moreover, it was not only the leftist deputies who arrived in the capital in April of 1906, committed to a program of land reform. The agrarian plank of the Kadets supported an "increase in the amount of land held by those who cultivate it themselves" through the distribution of state, imperial, and monastic lands, and where necessary, through the confiscation of the land of private owners, with compensation at just, not market, prices. The alienated land should be placed in a government reserve. The criteria for the transfer of land from this reserve to those in need would "be determined by the practices of land ownership and land use in various parts of Russia."

Even the Octobrists, the Kadets' major rivals to the right, had an agrarian plank which would permit "alienation of sections of private land, with just compensation under terms set by the legislative power," given "conditions of national gravity" and the insufficiency of all other measures aimed at improving peasant welfare. The latter should include governmental regulation of leases of small plots, reorganization of the activity of the Peasant Land Bank, state sponsored migration, and resettlement aid. Like all the other Russian parties, the Octobrists viewed the lands owned by the state and the imperial family as a "fund for satisfying the land needs of peasants and other ranks of small land holders."

Much of the arable included in the latter categories was already cultivated by peasants, in return for dues paid the state. Furthermore, a very large percent of the 400 million acres of land owned by the state in European Russia was located in forest regions or the polar tundra and was unsuitable for agriculture. In addition, the state held title to all of the land in Siberia, except for territories belonging to Cossack communities or "his Majesty's chancellery" (*kabinetski zemli*). Considerable sections of Siberian land had been settled, mostly by fairly recent migrants who had gone under government sponsorship or on their own hook. The newcomers were usually organized into village communities, which held their land in perpetual use in return for an annual rent. Since 1891 the administration had actively encouraged settlement in Siberia, while in his May 13 speech to the First Duma, Goremykin stated that the further development of migration to "the vast expanses of land suitable for cultivation . . . in the Asiatic possessions of the Empire" would be "one of the most immediate tasks" of the ministry.

Goremykin's remarks on migration reflected a growing awareness during Nicholas's reign that the severe problems of rural Russia demanded increased attention. However, Tsarist measures and ideas about these problems were along lines unalterably opposed to reiterated demands for more land for the tillers at the expense of private owners. The Tsar's views on the confiscation of private property were definite and unswerving. On January 18, 1906, Nicholas addressed a deputation of Kursk peasants with characteristic phraseology:

> I am very happy to see you. You brothers should know of course that all rights of private property are inviolable. That which belongs to the landlord belongs to him, while that which belongs to the peasant is his . . . under the same inalienable right. . . . It can be no other way; here there can be no argument. I want you to convey this to your villagers.

Nicholas went on to assure the Kursk delegation that he would not "forget the peasants, whose needs were so dear to him." Together with the new assembly he would judge the peasant issue in search of the best solution. "You can count on me, I will help you," Nicholas concluded, but then he repeated his earlier statement—"always remember that the rights of property are sacrosanct and must be inviolable." These words of the sovereign, published in *Pravitelstvennyi Vestnik* for general consumption, were similar to statements

Nicholas was to make to more than one noble delegation that same winter. On February 9 he advised a group of Vladimir nobles that measures currently being prepared by his subordinates to mitigate the land needs of the peasants would firmly uphold the rights of private property.[6]

These public statements were not simply words of warning, or soothing assurances, made for the reading public. Rather they were an expression of Nicholas's deeply held convictions and desires. He was very troubled about the situation in rural Russia and he sincerely wanted to sponsor measures to improve it. Yet, the last Romanov Tsar could be a very indecisive leader, and as he contemplated the staggering disruption which would accompany any program of drastic reform in rural Russia, he was filled with an understandable hesitancy. Of one thing he was certain, however; he would be receptive to no agrarian measures which violated the rights of private property.

Nicholas's concern about the peasant issue was not purely a response to the severe riots in the countryside during the revolutionary year. Since the turn of the century he and his administration had been under increased pressure from many sides to do something to improve the dismal state of Russian agriculture.[7] Early in 1902 the Tsar had appointed Sergei Witte, then Minister of Finance, as chairman of an interministerial commission to study the needs of agriculture. At almost the same time Nicholas delegated another group, from within the Land Section of the Ministry of the Interior, to draw up prospective measures which dealt with the peasant problem. Under Witte's commission, central officials, selected experts and specially organized local committees deliberated upon the agricultural question and drew up recommendations, which were eventually bound into fifty-eight volumes. To produce these volumes, over 600 local committees involving more than 11,000 individuals had met and it was the consensus of the majority of their reports that the commune (*obshchina*) should be abolished, or at least permit free exit for its members. Most committees favored making peasants into individual landowners who shared the same civil rights as other citizens.

There had been no specific actions taken as a result of the commission findings when, in March of 1905, Witte received sudden notice that his group was being discontinued. It was replaced by another commission, directed to examine particularly the system of peasant land tenure.

Headed by none other than Witte's arch rival, Ivan L. Goremykin, the new group contained a conservative majority, along with an influential minority who favored abolition of the commune. As a result the Goremykin Conference's recommendations were mixed. While defending communal land tenure and a separate legal status for the peasants, it also favored measures to aid the consolidation of strips into single plots within the commune, and the exit of some peasants from it. Nor should any further measures be taken to bolster communal tenure. The commission also proposed that a single body be instituted to unify agricultural policy. In line with that suggestion, the Chief Administration of Land Organization and Agriculture was set up in early May of 1905, a body eventually used by both Witte and Stolypin to help implement agricultural policies.

Meanwhile the administration showed characteristic indecisiveness and did not act on Witte's recommendation that the commune be abolished, a proposal he had aired regularly to his sovereign since 1898. However, it was not until the widespread agrarian rioting of 1905 that the commune, long considered an essential bulwark of stability in rural Russia, was finally judged to be expendable. By then most of Nicholas's advisors who were at all conversant with agriculture or economics had reached a similar conclusion. In part the changed view toward the commune reflected a growing recognition that it was detrimental to agricultural productivity. Some of its opponents argued that communal agriculture was incompatible with a modern industrial economy. In addition, the sporadic, but widespread, rural riots which had plagued the Tsarist government since the turn of the century, only to peak in 1905, put holes in the claim that the commune provided order in the countryside. These riots, coupled with a mounting crescendo of demands that the large estates be broken up, gave a new urgency to an issue long under consideration. However, there was still great uncertainty just how to proceed.

In a long rambling report of January 9, 1906, Witte ranged about the tense situation in rural Russia and threw out numerous suggestions for future programs and actions. At one point he speculated that if measures were enacted which enabled peasants to leave the communes with their allotments intact, peasant legal consciousness and attitudes toward the property rights of others might improve. This comment evoked a favorable marginal notation in the handwriting of the sovereign, but the Tsar's reaction to another suggestion was negative. Perhaps, conjectured his chief minister, stubborn resistance to any confiscation of private land could result in the landlords' loss of all their property later, under much worse circumstances. To avoid this it might be better to give up part of their lands in 1906, as they had after the emancipation. The underlined notation—"private property must remain inviolable"—left Witte with no cause for doubt. Nicholas's private directives to his subordinates were in accord with his public pronouncements of the same winter.[8]

As to Witte's other observation—that the government might facilitate free egress from the commune with private plots intact—three enactments already in effect were in harmony with that goal. A law of March 12, 1903, sponsored by Witte, had abolished the joint liability of commune members for payment of current direct taxes, as well as arrears accumulated by its members; henceforth, these debts were the responsibility of individual households. Then in August of 1904 Nicholas took advantage of the baptism of his heir to announce the cancellation of all arrears, whether for redemption dues or the state land tax on allotment lands, as of the day of his son's birth. The same act exempted the peasants from corporal punishment, thus removing a major means employed by the tax collectors to influence recalcitrant taxpayers. Then, on November 3, 1905, another decree cut the redemption dues in half for 1906, and promised their total elimination by January of

1907. The commune could no longer hold an individual because he had to pay his share of the redemption debt.[9]

The act of November 3, 1905, thus removed all financial obstacles to free exit from the commune. Henceforth, an individual householder was legally free to claim his share of the allotment lands, but the law had not yet provided any procedure for the separation process. On March 4, 1906, during Witte's tenure as chief minister, a decree providing temporary rules for "land settlement" commissions at the central, *guberniia* and *uezd* levels was issued. It would be the responsibility of these commissions to work out improved methods of land tenure and utilization. They were directed to cooperate with established institutions such as the Peasant Land Bank, as well as to explore new possibilities for government programs. In March of 1906 it was not yet certain what policies they would help carry into effect; eventually they were to be the organs which implemented the Stolypin land decree of November 6, 1906, the provisions of which were in accord with Witte's January 1906 suggestion about facilitating exit from the commune.[10]

As Witte and his associates discussed plans to improve Russian agriculture, it was the chief minister's conviction that their projects must be presented to the First Duma for consideration. His successor, Ivan Goremykin, was, however, very reluctant to let the deputies freely debate the land issue. The two had a heated exchange over the matter at the April Tsarskoe Selo conference, called by Nicholas to review a draft proposal for the 1906 revision of the Fundamental Laws of the Empire. Goremykin argued that the clause on private property was too broad as worded, since it would permit compulsory alienation of private property for "state or social needs." He insisted that the statement be edited so that the Duma "could not touch" private property. Witte countered that it would be a "great mistake" to announce to the peasants in advance that compulsory land alienation would not be permitted. Undoubtedly, the deputies would propose a measure recommending confiscation of private land for peasant use. Since it could not become the law without State Council and sovereign approval, let them propose it. Witte warned that adoption of Goremykin's recommendations would serve only to pit the Duma against the administration before the assembly convened. The elderly Goremykin was not swayed by the reasoning of his long time rival: "If you think that the Duma will raise the question of land division, then it is essential to block this clearly and definitely. . . . Let the peasants await help from the Tsar, not from the Duma. . . ."[11]

Witte's prediction that the First Duma was bound to propose the confiscation of private estates to the benefit of the peasantry proved accurate, while Goremykin's response to the proposal was in harmony with opinions the new chief minister had aired before a receptive Nicholas in early April of 1906. According to Kokovtsov, the decision to hold a firm line against all schemes for land confiscation was one of the few issues on which the Goremykin cabinet agreed completely. Since the First Duma met determined to pursue agrarian policies along exactly that line, the lines of battle were drawn before the assembly made its first public statement on the land issue in its Address to the Throne. That document addressed itself to the problem in no uncertain terms:

> The most numerous sector of the populace, the toiling peasantry, awaits with impatience the satisfaction of its acute need for land. The First State Duma would not execute its duty if it did not work out a law satisfying this vital need. It must achieve this purpose by the use of treasury, appanage, cabinet, monastic and church lands, as well as through the compulsory confiscation of privately owned lands.

Goremykin's response a few days later was even more blunt:

> In regard to . . . the peasant land question . . . the Council of Ministers feels duty bound to announce that the solution of this question on the principles proposed by the State Duma is absolutely inadmissible.[12]

Undeterred by the chief minister's outright rejection of its land reform statement, the Duma proceeded to discuss agrarian measures along principles outlined in its Address. Virtually everyone in the lower house was willing to support some kind of land confiscation, although there was considerable disagreement over the details. Of three land measures eventually introduced into the assembly, the first had appeared in the few day interim between adoption of the Duma Address and Goremykin's reply. The May 8 "Agrarian Project of the 42," a Kadet measure, did not have the endorsement of the party as a whole, and there were several prominent party leaders among its opponents. Nor was it a finished bill, in spite of the fact that the Kadets had begun work on their agrarian measure long before the chamber convened; rather it was a statement of premises on which to base a final bill.[13]

The Proposal of the 42 declared that "the firm guarantee of land to the agricultural population" was its overall aim. To achieve that goal the state must draw upon treasury, imperial, church and monastic lands and, to the "extent necessary," it must also resort to "compulsory alienation of privately owned lands" at state expense. Present owners should be compensated at a "just price" based on the "normal productivity for a given locality under conditions of independent cultivation." High land prices created by the current land shortage should not determine compensation figures. Alienated land would go into a state land fund for distribution to "land hungry and landless agricultural families" on the basis of a "consumption norm" sufficient to provide average necessities to a family. All families in an area whose property did not meet the local consumption norm would have the right to an allotment. Beneficiaries would be entitled to "long term use" of the land in return for payments based on its productivity. The land fund would be administered by central and local institutions. Section V of the proposal dealt with the rules for expropriating private lands. All arable property which lay fallow as of January 1, 1906, or which was customarily leased by peasants, or tilled by them with their own stock and equipment, was "subject to alienation without limit." Beyond that, in each locale the law must set an upper limit to acreage tilled with landowners' equipment. All land above that figure would be subject to confiscation: in cases of extreme need, or to avoid harmful strip farming, acreage under that figure might also be alienated. A list of exceptions included such specific items as land under hospitals, educational institutions, or agricultural processing plants. There was also a broad category aimed at the preservation of efficient units; farmlands of "exceptional character" should remain in private hands.

The Kadet's Project of the 42 was introduced as "material" to be turned over to a specially elected Duma agrarian committee, charged with the huge task of drawing up a specific bill. Chosen on June 6, 1906, the commission was to total no less than ninety-nine members, so as to allow representation of as many regions and political groups as possible. Also channeled to this large and unwieldy committee was a second agricultural project, the Trudovik "Project of the 104," which came before the Duma on May 23, 1906, just ten days after Goremykin made his famous speech. Its authors sought the eventual full scale nationalization of the land: "the land must belong to all the people . . . to be distributed for use, only to those who work it with their own labor." Every citizen would have the right to an allotment based on the amount he could cultivate, i.e., a "workers' norm." All landed property in excess of a set norm should go into a state fund; the norm would vary from one region to another and compensation rates for confiscated land would also be determined locally.

Just before the adjournment of the June 6 session, President Muromtsev announced that a third agrarian proposal, signed by thirty-three deputies, had arrived. Its Trudovik sponsors wanted it sent as supplementary material for the Duma agrarian commission, since they considered the project of the 104 deficient in certain respects. The new project, which came up for house discussion two days later, began with a very radical proposition: "All private landed property rights within the limits of the Russian Empire are henceforth completely abolished." The land, with its waters and resources, would belong to the total population, all of whom would have the right to use it, for agricultural and other economic purposes, as well as for the establishment of dwelling units. All citizens would have the right to obtain materials to provide them with essential heat and shelter. The measure, with its rather sweeping proposals for socialistic use and direction of the nation's resources, was not accepted by the First Duma, even as material for the agrarian committee.[14]

As these land measures came before the lower house, they gave rise to so-called "debates on directions" which were to be used by the agrarian commission in its work. Supposedly designed to provide guidelines for that group, the debates actually became a full-scale airing of the woes of rural Russia, rather than a discussion of legislative means to improve the situation. Frequently heated and arousing strong passions, the agrarian debates dominated the Duma schedule between May 15 and June 6. Yet, there was never any serious doubt that the Kadet project would be sent to committee. So was the first Trudovik project, although many influential Kadets considered it and the second Trudovik proposal very unrealistic. Almost two hundred deputies applied to speak on the issue, and well over a hundred did so. Towards the end of the second week of discussion, there were still 115 orators signed up, awaiting their turn at the tribune. The result was far more contributions than were necessary to exhaust the subject from all sides represented in the lower house, according to A. Kaufman, Kadet expert on the agrarian question. The peasant deputies "nearly all read their speeches," wrote Bernard Pares, and having done so, each would "proudly dispatch the draft to his constituents." The item those constituents wanted was more land, and each deputy wanted his voters to know that he had made a public appeal to satisfy that demand. Consequently there was much in the discussion which was repetitious and unconstructive; on the other hand, Kaufman observed, these discourses from representatives of all corners of the empire served also to point up the complexity of the issue for the drafters of the final bill.

Once again the deputies from the minority groups used the Duma floor to air their unique complaints against the Tsarist government. In the case of land reform, however, they also brought up a specific objection. The terms of a land reform bill based on the communal land tenure system of Great Russia were simply not appropriate for the border areas of the empire. Members of the Polish Kolo had objected to the establishment of any all-empire land law during preliminary discussions of the Kadet proposal. During the floor debates, similar objections were voiced by deputies from the Ukraine, the Baltic regions and Belorussia. All of them insisted that appropriate land reform measures could be decided upon, and put into effect, only by units of autonomous self-government. To many of these men, the concentration of land into a single land fund would be against the best interest of the agricultural population of their region. It would represent the "imposition of communal land tenures on the Western borderlands where private ownership prevailed." Underneath these objections was a fear that the distribution of an all-Russian land fund would be but another device promoting centralization, and further Russification of border areas.[15]

By the close of the three weeks devoted to the land question, the orators spoke to an almost empty chamber, with those few in attendance generally engaged in private conversation and paying little heed to the speaker. After May 24, President Muromtsev habitually skipped the sessions. On May 30, M. Vinaver gained approval of his motion that only one-half of each session be devoted to the land issue. Throughout there was great reluctance to apply available cloture provisions, although speakers were requested to limit their speeches to ten minutes. Registration to speak on the issue was closed on May 27, although an exception was made for late arrivals from the Caucasus.[16]

The assembly did have some relief, however unwelcome, from the monotony during two subsequent mid-May sessions which were distinguished by visits from representatives of the administration.[17] First to present the executive's viewpoint was A. S. Stishinskii, Minister of Agriculture. The latter gave a tactful speech stressing the legal aspects of confiscation; he described land confiscation as an exceptional measure, to be resorted to only after careful consideration of individual cases. A general confiscation of private land would be harmful to the economy, he insisted, while the amount of land thus made available for redistribution would provide only negligible increments for each peasant proprietor. The benefits gained would be too small to justify the breakup of the large estates, while many peasants would be deprived of employment on them. Stishinskii, whose reasoned arguments had statistical backing, made a decent personal impression on his listeners, regardless of their opinions of his arguments. His presentation was "calm in tone and valid in argument," wrote Kadet agricultural expert A. Kaufman, observing further that there was a marked contrast between Stishinskii's remarks and the polemical attack on the Duma land program made by the next speaker, V. I. Gurko, an experienced official in the Department of Land Affairs of the Ministry of the Interior.

Gurko recalled that he had been up all night before the May 19, 1906 session in order to prepare his talk. He was very tired when he reached the Tauride Palace the next day, where, to his dismay, he did not get the floor until late in the afternoon. The trying delay had increased the natural agitation which accompanied a maiden performance before the deputies. Yet, he assured the readers of his memoirs, once at the tribune he spoke in a "voice clear and strong and commanding"; his audience listened attentively and the "speech made a tremendous impression." Gurko attributed its impact as much to his data as to his method of presentation. This self-evaluation received corroboration in the May 19 diary entry of A. Polovtsov, whose author found Gurko an "especially talented orator."[18]

Unlike the Minister of Agriculture, Gurko chose a querulous, mocking tone with which to present his arguments. The cases put forth by the two men were very similar, however, while both of them also devoted some time to the administration plans for dealing with the peasant problem. Gurko claimed that much more could be achieved, at considerably less cost, if these programs were carried out; Duma schemes would be more expensive and less effective. Gurko's concluding remarks were a public announcement of an administration viewpoint which had been gaining increased acceptancy in the upper bureaucracy:

> Not by abolishing private ownership in land, but by securing for each peasant, private ownership of the allotment land now in his possession . . . shall the State Duma earn the gratitude of the Russian people.

Gurko's arguments did not convince his listeners, while the tone he adopted merely served to irritate them further. In his memoirs Izvolskii nicely summarized the basic clash between the ministry's position and the Duma stance: all the Duma land proposals stressed the need to expropriate the lands of the great proprietors. That demand appeared to meet the almost unanimous desire of the assembly, while the executive regarded it as "absolutely impossible." The Duma leadership, on the other hand, was equally recalcitrant about giving a hearing to administration measures. On June 12 the deputies learned that land proposals, designed to widen peasant landownership, had arrived from the Ministry of Agriculture. Duma action consisted of a cryptic announcement of their arrival and the measures were not sent to committee. The proposals were in line with Gurko's and Stishinskii's arguments before the Duma, as well as the Stolypin measures of the following fall.[19]

In addition to statements sent to the Duma, the administration publicly aired its plans for dealing with the agrarian issue in a "communique," which appeared in the June 20, 1906, issue of *Pravitelstvennyi Vestnik*.[20] The communique contained several promises about the projected expansion of traditional efforts to aid the peasants, such as the Peasant Land Bank and migration assistance. Much more significant, however, were those sections which revealed departures from previous policies. The opening paragraph, for example, contained a reference to measures already sent to the First Duma which would "improve and widen peasant land ownership, and change the nature of land tenure for peasants on allotment lands." This goal would be partially achieved by transferring all arable still owned by the state to land-poor peasants under favorable terms. In accord with remarks about changing the land tenure system, the communique contained sharp criticisms of the communal system, especially in areas where periodic redistribution of allotments was customary. Since the threat of redistribution deterred an enterprising peasant from efforts to improve his allotment, the administration proposed working towards elimination of the entire system. As an initial step, in communes where there had been no general redistribution for twenty-four years, present plots should be considered inalienably owned, and not subject to future reallotment. For other communes, inalienable ownership of individual plots, preferably consolidated into a single farm, should be the ultimate goal of the administration. Furthermore, peasants should be given the right to leave the commune with their allotments.

The communique was not limited to administration plans, in that about half of its contents consisted of another frontal attack on land confiscation measures. Goremykin's ministry reiterated its intention to "unswervingly preserve the property rights of all." The missive contained a warning to peasants—"If the rights of landowners were destroyed today, then tomorrow it could be the rights of the peasants." The executive branch urged the peasants to see the fallacy in the "widespread conviction . . . that it was necessary to subject all privately owned land to compulsory alienation." Buttressing its arguments with statistical data, the communique tried to convince the rural masses that land division would only be harmful to them. The document concluded with an appeal to rural Russians which had a traditional, paternalistic ring:

239

> The Russian peasantry must know and understand,
> that, not from disorder and force should it expect satis-
> faction of its needs, but from peaceful work and the con-
> stant solicitation of the Sovereign Emperor.

The decision of the ministry to publish an appeal to the
populace over the heads of the First Duma, while not in
violation of the constitution, was a tactless move, given the
obvious mood of the lower house. By so doing, the aged chief
minister "again gave evidence of his scorn for the national
assembly," in the judgment of his colleague from the Ministry of Foreign Affairs; however, to Izvolskii, it was the
"form of the communication, rather than its contents, which
roused the unanimous indignation of the deputies." There
is a good deal to what Izvolskii said. The communique did
not disparage the First Duma directly, while the administration's views on land division were already public knowledge. Yet the document infuriated the deputies, and it led to
considerable debate and indecision about the best response.
The Duma leadership was determined to assure the populace that the assembly stood firm for land reform, and that
the lower house had no connection with the communique.
After considering several alternatives, the chamber finally
adopted the suggestion that its agrarian commission be delegated to compose a "formula of transition" to serve as a
"counter-communique." Aside from instructions that the
formula be printed up for wide distribution, the commission
had no clear guidelines about its task. During the process
of drawing up the statement, the word "appeal" was at one
point substituted for the original title of "resolution." By
permitting this change in title, the First Duma embarked
upon the dangerous course of making a direct appeal for
public support. It was a tactic frequently urged by the Trudoviks, but until then the Kadet leadership had successfully resisted them.[21]

Ironically, when the vote came on the final wording, the
Trudoviks judged it as too moderate and opted to abstain,
rather than defeat the measure. It was not the first time
that the Kadets had failed to muster support from their

unpredictable allies. The first upset to the comfortable majority which had heretofore approved all Kadet measures had occurred on June 16, when the Trudoviks had refused to support the bill on the regulation of public assemblies. During the July 6 final vote on the agrarian appeal, the Kadets were also to lose the support of the Polish Kolo, since their allies to the right wanted guarantees for local autonomy on land reform written into the statement. Having lost these two important blocks of voters, the Duma appeal went through with a small majority. Opposed were some fifty from the right and left wings of the chamber, while a sizeable number of Trudoviks, Poles, and Octobrists abstained. A group of Trudoviks left the hall *en masse*, and there were others who followed suit as the hours wore on. Eventually, when the suggestion arose that the appeal be printed in *Pravitelstvennyi Vestnik*, it was found that the house lacked the quorum necessary to act on the suggestion.[22]

It was the first time in the history of the First Duma that a measure had squeaked through the lower house with a very slim vote. "The Duma had published its dissensions before the world," to use the apt words of Bernard Pares. Furthermore, it had done so during the debates and vote upon a public appeal, "precisely the measure which, of all others, most required firmness and solidarity" if it were to have the desired effect. Moreover, the debates which preceeded final passage, and the variations between texts of the appeal, revealed publically that even the Kadet ranks were far from unanimous in their support of the radical step. Paul Miliukov himself opposed it. The original suggestion that the house adopt such a statement came from a member of one of the small moderate splinter parties in the assembly, not from a Kadet, and there were many influential men in that party who viewed the appeal as a very risky tactic.

The final version of the July 6, 1906, appeal announced the First Duma's intent to stand pat in its support of a land measure based on the principle of compulsory alienation of private property, in return for just compensation. Beyond that, the assembly would "decline all propositions which were not in accord with that principle." Pointing out the promise in the October Manifesto that no proposal could become law without Duma approval, the document concluded with an appeal to the populace to "wait calmly and peacefully" for a carefully composed bill which would provide them with needed land increments.[23]

Thus, matters remained at an impasse between executive and assembly, but this time the First Duma had taken the step which would result in its demise. The narrow vote for the July 6 appeal, and the uncertainty reflected on the lower house floor before final approval, had not gone unnoticed in the imperial palace. Furthermore, there had been much revolutionary talk from the left benches in the Tauride Palace while the measure was under discussion. In addition to newspaper stories, Nicholas had access to his Minister of the Interior's personal account of the heated July 4 session, when the draft version of the agrarian appeal first reached the floor. Stolypin had spent that day in the ministers' box in the Tauride Palace taking careful notes. Located right next to the tribune, the box provided an excellent vantage point for gathering his own impressions. He was not pleased with what he observed. The radical tone of the proceedings, as well as the text of the appeal itself, merely served to confirm Stolypin's gradually crystallizing conclusion that, since it was impossible to work constructively with the First Duma, the time had come to dissolve it. Many of the minister's colleagues in the upper echelons of the bureaucracy heartily supported this view.

CHAPTER XI

Dissolution and Aftermath

Only four days were to elapse between Stolypin's July 4 visit to the First Duma and Nicholas's announcement that it had held its final session:

> On the basis of article 105 of the Fundamental Laws of 1906, we order the dissolution of the State Duma; a newly elected chamber will be convened on February 20, 1907. A special *ukaz* announcing the dates of the next elections will be issued.

With that cryptic decree, Nicholas finally took the step which some of his advisors had always regarded as his only option, given the bellicose character of the lower house. To Kokovtsov, for example, the issue was clear-cut: one had only to recall the drafts of laws debated in the Duma and "the applause with which the most radical of these projects were greeted to see clearly and without any prejudice" that the chamber was becoming a "source of open revolutionary propaganda." Moreover, the only "legal means to fight this propaganda," namely dissolution, "had suggested itself from the first moment" of the chamber's existence.[1]

Nicholas had hesitated to make such a drastic move, however, not because of any conviction that it might be possible to work constructively with the assembly, but because of his very real fears of the public reaction to dissolution. Meanwhile, his reluctance had been shared by several important men close to the Tsar, some of whom had been

243

exploring the possibility of another way out of the impasse between executive and legislature. In an effort to satisfy Duma demands that the Goremykin ministry be replaced by one which enjoyed its confidence, a series of parallel secret talks had been held between leaders of the parties which were most influential in the Duma and members of the bureaucracy or court. The aim of the latter was the appointment of a coalition ministry of progressive bureaucrats and party men. Some, possibly all, of the meetings had the advance sanction of the Tsar, and the negotiations can be regarded as serious. They failed because of a basic split. The Kadets wanted the future ministry to be responsible to the assembly, while the administration refused to give up the traditional system of ministerial responsibility to the sovereign. Beneath this disagreement was a well-founded conviction on the part of the executive that a parliamentary ministry would make demands judged impossible by the administration.[2]

These talks were already in progress when the government communique on the land question appeared in the July 20 issue of *Pravitelstvennyi Vestnik*. It was the chamber's response to the communique, the July 6 Duma appeal, which tipped the scale in favor of dissolution, whereupon the administration abandoned its attempts to form a ministry more palatable to the First Duma. The Kadet's failure to unite the house on the vote for the appeal to the public, coupled with the Duma position favoring land alienation, finally convinced Nicholas that he should dismiss the unruly chamber.[3]

The evening after the assembly had approved the final version of its appeal found the members of Goremykin's cabinet assembled at his pleasant house on the Fontanka. Upon arrival, his colleagues discovered that their chief was not at home. Earlier that day, they were told, he had received a sudden summons to Peterhof. Minister of Interior Stolypin had also been called to the Tsar's palace outside of the capital. The puzzled ministers had no recourse, but to make themselves comfortable and await further developments.[4] About nine o'clock Goremykin returned home in "an unusually gay and animated" mood, bearing the surprise news

of his release as chairman of the ministerial council; ultimately his two most conservative colleagues, Stishinskii
and Shirinskii-Shikhmatov, were to leave with him, while
the rest of his cabinet stayed on. Goremykin also informed
his colleagues that Nicholas had chosen P. Stolypin as their
new chief. The latter would retain his portfolio as Minister
of the Interior along with the top cabinet post. Pressed for
more information, Goremykin revealed that the dissolution
of the First Duma was set for the following Sunday, July 9.
They would shortly hear all the details from his successor,
but in the meantime, the elderly bureaucrat wanted only to
get some sleep. He thereupon left the room "as hastily as he
had arrived," leaving his associates to ponder the startling
news he had brought.

About a half hour later Stolypin arrived and gave them
an account of his audience with the Tsar. He assured them
that he had found the sovereign "quite calm," especially
when his mood was contrasted to the frightened, agitated
state of some in the court entourage. Convinced that dissolution had become urgent, it was indeed their sovereign's
intention to carry it out that very week end. Since Goremykin judged himself inadequate to cope with the events
which might ensue, Nicholas had asked Stolypin to assume
his post. The Tsar had been impatient with Stolypin's protests that he lacked the necessary experience, so much so
that he interrupted Stolypin's remarks with a request that
they pray together before a favorite ikon for help in the
"difficult, perhaps historic, moment."

Nicholas's diary entry for the next day revealed something of the trauma beneath his usual placid exterior: July
8, 1906 was a "busy, fatiguing day" which reminded him of
those terrible days before October 17 of the preceeding year.
The morning had been taken up with reports, the late afternoon by long talks with Goremykin and Stolypin.[5] There
had been much to decide and it had to be done quickly.
Having settled upon Duma dissolution, there was the matter of how to make the news public. There was also the
important issue of security measures to accompany the
dissolution decree.

Fear of renewed outbreaks of revolutionary violence had

been the major deterrent to dissolution each time the proposal had come up that spring. Nagging doubts about the reliability of the army, should it be faced with a popular outburst, had become major fears just a month before, when a rebellious incident had occurred in the Tsar's own beloved First Battalion of the Preobrazhenskii Guard. Nicholas had done his service in that unit, and he was still its titular commander. While order had been restored quickly, the populace as a whole, as well as the royal family, had been inclined to overestimate the significance of the incidence, in the opinion of Minister of War A. F. Rediger. The Dowager Empress, for one, had been shattered by the trouble in the Preobrazhenskii: "While the guard was faithful there was still hope, but now what . . . ?", she sorrowfully asked a friend shortly afterwards. Yet Rediger, himself, had to admit that the troops had encountered considerable difficulty in maintaining order in the nation that spring. Furthermore, no regimental commander could say with certainty that an incident similar to the one in the guard unit would not break out among his men.[6]

Actually the dissolution decree was to lead to no immediate incidents which tested the loyalty of the troops, and hastily taken precautions proved adequate, perhaps unnecessary. At the suggestion of the Governor of St. Petersburg, several cavalry regiments from the guard were called into the city from summer quarters nearby, and the entire *guberniia* was declared under extraordinary security. Polovtsov reported the city quiet, but full of troops, on the ninth of July. The city governor asked those ministers who resided in private quarters to move, temporarily, into official dwellings to aid security measures. Otherwise, they were urged to follow their customary weekend schedules, so as not to arouse the suspicions of the public.[7]

Early Sunday morning, July 9, the city of St. Petersburg was plastered with copies of the dissolution *ukaz*; the text was read from pulpits and posted throughout the empire. A copy on the locked doors of the Tauride Palace greeted the deputies as they began to gather for their scheduled Sunday session. They found the entry to their chambers blocked by police and soldiers and they were unable even to enter to retrieve personal possessions from the hall where they had met during the past three months. That same day the Tsar issued a manifesto containing the administration's case for its drastic action, along with a plea to the populace to maintain order. Although the language had a familiar paternalistic, laborious style, there were sections of it which sounded utterly archaic, even for Nicholas. "True sons of Russia!" it read. "The Tsar calls upon you, much as a father calls upon his children, to rally around him in order to renovate and regenerate our Holy Fatherland." As one observer wrote: "What a strange impression the phrases of that manifesto must have evoked in anyone living on the earth and not the moon."[8]

In addition to appealing to his subjects for support, the manifesto reiterated Nicholas's constant concern about raising their educational and economic status. As always the peasants were his special worry, and he assured them that additional land would be made available to poor households, but without doing harm to the property rights of others. The next Duma would play its proper role in approving administration measures for agrarian reform. Hopefully it would perform a more useful service to the country than the First Duma; hopes once placed on that body had proved vain. Moreover, it had gone beyond its proper domain as a legislature when it issued an illegal direct appeal to the populace.

This appeal had, of course, been the immediate cause for its dissolution, but the July 9 manifesto also contained brief mention of another action of the First Duma which had contributed to its demise. In early June the deputies had voted to send a three-deputy fact finding commission to Belostok to determine the complicity of local officials in a recent pogrom in that city. Having interviewed mainly pogrom victims, the commission reported back to the chamber on June 22. Their account had demonstrated, to their and most of their fellow deputies' satisfaction, that local officials were implicated in the origin of the pogrom, and in the excesses which occurred in Belostok. For instance, leaflets inciting a pogrom had been passed out among local troops. Only the respected and moderate Octobrist, M. A. Stakhovich, protested that the commission's evidence was one-sided and did not prove the guilt of the officials involved. However, even before the three deputies had returned with their damning indictment, the executive had been strongly opposed to the assembly's decision to send its delegates to investigate the conduct of Tsarist officials.[9]

The report from the investigators of the Belostok pogrom was the major item before the house on Friday, July 7, 1906. That same afternoon word had come from Stolypin that he wished to reply to Duma accusations about the pogrom on the following Monday, June 10. News of Stolypin's projected appearance in the Tauride Palace was prominent in the weekend press, and the fact that the Minister of the Interior was scheduled to appear in the chambers on Monday aided the administration in its efforts to keep dissolution plans a secret until the actual posting of the Sunday morning *ukaz*. The precautions of the executive proved remarkably successful.

A few suspicions that some action was in the offing were aroused when those presses known to publish socialist and revolutionary literature were sealed up on Saturday night. Then, about four o'clock the next morning, an employee on *Rech* informed Miliukov that a dissolution decree would arrive from the government press that very morning. A bit later the stunned Kadet leader jumped upon his bicycle, and took a ride through the sleepy unsuspecting city in order to round up his party's central committee. By eight o'clock, just two hours after the posting of the decree, they were all gathered at the Petrunkevich's. Caught off guard, and locked out of the Tauride Palace to boot, for once the Kadets were without a plan. Most of them had proceeded on the assumption that, if it came, dissolution would be announced from the tribune, thus providing the deputies with a dramatic opportunity to refuse to leave their places. Suddenly they had been presented with a *fait accompli* which seemed to leave little room for drama. It was essential to think up an alternative response, and quickly. After some discussion they agreed upon a protest manifesto, immediately comissioning Miliukov to draw it up. He adjourned to an empty room where he found a dusty piano top to serve as a table. He hastily composed a first draft and brought it back to his colleagues; by noon they had an amended version at hand, in readiness to present it to the deputies.[10]

Meanwhile, throughout the morning the uninformed deputies had been arriving at the Tauride Palace for their session. Since most of them departed upon reading the Tsar's *ukaz*, no crowd collected in front of the building and no incidents occurred requiring police action. About noon, however, many Duma members were seen boarding a train at the Finland station, and towards evening word came back to the capital that a large number of them had gathered at the Hotel Belvedere in Vyborg, Finland, about eighty miles northwest of the city. Then came the dramatic news of the famous Vyborg session, reportedly opened by Muromtsev with the announcement: 'The sessions of the Duma are hereby resumed.'[11] Muromtsev spoke before a total of some two hundred deputies, representing at least four distinct fractions of the assembly. In addition a few foreign students, journalists and non-deputy party leaders had collected at the Finnish hotel. Fear of police reprisals in St. Petersburg prompted the decision to meet across the Finnish border, where the local police had a reputation for being notably lax in their cooperation with Russian officials in search of political offenders.

Once assembled, there was a wide diversity of opinion among the deputies as to their next move, but finally, about midnight, they agreed that Miliukov's protest manifesto should become the basis for their response. A six-man joint committee, made up of Kadet, Trudovik, and Social Democrat representatives, set to work at once and labored for the rest of the night. The small committee rejected the idea of calling for a general strike, but the document did emerge the next morning with a plea for passive resistance: "Not a kopeck for the treasury or a single soldier for the army" until the Duma reconvened. Furthermore, no future foreign loan would be considered legal without that assembly's approval. There was considerable doubt, even among the Kadets, as to the practicality and advisability of these appeals to the public, but just as Muromtsev was about to open a general meeting to discuss the draft, news arrived that the Finnish authorities were under orders from St. Petersburg to close the sessions. The governor of Vyborg informed the Duma chairman that if the deputies persisted, they would be dispersed by troops. With no time to change the text of the Vyborg Manifesto, the document was circulated hastily, and many a deputy affixed his signature to it against his better judgment.[12]

The deputies decided to return *en masse* to St. Petersburg and many of them caught a train about noon the next day, fully expecting to be arrested as they left their coaches. Rumors that angry crowds of Black Hundreds were assembling to take reprisals against the protesters also spread among the frightened legislators. Among the non-deputies in the party were those two indomitable foreign observers of the First Duma, B. Pares and S. Harper. Both carried concealed copies of the Vyborg appeal across the border, the latter confessing understandably that he "shared the nervousness of the returning deputies." To everyone's surprise, however, there were neither rightist mobs nor Tsarist police in sight as they pulled into the station, and all of them returned to their lodging without mishap. Their uncertainty lasted almost a week, finally to be broken by a July 16 indictment against all the signers of the manifesto. Their case was not to come to trial until December of 1907, but once under indictment, they were deprived of their political rights. In other words, virtually all of the influential deputies in the First Duma would be unable to stand for reelection to its successor.[13]

The Vyborg Manifesto was the most revolutionary action ever sponsored by the Kadets and most of them were soon to regret it. Aside from its dramatic flair, it was of doubtful practicality. Direct taxes formed only a very small fraction of the imperial budget, while recruits were not due until October. Maurice Baring neatly summed up an even more basic disadvantage: "Everybody is agreed that their action is a fatal mistake, since they have no means of having any such measures carried out." The "half-revolutionary" action came under more scathing attack from a Russian student of the Duma: "Citizens, defenseless before troops or police," should refuse to pay taxes or give up draftees, "while the people's representatives were ready to hide under the nearest bench at the first word from the Vyborg governor." It was "some consolation" that these representatives proclaimed their solidarity with the populace in its protest, he concluded sarcastically.[14]

Once the excitement generated at the meetings at Vyborg began to abate, the accuracy of Baring's remark became painfully obvious. The Vyborg appeal fell flat, with its sponsors doing virtually nothing to encourage its implementation. Perhaps its most tangible result was the increased distrust on the part of the administration for the Kadet party. Subjected to even worse police harrassment than before, party meetings tended to be held away from the capital. In mid-July the Kadet central committee gathered in a *dacha* near Terioki, Finland which had been rented by the Miliukov family for the summer. The purpose of the meeting was to take a central party position on the controversial Vyborg Manifesto, which until then had only the endorsement of the party's Duma fraction. The central committee voted against sponsorship of the document, but the matter came up again at the party congress in September. The statement finally settled on by that group is a marvel of political weaseling. The party congress judged the "distribution of the Vyborg Manifesto essential in order to acquaint the population with the idea of passive resistance, but not with the aim of arousing the population to its immediate realization"! Miliukov later described the Vyborg appeal as a tactical step, which at the time seemed the least risky means of meeting the pressing demand from many of the deputies that they adopt some kind of protest to the high-handed dissolution of their assembly. He also stated that the document was defensible only from that point of view.[15]

In many respects the Vyborg plea and the events which led up to its hasty adoption can be viewed as the climax of the dilemma which plagued the Kadet leadership throughout the life of the First Duma. The party was caught up in the middle between an administration which ultimately opted to dissolve the lower house rather than concede to its demands, and the deputies on the left, many of them flamboyant Trudoviks, whose votes were necessary to the Kadets if they were to carry their program through the chamber. In addition, it became the mounting concern of the Kadets to prevent these Trudoviks from sponsoring rash actions on the Tauride floor. Unlike the Kadets, the Trudoviks had little respect for parliamentary forms or the laws governing the Duma. Certain that popular opinion was right behind them, they hoped to use the assembly to pressure the executive branch for desired concessions, while a few deputies to their left saw the Duma simply as a vehicle for furthering the cause of revolution. Beyond their unreliable Trudovik allies, the Kadets had to cope with some one hundred peasant deputies, most of whom were unsophisticated politically; interested primarily in the land question, frequently unruly in debate, the political loyalty of these peasant deputies was always uncertain. An unprecedented number of their class to sit in a national political assembly of a major state,[16] the peasant deputies likewise represented a sizeable percent of the votes in the chamber.

The task of guiding this diverse and inexperienced chamber, while never easy, became increasingly difficult as the sessions wore on. Frequently there was a highly emotional tone to the proceedings, and many a session lasted late into the night, leaving its participants physically and mentally exhausted. There seemed never to be enough time for careful consideration of complex issues. Tough tactical questions came up constantly and they usually demanded instant solutions, which had to satisfy groups with very different interests. The emotional involvement of so many of the deputies, filled as they were with deep convictions about their obligations to the Russian populace and the historic importance of their task, put them under additional strain. Their fatigue was increased by the fact that at every step they met seemingly unsurmountable obstacles from the administration.[17]

Taking into consideration these numerous and very difficult handicaps, in the early weeks the Kadet leaders succeeded surprisingly well in steering the First Duma along the lines they laid out. To do so, however, they had regularly to modify their actions to some degree to suit their allies on the left. Toward the close of the sessions, however, not only did the Kadets find themselves sponsoring actions of questionable wisdom, or constitutionality, they also lost their grip on the comfortable majority their measures had met earlier along. Ultimately, the Kadets' majority broke down at the same time that the First Duma embarked on the course which gave the administration specific cause for its dissolution.

Throughout, the Kadets had based their strategy in the First Duma on the hope that, faced with a chamber firmly united behind the Kadet program, the executive would find the assembly's demands irresistible. Concessions would follow, since the administration would be afraid to risk the popular outbreak which presumably would result from its refusal to make them. This strategy proved to be based on a gamble that did not succeed. Instead of concessions, a stalemate ensued until the Tsar sent the deputies home. After that precipitous act, the Kadets, subjected as never before to strong pressures from the left, hastily sponsored the Vyborg Appeal. It was another gamble which did not pay off. Widespread support of the appeal, which was absolutely essential for effective passive resistance, was simply not forthcoming. The manifesto landed with a dull thud, and the members of the administration took due notice of that fact.

It was not only the Vyborg Manifesto which failed to garner significant public response that summer. The widespread revolutionary outbursts called for by the Social Revolutionaries and Social Democrats, and so deeply dreaded by the administration, also failed to materialize.

In late July the Central Committee of the Social Democrats admitted frankly that "right after the dissolution of the First Duma, clear signs of a strike mood were not visible." Since even the "avant guard of the St. Petersburg proletariat" had not rallied to calls for a general strike, the party had called it off on the third day. Efforts to stir up trouble in military garrisons met with slightly more response at first, although there were no disturbances of sustained duration. The Social Revolutionaries sent their best orators to military units, where Social Democrats were also busy. Members of both parties were involved in a July 17 mutiny at the naval fortress of Sveaborg, which dominated the port of Helsinki. Mutineers there found support three days later at nearby Kronstadt, as well as on the cruiser *Pamiat Azova*, then sailing off Reval.[18]

It had been the *Pamiat Azova* which carried the youthful Nicholas on an extensive cruise to the Far East in 1890, and this made it somehow a bit more shocking that a mutiny had broken out on the ship. When the Tsar wrote his mother about the "disgusting things" which had happened on the cruiser and at the Baltic naval bases, he reported himself "tired in mind, but fit in body." Yet, he was typically able to hide his emotions from his subordinates. Izvolskii has left a moving account of an interview that he had with Nicholas during the revolt on Kronstadt. As the two men talked, the cannonade from the nearby fortress echoed in their ears. Both knew full well that those cannons could prevent the sovereign and his family from an escape by sea, should the situation become too precarious. When the Foreign Minister expressed surprise at seeing Nicholas so unmoved, the Tsar turned, and with a characteristic expression of "extraordinary gentleness" replied simply:

> If you see me so calm, it is because I have the firm, the absolute conviction that the fate of Russia, my own fate and that of my family, is [sic] in the hands of God, Who placed me where I am. Whatever happens, I will bow to His will, conscious of never having had a thought other than that of serving the country that He confided to me.

That very night, Izvolskii learned later, the revolt at Kronstadt had been subdued: the disturbances at Sveaborg and on the *Pamiat Azova* proved equally short lived.[19] Afterwards the revolutionaries kept up their barrage of propaganda in military units, but to little avail.

"We all expected trouble," wrote Samuel Harper, but events soon demonstrated that the "Russian bureaucracy had gauged the situation better than had the Russian liberals or we outsiders." Records of agrarian riots, which had peaked in the spring, indicated a continuing downward trend after the dissolution decree. Certainly there was no widespread peasant response to the Tsar's decision, although land and crop seizures, arson and looting still went on. Many such incidents had no connection with the fate of the Duma. Village Russia often had only the vaguest of ideas about events in the capital. Witness a mid-August memorandum from Samara province reporting many villagers still awaiting the arrival of a "Duma surveyor" to parcel out all the gentry land![20]

Although agrarian uprisings were abating, there was a marked upswing of terrorist activity in comparison with the lull which had occurred during the life of the First Duma. The outrages came from the extreme left and right. Members of the Union of the Russian People assassinated two Jewish Kadet deputies, M. I. Gertzenstein and G. B. Iollas, as well as the Trudovik A. L. Karavaev. An attempt on the life of ex-minister Sergei Witte failed. The party also organized "tea rooms" and "combat teams" for propaganda uses, and it sponsored a barrage of telegrams decrying the rebellious and treasonous First Duma. From the extreme left, the Social Revolutionaries and the anarchists mounted a new terrorist campaign; it had been official central policy of the SR's not to engage in terrorist acts while the First Duma was in session. Hoping to create panic and to hinder the government in its functions, their "expropriations," a euphemism for robbery, and attempts on the lives of officials became common events. The SR's and anarchists were to claim more than 4,000 lives during 1906 and 1907; they lost a comparable number of their own members, most of whom were SRs.[21]

The victims of these outrages were primarily men from lower ranks of Tsarist officialdom, aside from a few highly placed exceptions. The hated military prosecutor, V. P. Pavlov, whose attempt to speak in the First Duma had aroused such bellicose protests, was one. Another, General G. A. Min, Commander of the Semenovskii Guard and pacifier of the Moscow revolt of December, 1905, met violent death at the hands of an SR school mistress on August 13, 1906. Just the day before Min's death, Chief Minister P. Stolypin's official summer residence, a pleasant villa on Aptekarskii Island in the Neva estuary, was bombed by SR Maximalists. V. Gurko, who happened to be one of the first to arrive after the explosion, found much of the house "in ruins; the facade . . . entirely demolished." Among the heaps of debris was his chief, covered with ink spots; he had been at his desk when the explosion hit and his large bronze inkstand had flown off of it. Aside from that, Stolypin's study suffered no damage, but it was the only room left completely unharmed. His young son and teenage daughter both suffered injuries, and for a time it looked doubtful if the girl could recover without a foot amputation. The thirty-two dead included the perpetrators of the crime and some twenty persons who had been waiting in an anteroom to see the minister; the explosion occurred on the day the minister customarily received petitioners. Stolypin's great personal courage and enormous composure immediately after the tragedy contributed much to Nicholas's new chief minister's rapidly rising image in the capital.[22]

Among those who were increasingly impressed by Stolypin's character and talents was the Tsar. "Thank God," he wrote on August 12, 1906, Stolypin "remains unharmed." Understandably shaken by the disaster at his minister's villa and the funeral of General Min the same week, a fortnight later he exclaimed to his mother: "There can be no peace or safety in Russia before these monsters are exterminated." The Tsar had reason to be afraid for his own life as well, since some of the terrorists had hoped to include Nicholas and certain members of the court circle among their victims. That autumn found the Social Revolutionary's

Abram Gotz in prison after his arrest at the Tsar's palace, where he had been "studying the pattern of the Tsar's movements" in order to plan an attempt against him. In August Nicholas informed his mother that several "anarchist scoundrels," encouraged by the assassination of General Min, had been arrested at Peterhof for their plotting. Safety precautions prevented Nicholas from taking his usual rides, and he was confined to the palace grounds. "This at one's own home, at Peterhof, usually so peaceful," he complained bitterly. To avoid some of the annoyance and "humiliation" he suffered that fall, the Tsar took his family on a Baltic cruise. Once at sea, they changed moorings regularly and kept their location a secret. It was a refreshing change in spite of the fact that a courier arrived daily by torpedo boat with official reports. Furthermore, the squadron of ships on guard nearby provided a constant reminder of the dangerous times. Still their very presence was also reassuring, while the beams from their searchlights, as they plied the surface of the water, were "a most beautiful sight. I cannot tell you how much I enjoy being able to live a little while for myself," Nicholas confessed sadly.[23]

The terrorists failed to obliterate their top victims, but their renewed activity led to a drastic response on the part of the administration. On August 19, 1906 an imperial *ukaz*, sponsored by Stolypin, announced that special courts-martial would be set up in areas under extraordinary security. By the end of 1906 approximately three-fourths of the empire fit into that category. Promulgated under article 87 of the Fundamental Laws, which permitted emergency legislation by the executive between Duma sessions, the decree gave governor-generals, or officials with similar power, the right to refer crimes against the public order to these special military courts. Preliminary investigations could be waived and the verdict delivered in forty-eight hours; the sentence, frequently death, was to be carried out at once. On August 27, 1906, Minister of War Rediger warned the commanders of the military districts that those who dodged their obligations to apply the new regulations would answer "personally before his majesty." Furthermore, once a case had been tried before a court-martial, local commanders should take care not to send requests for pardons to the sovereign. These extreme measures were necessary in order to secure freedom to live and work in the empire, Rediger explained. Kokovtsov concurred with Rediger's view at the time and he later defended the special courts in his memoirs: the courts-martials, so heavily criticized by the Second Duma, undoubtedly "played the chief part in reestablishing order and confidence" in the country. Moreover, at the time of the adoption of the August 19 *ukaz*, "all the ministers agreed to it."[24]

Nicholas's remarks in a letter written late that September support Kokovtsov's judgement: "The country seems to be becoming sober again," and he could see a "healthy reaction in favor of good order." As to the special courts which handed down harsh sentences for "looting, robbery, and murder," Nicholas believed that they were "doing some good" and their salutary effects already becoming evident. "It's distressing to have them, but unavoidable," he concluded. In December of the same year Nicholas expressed similar sentiments in a letter to General Dubasov, Governor-General of Moscow, who had just survived a second attempt on his life: "You know me; I am a gentle man; I write you with complete conviction about the correctness of my opinion. It is painful, but true, to our sorrow and shame, that only the execution of a few will prevent a sea of blood —and has already prevented it."[25]

The role played by Stolypin in the reestablishment of order contributed significantly to the rapid rise of his star at the palace. Like all of Stolypin's associates, Nicholas had been notably impressed by his minister's composure and courage after the bombing of his villa, and by October the sovereign would also write in glowing terms about his new appointee's character, intelligence, and administrative ability.[26] Stolypin had not been long in office as chief minister when Nicholas made that highly favorable evaluation. A man of strong convictions who was not afraid to act upon them, Stolypin had quickly made his presence felt throughout the administration. After the interlude of Goremykin's government of indecision, it was a remarkable change. Goremykin's successor took office with definite ideas about the kind of reforms essential to the renovation of his country. To achieve his positive goals, however, he considered it necessary to restore order first. Thus, he recommended that the administration set up the harsh courts-martial, which he always regarded as a temporary necessity. Ultimately Stolypin's positive measures would be of more long-run importance than the special military courts. The latter were abolished the following April (1907), but the image of Stolypin as the executioner of political prisoners would be long-lasting. In 1907 Rodichev coined the phrase "Stolypin's necktie" for the noose used in hangings, while according to a 1969 account of Soviet labor camps, railroad coaches transporting prisoners in the Soviet Union are still dubbed "Stolypin's."

Like the *ukaz* establishing the courts-martial, the positive measures announced that fall appeared as special emergency legislation under article 87. A decree of August 12, 1906, transferred some imperial family lands to the Peasant Land Bank, and on August 27, all the arable in the State Domains was made available for sale under easy terms to peasants. A decree of September 19, 1906, placed the unpopulated arable owned by the Tsar in the Altai region at the disposal of the Ministry of Agriculture for distribution to settlers. The payments due on outstanding and future loans made through the Peasant Land Bank were greatly lowered by a decree of October 14, 1906. Henceforth, the bank had to be subsidized, since it charged a lower rate of interest than it had to pay out on its own bonds.[27]

A law of October 5 extended the personal freedom of peasants and removed many of the special limitations suffered by that class. Henceforth, a peasant could choose his place of residence freely, and he would no longer be dependent upon the head of the household or the commune for obtaining a passport. Passports would be issued without a time limit, thus removing the possibility of a peasant becoming a passportless outlaw, who had no choice but to return to his village. The *ukaz* broke the juridical power of the commune over the individual member, and brought the Russian peasant much closer to judicial equality with his urban counterparts. Greater mobility for the peasants was equally important, since it would then be possible to change place of residence, choose an occupation, enter the civil service or an educational institution without the approval of the commune.

In addition to the law extending the legal rights of peasants, the autumn of 1906 saw the first of several comprehensive laws on village land tenure, eventually known collectively as the Stolypin land reforms. An *ukaz* of November 6, 1906, facilitated free egress from the commune; many of the clauses of the decree were similar to the administration land bill presented to the First Duma, and it was in harmony with views about land reform expressed by representatives of the administration during its struggles with that legislature. In communes which had not had a redistribution of allotments for twenty-four years, each peasant household was henceforth entitled to the lands then in its possession, under terms of permanent private ownership. In communes which had undergone redistribution in the past twenty-four years, each household could also claim the allotments to which it was entitled as private property; it could purchase holdings exceeding its share at the price at the time of the emancipation. A seceding peasant could request his share as a consolidated plot if he so desired. Departing commune members did not lose their rights to use communal pastures and forests.

The principles of this *ukaz* were not original with Stolypin, and they reflected ideas which had been discussed by capital bureaucrats before he made his entry into their milieu. They were also in accord with views on the desirability of individual privately owned farms which Stolypin had held since his days as Governor of Grodno, just after the turn of the century. At first impressed by the economic advantages of the *khutor* system, by 1905 he also regarded the establishment of small landed proprietors as a necessary means of providing political stability in rural Russia. There were many men in high bureaucratic circles who had long held similar opinions, but until Stolypin assumed the post of chief minister, all projects for breaking up the communal system had remained in the planning stages. It was under Stolypin that the principles were inaugurated into specific legislation and eventually expanded.

Only on one important measure, namely easing the legalized restrictions against Jews, did the new chief minister meet staunch resistance from the sovereign. Stolypin presented his proposals to ease these irksome restrictions to Nicholas in October; he had the support of the ministerial council for his measures. After a two-month delay Nicholas notified him that he could not approve the proposals in spite of "convincing arguments" in their favor. The Tsar had decided on rejection because an "inner voice" told him not to "accept responsibility" for the bills. "So far my conscience has not deceived me," he explained further, thus he would follow its dictates once again, remaining ready to answer for his decision at any time.[28]

Stolypin wisely dropped the issue. Like all of Nicholas's ministers, he was soon to learn that on those measures where the Tsar took a firm position, it was best to give in. Failure to do so could only result in loss of favor with the sovereign. In that case, Stolypin rightly surmised, it would be impossible to proceed with any of his program. It was preferable to relinquish part of it rather than jeopardize the whole package, not to speak of his own rapidly rising career. He could be secure in his new post as long as he remained in the good graces of Nicholas II. Fear of dismissal hung constantly over his head, as it did over all of Nicholas's high appointees. Nicholas did not have a set of fixed policies which he wanted his ministers to put into effect, but it was not possible to remain in office if one pushed too hard for policies which were in opposition to the Tsar's wishes.

CHAPTER XII

A Summing Up

The first anniversary of the October Manifesto found Nicholas II in much firmer control of his empire than on the day of the document's proclamation. In Peter A. Stolypin, he had discovered an able and determined chief minister, and as yet Nicholas had seen no cause for disillusionment with his new appointee. Certainly the future looked brighter than it had even a few months previous. His regime had survived the terrible fall of 1905, as well as the onslaughts of the First Duma, while the decision to terminate that turbulent body had led to no widespread or long term protests. Yet, as Nicholas sat at his desk on October 17, 1906, in readiness to make the customary entry in his diary, all of the events that had preceeded his reluctant decision to sign the October concessions swiftly passed through his mind. His emotions welled up in him and he wrote briefly: "The first anniversary of the crash and the agonizing hours of last year. Thanks be to God that we have survived it all."[1]

The first organized protests had come from the nation's *zemstvo* representatives, meeting in private homes in Moscow in November of 1904. Their eleven "theses," which had the endorsement of all except a small minority of the delegates, included requests for a legislative assembly, legal equality for all Tsarist subjects, and guaranteed civil rights. Members of some of Russia's oldest and most distinguished families had been among the leading lights at the gathering, and their sponsorship of such bold requests had shocked the sovereign. The next concerted reform drive had been the Union of Liberation's banquet campaign of November-December, 1904. Ostensibly to celebrate the fortieth anniversary of the legal reforms of 1864, the banquets were really occasions to pass resolutions seeking an elected assembly and other constitutional reforms. News of the December 20 surrender of Port Arthur, after 148 days of desperate defense, arrived right on the heels of the banquet campaign and served to further discredit the regime. On a personal level, suspicions that the long-awaited heir suffered from the dread hemophilia became a certainty sometime that same fall.

Before January 9, 1905, the protests had embraced primarily the educated upper layer of Tsarist society, but with the tragedy of Bloody Sunday the movement moved into the city streets. On that bleak winter day Tsarist troops fired on unarmed workers, assembled by the many thousands, after they refused to turn back from a march to the Winter Palace with a petition for "Little Father Tsar." The procession bore a religious flavor, the language was loyal in tone, but the demands were radical. Once again the matter of a popularly elected assembly—this time with constituent functions—was among them. Official records of the massacre admit to over a hundred dead and about three hundred wounded; the figures for those rescued or buried by friends were of course missing from the tally. Bloody Sunday was followed by widespread strikes and a rapidly burgeoning union movement.

As the Russian winter of 1905 pursued its relentless course, the situation in the empire continued its downhill direction. February saw the heavy casualties of the battle of Mukden, and the first assassination of a member of the royal family since 1881. By mid-spring rural Russia was ablaze with riots. In the war theatre, the tragicomic May 14 defeat of the Baltic fleet in less than twenty-four hours, after an eight-month journey, added new humiliations.

Meanwhile there had been few concrete concessions from the palace, although vocal opponents of the outmoded autocracy had become angrier and bolder. Requests turned into demands. The administration had lost the respect of its citizens, and its officials were unable either to prevent or control the popular outburst. Several hesitant statements promising basic changes in the future had come from the sovereign; frequently these were accompanied by contradictory appeals, warning against sedition and urging loyalty to the administration. These promises were too vague and they came too late, after the demands had escalated. For example, by the time that the February, 1905, rescript reached fruition in the August, 1905, Bulygin Duma law, which provided for a consultative assembly, the concession only met with contempt from the public. Two months later Nicholas heeded the urging of Sergei Witte, that it was time to promise a legislative assembly and civil liberties in order to break the back of the revolts. The October Manifesto followed. Both Witte and Nicholas viewed the concessions therein as purely a necessary evil, and neither was a true proponent of the constitutional reforms which they sponsored.

Just a few days before signing the October Manifesto, Nicholas had appointed Witte as chief minister. Long a proponent of modernization of the autocracy through rational reform from above, Witte suddenly found himself a reformer in the midst of chaos. A. F. Rediger, Minister of War in the Witte cabinet, recalled the "terrible circumstances" of Witte's early ministry. Fearing for their lives, the ministerial council did not meet openly, or even at a regular site until their chief moved into quarters at the Winter Palace later in the month.[2] His first six weeks in office were marked by more violent protests than had preceded the October announcement. The administration resorted to traditional methods of force to suppress them, combined with a series of Witte-sponsored quick concessions, and by mid-January a tenuous control had been achieved. In the meantime work was begun on the constitutional changes made necessary by the October promises. The deliberate decision, backed heartily by Nicholas and the majority of his advisors, to keep so many important powers of the administration beyond the control of the future assembly angered the opposition, who rightly viewed the new statutes as a reneging on the Tsar's October reforms. The Tsar himself played an important role in the conferences where these statutes were approved, and the final versions contained no provisions to which Nicholas raised specific objections, if he refused to drop them.

The Tsar's contributions to the discussions were characteristic, in that he frequently spoke in favor of protecting the prerogatives of his office. He had made the October concessions in the midst of mass riots, and as the extreme danger to his throne abated, he saw a chance to retrieve some of his losses. However, in spite of all the powers ultimately reserved to the executive branch, Nicholas was never comfortable with the post-1905 constitution, and his administration never really made an effort to put it into effect. Furthermore, he would always resent the persuasive and overbearing minister who urged him to adopt it. A few years later Nicholas was strolling through the Hall of Portraits with a lady-in-waiting to the Tsaritsa. "This place reminds me of evil days," he observed grimly. "I felt all the time that this person [Witte] was trying to lead me into a wrong path, but I had not enough strength to oppose him."[3] It had not, however, been purely a matter of strength of will. Nicholas had followed Witte's advice in desperation, and at the time neither he, nor anyone else in the administration, had an alternative plan to save his tottering throne. Once the crisis was over, it was typical of the Tsar to forget that Witte's plan had achieved its immediate objective, and to be aware only of the long term consequences.

The relationship between Witte and Nicholas during the former's six-months term as chief minister, as well as the enormous mutual hostility which was to follow the association, reveals much about the last Tsar of Russia. Nicholas was always very uncertain of his ability to cope with the huge responsibilities that he had inherited, and he tended to resent people of obviously superior talents, especially if they were also blessed with the self-confidence he so sorely lacked. Moreover, in spite of his grave doubts about his capabilities, Nicholas was determined to keep the reins of rule tightly in his hands. He truly believed that since he had inherited his weighty office from his father, he should turn it over to his heir with its autocratic powers intact. A very stubborn man, especially when it came to the prerogatives of that office, it was, however, possible to persuade the Tsar to adopt a measure which went against his preconceptions, if he could be convinced that it was desirable, or necessary. Frequently, he would later repent his decision and turn against its original proponent.

On the other hand, if Nicholas objected to a specific proposal, it could not be put into effect. The most cryptic negative remark on the margin of a report could be sufficient warning to a minister that he was well advised to give up the idea expressed therein, if he wanted to retain his post. Nicholas was prone to retire his subordinates without advance warning, and without giving them a chance to present their side before retirement took effect. And while loss of post need not have any connections with a man's policies, or his recommendations for future measures, there was frequently a direct causal relationship.

The last Tsar of Russia was important as an essentially negative factor in his administration. He had no fixed policies, or even goals, which he wanted his subordinates to put into effect. Policies came from those particular ministers, or advisors from outside the ministry, who happened to have the Tsar's ear at the time. The result was a capricious choice of measures, and a lack of continuity or overall plan. It is not correct to say, however, that Nicholas accepted the advice of the last man who spoke to him—his reign was too full of ministers whose recommendations were rejected in spite of their favored position at the time. In accepting a particular proposal, Nicholas tended to be guided by his instinctive, or emotional, reaction to it. He often sought divine guidance before making a decision, and he had a firm faith that the Almighty constantly guided his actions as emperor of the realm which He had entrusted to him. Beyond that faith lay a fatalistic conviction that personal initiative played a very minor role compared to those higher forces which directed the course of events. Consequently, Nicholas bore his office with a sort of "mystical resignation," which made him follow life and not try to lead it. He hated most of the duties which it entailed, and the tutor to the royal children was probably right in his judgement that Nicholas would have been happy to live as a private individual.[4]

Hesitant, uncertain, stubborn, and afraid, Nicholas had been endowed neither by nature or experience for his tremendous job. The problems facing his country were enormous, and he could not grasp the complex modern changes which were sweeping over it. A host of domestic problems called for solution, and at the same time he had inherited a throne committed to maintaining Russia's traditional role as a great power. Increased competition from more advanced western industrial nations made this an appallingly difficult task for the more backward Russians. They too had embarked on a program of industrialization, but they remained far behind their leading competitors. Moreover, with early industrialization had come many of the dislocations, and as yet few of the benefits to society, which eventually accompany that development.

While there were many men in Nicholas's administration with a much better grasp of the modern world than he, there were few advocates of parliamentary government among the upper bureaucracy. Unlike most members of the Tsarist opposition, who believed that the necessary changes in the country could be achieved only after basic democratic political reforms, most Tsarist bureaucrats advocated reform from above. They thought that the Russian public, with its high rate of illiteracy, was not ready for participation in the affairs of the administration. Once faced with the prospects of governing with a popular assembly, they concentrated their efforts on clipping the powers of that body in advance. Many bureaucrats viewed the arrival of the First Duma deputies with distrust, even horror. The demands expressed by the most moderate wing of the opposition movement seemed dangerous and preposterous; apprehensions that these demands, and many others which were even more radical, would soon be heard from the Tauride floor proved accurate.

There was never to be any cooperation between the First

267

Duma and the administration. Neither side in the struggle was willing to make concessions. There were almost no supporters of the administration in the chamber, and those few voices which spoke for moderation were lost in the noisy clamor. The bulk of the eager deputies, many of them uneducated and all of them inexperienced as national legislators, wanted instant basic change in the political system and in the daily lives of their constituents, and they put great pressure on the Duma leadership to work for these changes. The Duma leaders, largely followers of western liberal political theory, were interested primarily in basic political reforms. They had no interest in the pressures felt by the administration as it tried to cope with internal dissension, the realities of international power politics, and the budget deficits which followed the Russo-Japanese War. Like all the members of the opposition, they tended to place all the blame for the situation on the policies of the Tsarist government, and they minimized the provocations committed by revolutionaries, and the element of uncertainty and fear which dominated within the administration.

One of the major demands put forth by the First Duma was a total amnesty of political prisoners. In addition, the assembly wanted the administration to abrogate all of its emergency legislation, and to abolish the death sentence. These demands were sent to a government which had just spent over a year fighting for its life, and the chief means employed in that battle were exactly those which the Duma sought to abolish. To put the viewpoint of the administration in perspective, one cannot resist the temptation to raise a parallel recently suggested by George F. Kennan. It is in the nature of regimes to resist overthrow, Kennan remarked, adding that he shuddered to think of the reaction of the United States establishment to a situation when the assassination of public officials ran at a rate of over 1,500 a year, as it did in Russia in 1906.[5]

As one examines the two sides during this bitter clash, the outcome can only be understood if the difficulties under which each had to operate are taken into consideration. In the summer of 1906 Paul Miliukov referred to the First Duma as "that beloved child of whom all is expected." Shortly before that, he dubbed the new assembly "a hot house plant of a national legislature," and pondered whether it could "survive on a Russian city street" where administrators like Goremykin could flourish. In these two statements the Kadet leader caught the essence of the problem for the Duma leadership, trying to steer a course between a rigid administration and the wants of the in-experienced deputies, so full of optimism about their cham-ber's options, and its popular backing. Even Minister of War Rediger would write years later that the First Duma felt called upon to renovate Russia because the populace put such great hopes in it. Furthermore, in his estimation the masses largely approved what they heard from the Tauride Palace, with only a few educated citizens becoming disenchanted with the proceedings.

In response to this pressure and regarding themselves as broadly representative of the will of the people, the Kadets sponsored a program they knew was unacceptable to the administration. They succeeded in mustering majority sup-port for this program for most of the life of the First Duma; there is considerable evidence that a less radical program would not have done so. In adopting this program, the Kadets gambled that the administration would give in, when faced with the moral force evoked by the assembly, and behind that, the threat of popular revolution. The tactic failed, and Rodichev's claim that the First Duma was an ikon which the administration would not destroy proved incorrect. The fiasco of the Vyborg Manifesto further demonstrated that, while the people may have expected much from the Duma, there would be little popular response to its demise. The Kadets were to change their tactics in the Second Duma. The slogan became "preserve the Duma"; the opposition would use the chamber to push for moderate changes, but avoid head-on clashes with the executive branch. As Miliukov was to put it, the strategy changed from assault to peaceful coexistence.[6]

The dissolution of the First Duma occurred after the

chamber refused to give up a land reform program, which included the confiscation of private estates as one of several measures to relieve the land hunger of the peasants. The administration came out with a categorical refusal to consider such a measure, and proceeded to work on the problem along other lines. Several economic arguments were advanced against alienation of private estates. Nicholas himself completely opposed the measure on principle, and furthermore, it should not be forgotten that the traditional support for the monarchy had been the landed class. It is hardly surprising that the regime chose not to consent to a program which was against the interests of that class, at a time when it was faced with mass discontent. Just two months previous to the Tsar's dissolution decree, the first national Congress of the Representatives of the Nobles' Associations came out with a categorical rejection of any measures which provided for compulsory confiscation of private landed property.[7]

The famous writer, Vladimir Nabokov, Jr., has aptly characterized 1905 as a "year of difficult decisions and liberal hopes."[8] The first half of the phrase fits both sides in the struggle. However, the hopes of the elder Nabokov and his liberal associates, at first so high, remained unrealized at the time of Duma dissolution. Many students of the opposition in Russia tend to share the view of the reformers that the revolution of 1905 ended in failure. A constitutional system, with a strong legislative branch, had not been achieved, and the likelihood of more arbitrary actions on the part of the administration remained a certainty. The Tsar and his advisors had seen to that, when they inserted clauses carefully protecting the regular and emergency powers of the executive into the 1906 Fundamental Laws.

On the other hand, as Nicholas thought over all the bitter experiences he had suffered during the revolution, he was painfully reminded that many important changes had occurred in the autocracy which he had inherited from his father. Some of them might have come eventually without the 1905 revolution; others he could relate directly to that event. For example, the Stolypin land reform, which had as its ultimate goal the breakup of the communes into private homesteads, was in accord with the ideas of many influential bureaucrats, who had studied the problems of rural Russia. There can be no doubt, however, that the enormous pressure for land reform, and the riots in the provinces, hurried the administration into its decision that the commune, once considered the bulwark of order and the autocracy in rural Russia, was expendable. Under Witte's administration, some of the preliminary legislation preparing the ground for the Stolypin reforms had been announced, although it was not certain at the time what measures would follow. The decree which had the most immediate application was the November 3, 1905, cancellation of the redemption dues. In addition, the terms under which peasants could purchase land through the auspices of the Peasant Land Bank were considerably relaxed. The next autumn saw a significant change in the status of the peasants, after a decree of October 5, 1906, provided that they could change their residence and choose an occupation without the approval of the commune. These, along with the law's other provisions, meant that henceforth, the peasants had virtually the same civil rights as the rest of the population.

Stolypin had not been able to persuade Nicholas that the discriminatory laws which put the Jews under a different status than their fellow citizens should be changed. However, the restrictions placed on another of the empire's religious minorities, the Old Believers, had been greatly lessened by an *ukaz* of April 17, 1905. It had been the first Tsarist measure of the revolutionary year which brought concrete reforms. Actually its provisions were to benefit members of other non-Orthodox religions, as well as the Old Believers. Henceforth, it was possible to leave the Orthodox Church and join another Christian faith with no penalties or loss of rights. The law also removed many of the burdensome restrictions against the open practice of their faith, which had hindered the non-Orthodox. Many sealed houses of prayer were opened, and a general permission to build new buildings granted. Old Believers were declared eligible for public office.

The edict of religious toleration was issued just at the time when the administration found itself plagued by the strike movement which followed the Bloody Sunday tragedy. By then it was obvious that the attempts of the government to ease labor unrest through government-sponsored unions had ended in failure; the leader of the January 9 workers' march had after all been Father George Gapon, head of the largest of these official unions. After considerable deliberation on the question of labor legislation, two important decrees were eventually issued. The first, that of December 2, 1905, repealed penal clauses against those who participated in strikes with purely economic goals. The March 4, 1906, law on societies and associations legalized those labor unions which aimed at promoting the economic interests and improving the working conditions of their members.[9]

Of benefit to some of the minority groups was the abolition of edicts which forbade printing in certain native languages. In February of 1905 the Tsar gave permission to print the gospels in Ukrainian for the first time since 1876. Recognition from the empire's Academy of Science that Ukrainian was a linguistically independent language paved the way towards its use as a language of instruction and as a subject of study. Linguistic concessions were also made to the Poles. Henceforth, religious instruction for the Roman Catholic Poles could be conducted in their own language in government schools. Private schools could be established which used Polish as the language of instruction, with the proviso that Russian history, geography and language be taught in Russian. The results of these concessions were not what Nicholas had hoped. They acted as a stimulus to national aspirations, as reflected in the spate of anti-administration literature, now in the native tongues, which flowed from the presses in the borderlands.[10]

All of these decrees loosened rigid and antiquarian aspects of Nicholas' government to some degree, but the most important change which ensued from the revolution of 1905 was the Duma. The limitations on that assembly, which were built into the Duma statute and the Fundamental Laws of 1906, infuriated the opposition, and greatly hampered the actions of the lower house. The fact remains, however, that from that time forward the Tsarist government was subjected to severe and searching criticisms from the Tauride Palace floor, whenever the Duma was in session. For an autocracy which had legally forbidden discussion of national affairs in the press, and which had staunchly resisted all attempts at public participation in the central administration, this was a disconcerting change. True enough, the press laws had been unevenly enforced, and there had been many ways to circumvent them; yet the possibility of keeping the press in line had been there when the censors chose to invoke it. Once the Duma was called into existence, there was no legal way to curb the tone of the proceedings, which were immediately aired in the empire's press in great detail. The administration could still hamper the press, but after the 1905-1906 press regulations, it was much more difficult. Preliminary censorship had been abolished, and all press offenses were supposed to be handled through standard judicial procedures. And regardless of those regulations which still existed as a potential threat to the freedom of the press, the fact remained that from 1905 on the periodical press in Russia was replete with pungent criticisms of the regime.[11]

The Tsar paid little attention to the contents of the opposition press, since he regarded it as the vehicle of the intelligentsia, that minority of the populace, which was so bent on corrupting the loyal majority. Still the attacks on his administration were a constant irritant. Moreover, the criticisms voiced in the press and in the lower house helped to prevent the regime of Nicholas II from reverting entirely to pre-1905 methods of rule. It might evade the restrictions placed on the executive by the new constitution, but it could not ignore the lower house entirely.

In the above respects the revolution of 1905 had led to important changes in the lives of Nicholas's subjects, as well as in the method of rule and governmental structure of the Russian Empire. The Tsar never adjusted to the new system, in part because it went against all of those principles which had been instilled in him from birth, principles he truly believed in. Most members of the opposition were also disappointed. Autocratic Russia had not been transformed into a true constitutional monarchy, or a democratic republic, like those western models which so many of them hoped to introduce into their country.

The Manifesto of October 17, 1905

BY THE GRACE OF GOD

WE, NICHOLAS II, Emperor and Autocrat of All the Russias, Tsar of Poland, Grand Duke of Finland, &c., &c., &c.

Declare to all our loyal subjects: Unrest and disturbances in the capitals and in many parts of Our Empire fill Our heart with great and heavy grief. The welfare of the Russian Sovereign is inseparable from the welfare of the people, and the people's sorrow in His sorrow. The unrest, which now has made its appearance, may give rise to profound disaffection among the masses and become a menace to the integrity and unity of the Russian State. The great vow of Tsarist service enjoins Us to strive with all the might of Our reason and authority for the speediest cessation of unrest so perilous to the State. Having ordered the proper authorities to take measures to suppress the direct manifestations of disorder, rioting, and violence, and to insure the safety of peaceful people who seek to fulfill in peace the duties incumbent upon them, We, in order to carry out more successfully the measures designed by Us for the pacification of the State, have deemed it necessary to coordinate the activities of the higher Government agencies.

We impose upon the Government the obligation to carry out Our inflexible will:

1. To grant the population the unshakable foundations of civic freedom based on the principles of real personal inviolability, freedom of conscience, speech, assembly, and association.

2. Without halting the scheduled elections to the State Duma, to admit to participation in the Duma, as far as is possible in the short space of time left before its summons, those classes of the population which at present are altogether deprived of the franchise, leaving the further development of the principle of universal suffrage to the newly established legislature.

3. To establish it as an unbreakable rule that no law can become effective without the sanction of the State Duma and that the people's elected representatives should be guaranteed an opportunity for actual participation in the supervision of the legality of the actions of authorities appointed by Us.

We call upon all the loyal sons of Russia to remember their duty to their country, to lend assistance in putting an end to the unprecedented disturbances, and together with Us to make every effort to restore peace and quiet in our native land.

Issued at Peterhof on the seventeenth day of October in the year of Our Lord, nineteen hundred and five. The original text signed in His Imperial Majesty's own hand.

NICHOLAS

Foreign Precedents for
the Fundamental Laws of 1906

There were certain similarities between the Fundamental Laws of the Russian Empire (1906) and constitutions then in effect in the western world and Japan. There is evidence that Tsarist officials responsible for drafting the Fundamental Laws sought ideas in other constitutions, but it is not generally possible to give the exact origin of a particular clause. The matter is further complicated by the fact that frequently a clause in one constitution, say the Japanese, was itself a partial borrowing, or an amalgam, from other models. For instance, the constitutions of Japan (article 8), Prussia (article 63), and Austria-Hungary (article 14) all contain clauses much like the famous article 45 (87) of the Russian Fundamental Laws, which gave the monarch the power, "should extraordinary circumstances demand" it, to issue legislation when the State Duma was not in session.* Each of these four articles specifically stated that an edict thus issued could not legally remain in effect without subsequent approval by the legislature. However, there was variation as to how long the monarch could wait to submit the decree after the assembly met again—from "immediately" in the case of Prussia, to "within four weeks" (Austria), to "within two months" (Russia), to simply "at its next session" (Japan). While the Austrian and Russian clauses expressly excepted any alteration of the fundamental laws from the scope of the sovereign's emergency powers, there was no such explicit proviso in the Japanese clause. The corresponding Prussian statute merely stated

277

that emergency ordinances must not "contravene the constitution." The Austrian clause further exempted any edicts which imposed a "lasting burden upon the public treasury" from the monarch's emergency legislative powers, but no such proviso was in the Russian clause. On the other hand, according to another article of the Japanese constitution (article 70), the emperor could take "all necessary financial measures" in order to maintain public safety; these measures had to be submitted for subsequent approval by the Diet. With the exception of the Japanese clause, all of the articles granting the monarch the right to issue legislation between assembly sessions mentioned that edicts should be worked out in conjunction with the ministry. Thus, this one example points up the complexity of pinpointing the exact origins of the Russian Fundamental Laws, and article 45 was not simply a copy from any one constitution.

The emergency legislative powers conferred upon these monarchs took on additional significance because of the executives' control over the timing of assembly sessions. The Russian Tsar was to convene the State Duma annually; he could "determine the length of an annual session" (i.e., he could prorogue the chamber), and set the intervals between sessions. Each Duma was to last five years, but the Tsar could "dissolve the State Duma and release its members from their five-year term" at any time, provided that the dissolution decree announced new elections and set the date for the new chamber's opening (articles 56, 57, 63). According to the Prussian Constitution, the king could similarly dissolve the assembly, but there was a specific limit set—within ninety days—for the convening of the new house (article 51). The Imperial German Constitution also contained the ninety-day limit: moreover, the Kaiser could only dissolve the lower house if he obtained a "resolution of the Bundesrat," the upper house, to that effect. The German Emperor's control over the Reichsdag was considerably more restricted by the constitution than the Tsar's power over the Duma. The former could not prorogue the Reichsdag for more than thirty days, nor more than twice during the same session without the consent of the assembly itself (articles 24, 25, 26). The Meiji Constitution gave the Emperor the power to open, close, prorogue, and dissolve the Japanese Diet; upon dissolution a newly elected chamber had to assemble "within five months" (articles 7, 45). The Austrian Emperor had no such time limit set by statute; the law simply stated that "a new election shall be held" after dissolution occurred (articles 18, 19).

The statutes governing election to these legislative bodies varied in detail, as well as in principle. Both the Russian and Prussian electoral laws provided for indirect, multistage elections based on a class system which gave heavier representation to wealthier voters. Germany and Japan, on the other hand, both had direct one-stage national elections. Until an amendment of January 26, 1907, which established universal male suffrage in the Austro-Hungarian Empire, residents of that multinational empire had a restricted franchise which was not uniform throughout the country. Voting occurred under a complicated class system which favored the wealthy; separate classes were allotted specific numbers of representatives to the imperial assembly.

In none of these states was the parliament given effective control over the ministry, since in every case it was the monarch who appointed and dismissed ministers, without consultation with the legislators. The former were responsible only to the monarch. Moreover, effective financial control of the executive by the legislature was specifically limited in both the Russian and Japanese constitutions. In these states, as long as the assembly failed to approve the annual budget proposals submitted by the executive, the budget approved the previous year remained in effect (article 71 for Japan; 74 for Russia). In a similar limitation on the legislature's power, if the Russian Duma refused to approve the administration's application for an annual recruit levy by May 1, the executive could draft "no more than" the number of recruits which had been approved the previous year (article 77). This provision was not in any of the other four constitutions analyzed.

All five of these constitutions were granted between the years 1848 and 1906 by monarchs reluctant to share sovereignty with elected representatives of the people. It is hardly surprising that they contain many similar devices designed to restrict the powers of new elected assemblies and to reserve considerable options for the sovereign.

*Moreover, according to Tomio Nakano, eighteen of the twenty-five states in the German Empire "vested ordinance power in the executive." T. Nakano, *The Ordinance Power of the Japanese Emperor.* Chapter XV of Nakano's study contains an analysis of the European origins of the Japanese constitution of 1889. See also George M. Beckman's *The Making of the Meiji Constitution.* The Meiji Constitution, along with the constitutions of Russia, Germany, and Austria-Hungary, is included in Herbert F. Wright's handy compilation, *The Constitutions of the States at War: 1914-1918.* The constitution of the kingdom of Prussia, translated and edited by James H. Robinson, was published in the September, 1894 supplement to the *Annals* of the American Academy of Political and Social Science. For a discussion of the Imperial German Constitution and its origins see Otis H. Fisk's *Germany's Constitutions of 1871 and 1919: Texts with Notes and Introductions.*

Notes

NOTES TO CHAPTER I

1. There is a complete text of the October Manifesto in Appendix A of this study. PSZRI No. 26803. Parallel English and Russian texts are in the appendix to Ivar Spector's *The First Russian Revolution: Its Impact on Asia* (Englewood, N.J., 1962).

2. Maurice Baring, *A Year in Russia* (New York, 1907), p. 27.

3. Alexander Kerensky, *Russia and History's Turning Point* (New York, 1965), pp. 55, 58.

4. Sergei R. Mintslov, *Peterburg v 1903-1910 godakh (St. Petersburg During the Years 1903 to 1910)* (Riga, 1931), pp. 166-173 *passim*.

5. Donald Treadgold, "The Constitutional Democrats and the Russian Liberal Tradition," *The American Slavic and East European Review*, X: (April, 1951), pp. 92-93; Paul Miliukov, *Political Memoirs*, ed. by Arthur P. Mendel (Ann Arbor, Michigan, 1967), pp. 49-50, 66. The words attributed to Miliukov actually were recorded by V. A. Maklakov. Miliukov later stated that he could not recall his exact words, but that Maklakov's quote caught the essence of his reaction that day.

6. Cited from *Izvestiia soveta rabochikh deputatov (News of the Council of Worker's Deputies)* in Bertram Wolfe's *Three Who Made a Revolution* (Boston, 1955), p. 323.

7. From *Proletary (The Proletarian)* (October 25, 1905), in *Little Lenin Library*, Vol. 6 (New York, 1934), pp. 26-27.

8. Vladimir Zenzinov, *Perezhitoe (Experiences)* (New York, 1953), pp. 201-203.

9. Vladimir S. Woytinsky, *Stormy Passage* (New York, 1961), pp. 42-43.

10. Zenzinov, *Perezhitoe*, p. 218.

11. VPS, Vol. I, pp. 641, 375; Simon Kaplan, *Once a Rebel* (New York, 1941), pp. 207-210 *passim*.

12. VPS, Vol. I, pp. 196-200 *passim*, 207, 608-609.

13. Alexander Guchkov, "Types of Russian Oratory," *Russian Review*, 3: (London, 1914), p. 143; From *Izvestiia moskovskoi gorodskoi dumy (News of the Moscow City Duma)*, October 18, 1905 as cited in Louis Menashe's Ph. D. dissertation, "Alexander Guchkov and the Origins of the Octobrist Party: The Russian Bourgeois in Politics, 1905" (New York University, 1966), p. 125.

14. Sergei Kryzhanovskii, *Vospominaniia (Memoirs)* (Berlin, n.d.), pp. 53-57.

NOTES TO CHAPTER II

1. Bing, *Secret Letters*, p. 185; Nicholas, *Dnevnik*, p. 222.

2. Bing, *Secret Letters*, pp. 182-183.

3. Sidney Harcave, *First Blood* (New York, 1964), pp. 112, 167; Kerensky, *Russia and History's Turning Point*, pp. 59-60; Woytinsky, *Stormy Passage*, pp. 19-20; Sidney Harcave, "Jewish Political Parties and Groups and the Russian State Duma From 1905 to 1907," (Unpublished Ph. D. dissertation, University of Chicago, 1943), pp. 50-51.

4. VPS, Part I, pp. 124, 545; John S. Curtiss, *Church and State in Russia* (Columbia University Press, 1940), p. 207; Vladimir Gurko, *Figures and Features of the Past* (Laura Matveev Translator, Stanford University Press, 1939), p. 419.

5. For a good description of the conditions of Russian factory workers see Theodore Von Laue's articles: "Russian Labor Between Field and Factory, 1892-1903," in *California Slavic Studies*, 3:(1964), pp. 33-65; and "Russian Peasants in the Factory" in *The Journal of Economic History*, 21:(March, 1961), pp. 61-81.

6. Alexander Gerschenkron, *Continuity in History and Other Essays* (Harvard University Press, 1968), pp. 229-230; For the industrial crisis see also Theodore Von Laue's *Sergei Witte and the Industrialization of Russia* (Columbia University Press, 1963), and Peter I. Lyaschenko's *History of the National Economy of Russia*, trans. by L. M. Herman (New York, 1949).

7. Bernard Pares, *Russia and Reform* (London, 1907), pp. 459, 471-475.

8. See Harcave's *First Blood*, pp. 174, 152-156, 180-186, for the labor movement.

9. VPS, Part I, p. 426; Kaplan, *Once a Rebel*, pp. 195-196. For the railroad strike see Walter Sablinsky's article "The All-Russian Railroad Union and the Beginning of the General Strike in

October, 1905" in Alexander and Janet Rabinowitch (eds.) *Revolution and Politics in Russia* (Indiana University Press, 1972).

10. VPS, Part I, p. 44.

11. Gurko, *Figures and Features of the Past*, p. 393.

12. Harcave, *First Blood*, pp. 185-186.

13. George Khrustalev-Nosar, "The Council of Workmen's Deputies," *Russian Review* 2: (London, 1913), p. 90; Henry Nevinson, *The Dawn in Russia* (London, 1906), pp. 25-28 *passim*.

14. VPS, Part I, pp. 422, 504.

15. Anna M. Pankratova, *Pervaia russkaia revoliutsiia 1905-1907 gg. (First Russian Revolution of 1905-1907)* (Moscow, 1951), p. 78.

16. Geroid T. Robinson, *Rural Russia Under the Old Regime* (University of California Press, 1967), pp. 174-176.

17. "Zapiski A. F. Redigera o 1905 g." (Comments by A. F. Rediger about 1905), *Krasnyi Arkhiv* (Red Archives), 45: (Leningrad, 1931), pp. 91-92.

18. For the liberal reform movement see George Fischer's *Russian Liberalism from Gentry to Intelligentsia* (Harvard University Press, 1958); Robert Charque's *The Twilight of Imperial Russia* (London, 1965); and Donald W. Treadgold's *Lenin and His Rivals* (New York, 1955).

19. Gurko, *Figures and Features of the Past*, pp. 366-367.

20. Louis Menashe, "Alexander Guchkov and the Origins of the Octobrist Party," pp. 100-101, 114.

21. *Ibid.*, pp. 112-124, *passim*.

22. For the Tsar's private life see the account by the tutor to the royal children: Pierre Gilliard, *Thirteen Years at the Russian Court*, trans. by F. Appleby Holt (New York, 1970); and the vivid modern portrayal by Robert K. Massie, *Nicholas and Alexandra* (New York, 1967).

23. Witte, TN I, p. 70; Gurko, *Figures and Features of the Past*, p. 380.

24. For the court circle see Alexander Iswolsky's *The Memoirs of Alexander Iswolsky*, trans. by Charles L. Seeger (London, 1920), and A. A. Mossolov's *At the Court of the Last Tsar*, trans. by E. W. Dickes (London, 1935).

25. Grand Duke Alexander of Russia, *Once a Grand Duke* (Garden City, N.Y., 1932), p. 169; Gilliard, *Thirteen Years at the Russian Court*, pp. 167-168.

26. Bing, *Secret Letters*, p. 132; Nicholas, *Dnevnik*, pp. 107, 213.

27. Mossolov, *At the Court of the Last Tsar*, p. 12.

28. Bing, *Secret Letters*, pp. 185, 202-203.

29. Cited in Curtiss, *Church and State in Russia*, pp. 186-187.

30. *Polnoi sobranie rechei Imperatora Nikolaia II: 1894-1906 (Complete Collection of the Speeches of Emperor Nicholas II, 1894-1906,* (St. Petersburg, 1906), p. 58.

31. Baroness Sophie Buxhoeveden, *The Life and Tragedy of Alexandra Feodorovna, Empress of Russia* (New York-London, 1929), pp. 108-110.

NOTES TO CHAPTER III

1. Witte, TN I, p. 233.

2. Iswolsky, *The Memoirs of Alexander Iswolsky*, p. 114.

3. In addition to Witte's and Iswolsky's memoirs see the following interpretations of Witte's career and abilities: Theodore Von Laue, *Sergei Witte and the Industrialization of Russia* and Vladimir Gurko, *Figures and Features of the Past*.

4. Witte, TN I, p. 334.

5. For details of this policy dispute see John A. White, *The Diplomacy of the Russo-Japanese War* (Princeton University Press, 1963), pp. 11-30.

6. Quoted by White in *Ibid.*, p. 234.

7. Iswolsky, *Memoirs*, pp. 129-130.

8. Polovtsev, "Dnevnik A. A. Polovtseva, 1905 g." (Diary of A. A. Polovtsev for 1905) *Krasnyi Arkhiv*, 4: (Leningrad, 1923), p. 63.

9. Witte, TN I, pp. 494-495; Gurko, *Figures and Features of the Past*, pp. 359-360, 394-395.

10. Polovtsev, *Dnevnik*, p. 66.

11. The Bulygin Duma Law and Electoral Statute are in PSZRI, Numbers 26661 and 26662. An almost complete English translation is in Marc Raeff's *Plans for Political Reform in Imperial Russia, 1730-1905* (Englewood Cliffs, N.J., 1966).

12. Witte, TN II, pp. 26-27, 310.

13. From Witte's memorandum in *Krasnyi Arkhiv*, 11-12: (Leningrad, 1925), pp. 61, 57.

14. Witte, TN I, p. 300.

15. *Ibid.*, p. 276.

16. Bernard Pares, *A Wandering Student* (Syracuse University Press, 1948), p. 130. The actual author of the original draft was the younger Prince A. D. Obolenskii. He was a house guest at Witte's at the time and the two men both worked on the final version. It should also be noted that Witte urged the Tsar not to issue the concessions in the form of a manifesto under Nicholas's signature. Witte thought that an imperial manifesto would arouse the populace's hopes unduly, and associate the sovereign too closely with the outcome of the reforms. Witte's advice notwith-

standing, Nicholas opted for the manifesto; almost simultaneously with it, there appeared a lengthy report signed by S. Witte which elaborated on the concessions. The official report and the manifesto appeared in the government newspaper, *Pravitelstvennyi Vestnik (Government Messenger)*. Reprints of the documents are found in Witte's memoirs, and English versions are in Harcave's *First Blood*. For a good discussion of the drafting of the Manifesto see the Ph. D. dissertation of Howard D. Mehlinger, "Count Sergei I. Witte and the Problems of Constitutionalism in Russia, 1905-1906," (University of Kansas, 1964).

17. Witte, TN II, p. 8.

18. Mossolov, *At the Court of the Last Tsar*, pp. 89-90; Rediger, "Zapiski A. F. Redigera o 1905 g," pp. 88-89.

19. Bing, *Secret Letters*, pp. 184-185, 190.

20. The decree announcing the reformed Council of Ministers is in PSZRI No. 26820. For interesting interpretations of Witte's term as chief minister see Theodore Von Laue's "Count Witte and the Russian Revolution of 1905," *American Slavic and East European Review*, 17: February, 1958), pp. 25-46; and Howard D. Mehlinger and John M. Thompson, *Count Witte and the Tsarist Government in the 1905 Revolution* (Indiana University Press, 1972).

21. Vladimir Kokovtsov, *Out of My Past*, trans. by Laura Matveev (Stanford University Press, 1935), pp. 32-34.

22. Gessen, Iosif V. "Reminiscences." An English translation, in typescript, of I. V. Gessen's memoirs. (In the Hoover Archives, n.d.), pp. 27-28.

23. The dialogue at Witte's press interview is in *Krasnyi Arkhiv* 11-12: (Leningrad, 1925), pp. 99-105; Witte, TN II, pp. 52-53.

24. Mehlinger, "Count Sergei Iu. Witte," pp. 164-165; R. W. Postgate, *Revolution From 1789 to 1906* (New York, 1962), p. 382.

25. For Witte's efforts to get liberals in his cabinet see: Geoffrey A. Hosking, *The Russian Constitutional Experiment: Government and Duma, 1907-1914* (Cambridge University Press, 1973), pp. 16-17; "Count Witte Invites Public Men to Join His Cabinet," an account from the memoirs of D. N. Shipov, is translated in the appendix to Vladimir Gurko's *Figures and Features of the Past*, pp. 703-710; W. Harrison, "The Octobrists and the Russian Revolution of 1905," *Durham University Journal*, 24: (March, 1963), p. 50.

26. Bing, *Secret Letters*, p. 188.

27. PSZRI, Number 26835; Witte, TN II, pp. 108-109; Gurko, *Figures and Features of the Past*, pp. 416-417.

28. PSZRI Numbers 26871, 26872, 26873, 26969. The English text of the debt cancellation decree is in Basil Dmytryshyn's

Imperial Russia: A Source Book: 1700-1917 (New York, 1967), pp. 315-316; Margaret Miller, *The Economic Development of Russia, 1905-1914* (London, 1967), p. 101; Harcave, *First Blood*, pp. 251-252.

29. PSZRI Number 26962. For a discussion of the press in Tsarist Russia see Jacob Walkin's *The Rise of Democracy in Pre-Revolutionary Russia* (New York, 1962); and Benjamin Rigsberg, "Tsarist Censorship Performance: 1894-1905," *Jahrbücher für Geschichte Osteuropas, 17:* (1969), pp. 59-76.

30. Baring, *A Year in Russia*, p. 119; Mintslov diary, pp. 191, 201-202.

31. For a brief summary of restrictions on Finnish autonomy see Michael T. Florinsky, *Russia: A History and Interpretation* (New York, 1953), pp. 1158, 1180.

32. The peasants' remark is cited in Robinson, *Rural Russia Under the Old Regime*, p. 174; Mintslov diary, p. 198.

33. VPS, Vol. I, pp. 601-602, 535.

34. Rediger, "Zapiski A. F. Redigera o 1905 g.," p. 90; *Vtoroi period revoliutsii (Second Period of the Revolution)*, (January-April, 1906), Vol. I, Part I, p. 900.

35. Documents on the Post-Telegraph Union are in VPR, Vol. I, pp. 111-123. See also the Ph. D. dissertation by Wayne Santoni, "P. N. Durnovo as Minister of Internal Affairs in the Witte Cabinet," (University of Kansas, 1968), pp. 217-219, 279-282.

36. Bing, *Secret Letters*, pp. 187, 192.

37. VPS, Vol. I, pp. 394-395.

38. VPS, Vol. I, pp. 554-555.

39. Bing, *Secret Letters*, p. 187.

40. Eve Broido, *Memoirs of a Revolutionary*, trans. and ed. by Vera Broido (New York, 1967), p. 125; VPS, Vol. I, pp. 592-593.

41. VPS, Vol. I, p. 387. For a vivid account of methods used in "Storming the Censorship Bastilles" see Chapter 13 of Leon Trotsky's *1905*, trans. by Anya Bostok (New York, 1972).

42. From Witte Letter of December 21, 1905, printed in *Byloe* 9: (March, 1918), p. 3.

43. For documents on the November strike see VPR, Vol. I, pp. 361-369; Gurko, *Figures and Features of the Past*, p. 419.

44. Nevinson, *The Dawn in Russia*, p. 38; Woytinsky, *Stormy Passage*, pp. 57-59; *Vtoroi period revoliutsii*, January-April, 1906, Vol. I, Part I, pp. 178-179.

45. Bing, *Secret Letters*, p. 195.

46. VPR, Vol. I, pp. 25-26, 62; "Tsarskoselskiia soveshchaniia: Protokoly" (Tsarskoe Selo Conference: Protocal), *Byloe* 3: (1917), pp. 248-249.

47. Broido, *Memoirs*, p. 125; Kaplan, *Once a Rebel*, pp. 212-213.

48. Zenzinov, *Perezhitoe*, p. 258. For the December revolt and

the role of the revolutionary parties in it see J. L. H. Keep's *The Rise of Social Democracy in Russia* (Oxford University Press, 1963).

49. VPR, Vol. I, p. 78.
50. *Vtoroi period revoliutsii*, January-April, 1906, Vol. I, Part I, p. 631; VPR, Vol. I, p. 99.
51. Mintslov diary, p. 163.
52. *Vtoroi period revoliutsii*, January-April, 1906, Vol. I, Part I, pp. 815-817.
53. Gurko, *Figures and Features of the Past*, p. 445; *Vtoroi period revoliutsii*, January-April, 1906, Vol. I, Part I, pp. 818-819, 915.
54. PSZRI Number 26998.
55. Kaplan, *Once a Rebel*, p. 229; Mintslov diary, 207, 215.
56. Baring, *A Year in Russia*, p. 61.

NOTES TO CHAPTER IV

1. See Robert K. Massie's *Nicholas and Alexandra* for a literate description of life at Tsarskoe Selo, pp. 111-119.
2. Nicholas S. Tagantsev, *Perezhitoe: Uchrezhdenie gosudarstvennoi dumy v 1905-1906 gg. (Experiences: The Institution of the State Duma in 1905-1906)*, (Petrograd, 1919), p. 87. The record of the July Peterhof meetings was published as: *Petergofskoe soveshchanie o proekte gosudarstvennoi dumy podlichnym presedatelstvom Ego Imperatorskago Velichestva; Sekretnye protokoly (The Peterhof Conference About the Draft Project of a State Duma Under the Personal Chairmanship of His Imperial Majesty: Secret Protocols)*, (Berlin, n.d.), p. 8. Cited hereafter as PS (July). For an article about the sessions in English see Sir Bernard Pares' "The Peterhof Conference" in *Russian Review* 2: (London, 1913), pp. 87-120. In his memoirs I. V. Gessen, co-editor of the Kadet newspaper *Rech*, says that he obtained a copy of the stenographic report of the meetings from the historian, V. Kliuchevskii, who was in attendance; Gessen later published these reports in Berlin. See the English typescript of Gessen's "Reminiscences" in the Hoover archives, p. 20.
3. Sergei E. Kryzhanovskii, *Vospominaniia* (Berlin, n.d.), pp. 34, 39.
4. Polovtsov, "Dnevnik," p. 104.
5. Tagantsev, *Perezhitoe*, pp. 12-14.
6. Kryzhanovskii, *Vospominaniia*, p. 34.

7. PS (July), pp. 9-12.

8. *Ibid.*, p. 33.

9. *Ibid.*, pp. 15-19, 102.

10. PSZRI Numbers 26661 and 26662. English translations of the main provisions of the Bulygin Duma laws and the accompanying manifesto are in Marc Raeff's *Plans for Political Reform in Imperial Russia: 1730-1905* (Englewood Cliffs, N.J., 1966).

11. The five conservatives were Senators A. A. Bobrinskii, A. A. Shirinskii-Shikhmatov, A. A. Naryshkin, and State Council Members A. P. Ignatiev and A. S. Stishinskii. Debate on their suggestions is on pages 88-96 in PS (July). Of the five, two—Shirinskii-Shikhmatov and Stishinskii—would receive ministerial Portfolios (Ober-Procurator of the Holy Synod and Land Affairs, respectively) in the Goremykin cabinet, which was to replace the Witte government before the First Duma convened.

12. *Ibid.*, pp. 155-156.

13. *Ibid.*, p. 157.

14. *Ibid.*, pp. 115-117, 120-124, 145.

15. *Ibid.*, pp. 201-202.

16. *Ibid.*, pp. 206-207, 193-194, 205.

17. *Ibid.*, pp. 185-187, 191-192, 207-208.

18. *Ibid.*, p. 197.

19. Debate on literacy requirement, *Ibid.*, pp. 209-212.

20. The Russian text of the Bulygin manifesto is in N. S. Tagantsev's *Perezhitoe*, along with two draft projects; the first was drawn up by Tagantsev, the second by the moderate *zemstvo* liberal and Octobrist, Count E. V. Geiden. The final version, drawn up by a special commission which met on July 30, 1905 under the chairmanship of K. Pobedonotsev, was an amalgam of the drafts. In his book Tagantsev cites the exact source of each clause in the document. According to Tagantsev, Pobedonotsev signed the final document, but did not contribute to it: "It was evident that the whole undertaking and its fulfillment appeared to him as something impious," Tagantsev wrote. pp. 36-46.

21. The phrase is in Tagantsev's *Perezhitoe*, p. 17. Ironically, Ivan Petrunkevich would give the initial speech from the floor in the First Duma, a passionate appeal for complete amnesty for political prisoners. He was a floor leader for the Constitutional Democrats in the Duma, but not the president.

22. *Ibid.*, pp. 98-99.

23. *Ibid.*, pp. 24-25, 152.

24. Tagantsev, *Perezhitoe*, p. 27; PS (July), p. 112.

25. Kryzhanovskii, *Vospominaniia*, p. 36. Since the final law under which the First Duma elections took place kept the principles of the Bulygin electoral law, a more detailed analysis of the

statute follows in connection with the discussion of the December
11, 1905 modifications of the August law.
26. Nicholas, *Dnevnik*, p. 213.
27. Kryzhanovskii, *Vospominaniia*, pp. 40-41.
28. From an August, 1905 pamphlet of the Central Committee of
the Social Democrats. VPS Vol. I, pp. 7, 3; Miliukov, *Memoirs*, pp.
44-46.
29. Kryzhanovskii, *Vospominaniia*, pp. 48-49.
30. For Witte's version of the December conference see TN II,
pp. 111-114. Tagantsev and Kryzhanovskii both attended the
sessions and their memoirs contain some interesting sidelights
on them. For the record of the conference see "Tsarskoselskiia
soveshchaniia pod lichnym e.i.v. predsedatelstvom, dlia razsmo-
treniia predpolozhenii soveta ministrov o sposobakh osushchest-
vleniia vysochaishikh predukazanii, vozveshchennykh v punkte
2 manifesta 17 oktiabria 1905 goda: Protokoly" (1917), ("Tsarskoe
Selo Conference under the Personal Chairmanship of His Imperial
Majesty to Review Preliminary Proposals of the Council of
Ministers on How to Carry out His Imperial Orders in Regards
to the Second Point of the October 17, 1905 Manifesto), *Byloe*
3: (Petrograd, 1917), pp. 235-265. Cited hereafter as TS (December).
31. D. N. Shipov, *Vospominaniia i dumy o perezhitom (Recollections and Thoughts About the Past)*, (Moscow, 1918), p. 380;
For the defense of universal suffrage see TS (December), pp.
238-244.
32. Kryzhanovskii, *Vospominaniia*, p. 70.
33. Tagantsev, *Perezhitoe*, p. 94; Kryzhanovskii, *Vospominaniia*, pp. 72-73.
34. Witte's remarks, TS (December), pp. 258, 245, 248, 252.
35. *Ibid.*, pp. 248-249, 244, 252-253.
36. Tagantsev, *Perezhitoe*, p. 91; Bing, *Secret Letters*, p. 199.
37. TS (December), p. 258; Bing, *Secret Letters*, p. 199.
38. PSZRI Number 27029 (December Electoral Law); Number
26662 (Bulygin Electoral Law). The codified version of these laws
and the separate laws for the border regions are in *Svod zakonov
rossiiskoi imperii*, St. Petersburg, 1906. English translation of the
Bulygin statute in Marc Raeff's *Plans for Political Reform in
Imperial Russia: 1730-1905*. See also Samuel N. Harper's *The New
Electoral Law for the Russian Duma* (University of Chicago Press,
1908), and Alfred Levin's *The Second Duma* (Yale University
Press, 1940). For a useful collection of many of the major docu-
ments of the era, including the electoral laws, see F. I. Kalinychev's
Gosudarstvennaia duma v Rossii v dokumentakh i materialakh,
Moscow, 1957.
39. Miliukov, *Memoirs*, p. 86; VPR, Vol. I, p. 504.

NOTES TO CHAPTER V

1. *Vtoroi period revoliutsii*, January-April, 1906, Vol. I, Part I, pp. 77-78.

2. Shipov, *Vospominaniia*, p. 408; Harrison, "The Octobrists," *Durham University Journal* (March, 1963), p. 54.

3. Miliukov, *Memoirs*, p. 65.

4. Tagantsev, *Perezhitoe*, p. 144; For the record of the February conference see "Protokoly sekretnago soveshchaniia v fevrale 1906 goda pod predsedatelstvom byvshago imperatora po vyrabotke uchrezhdenii gosudarstvennoi dumy i gosudarstvennago soveta," ("Protocol of the Secret Meeting, February, 1906, Under the Chairmanship of the Former Emperor in Order to Draw Up Statutes for the State Duma and the State Council"), in *Byloe* 5-6; Petrograd, 1917), pp. 289-318. Cited hereafter as TS (February).

5. Witte, TN II, p. 4; TS (December), p. 245; TS (February), p. 293.

6. For an interesting description of the State Council by a man who worked in the Imperial Chancellery, the office attached to it, see V. Gurko's *Figures and Features of the Past*.

7. Polovtsov, *Dnevnik*, pp. 67, 84.

8. Gurko, *Figures and Features of the Past*, p. 23; Tagantsev, *Perezhitoe*, p. 144.

9. TS (February), pp. 302-303.

10. Tagantsev, *Perezhitoe*, p. 152.

11. Parallel texts of the final version of the February 20, 1906 Manifesto and the Solskii Commission proposal are in Tagantsev, *Perezhitoe*, pp. 122-127. The Duma and State Council Statutes are in *Svod zakonov rossiiskoi imperii* (St. Petersburg, 1906).

12. Cited from Shipov's memoirs by L. Menashe in his "Alexander Guchkov and the Origins of the Octobrist Party," p. 196.

13. The record of the April conference, "Tsarskoselskiia soveshchaniia pod lichnym e.i.v. presedatelstvom po peresmotru osnovykh gosudarstvennykh zakonov: protokoly" ("Tsarskoe Selo Conference under the Chairmanship of His Imperial Majesty for the Review of the Fundamental Laws: Protocol"), is in *Byloe* 4: (Petrograd, 1917), pp. 188-245. Cited hereafter as TS (April). Nicholas' remark is on page 189.

14. TS (April), pp. 191-192, 194-195.

15. *Ibid.*, p. 189; Witte TN II, pp. 259-260.

16. "Third element"—the term applied to individuals hired by organs of the central and local government, especially the *zemstvos*. The other two "elements" were the Tsarist bureaucracy and the elected representatives of local government. The third element included teachers, agronomists, statisticians, etc., many of whom were active in the reform movement; TS (April). Nicho-

las' speech is on pages 204-205 and the debate follows, pp. 205-209.

17. PSZRI, Number 27805. An English translation of the Fundamental Laws of April 23, 1906 is in Basil Dmytryshyn's *Imperial Russia: A Source Book, 1700-1917*, pp. 316-324. Article 4 in the 1906 version corresponded to article 1 in the former code. See Appendix B for a discussion of other constitutions which had provisions similar to the Fundamental Laws of 1906.

18. The law of April 23, 1906 merely listed in two articles the appropriate numbers of the regulations for the Imperial family which were retained from the old code. The 1906 edition of *Svod zakonov rossiiskoi imperii*, however, included all of these articles and incorporated them into the new law. For this reason the article numbers in the two 1906 versions do not correspond; article 87 in the *Svod* is article 45 in *Polnoe Sobranie*.

19. Fundamental Laws, articles 56-77; Dmytryshyn, *Imperial Russia*, pp. 322-324.

20. Michael T. Florinsky, *Russia: A History and an Interpretation*, Vol. II, p. 1187, and Alfred Levin, *The Second Duma*, p. 16. The Duma budget law is in *Svod zakonov rossiiskoi imperii*; it is also incorporated into the Fundamental Laws.

21. TS (April), pp. 189-190 and TS (February), p. 312; Witte TN II, p. 268.

22. Kokovtsov, *Out of my Past*, pp. 101-102; Kryzhanovskii, *Vospominaniia*, p. 75 footnote.

23. TS (April), debate on recruits, pp. 240-244. Tagantsev, *Perezhitoe*, p. 204.

24. *Polnoe sobranie rechei Imperatora Nikolaia II*, p. 73.

25. Harcave, "Jewish Political Parties," pp. 89-90.

26. For Kadet election strategy see Judith Zimmerman's unpublished Ph. D. dissertation, "Between Revolution and Reaction: The Russian Constitutional Democratic Party: October 1905 to June 1907," (Columbia University, 1967) pp. 165, 173-174; George Rhyne, "The Constitutional Democratic Party from its Origins Through the First State Duma," (Unpublished Ph. D. dissertation, University of North Carolina, 1968), p. 223. See the fifth chapter of S. M. Sidelnikov's *Obrazovanie i deiatelnost pervoi gosudarstvennoi dumy (The Origins and Activities of First State Duma)*, (Moscow, 1962) for an analysis of the elections. As he is careful to point out, the dearth of accurate statistics and the large number of candidates running without a party label make all conclusions very tenuous.

27. See Rhyne's dissertation, "The Constitutional Democratic Party," pp. 216-219, for a fuller discussion of administrative interference in the elections.

28. Harcave, "Jewish Political Parties," p. 98.

29. The Kadet program is in Basil Dmytryshyn's *Imperial*

Russia: A Source Book, pp. 338-343; Zimmerman, "Between Revolution and Reaction," pp. 166-170.

30. This discussion of the Jews and the elections is based on Sidney Harcave's dissertation, pp. 31-34, 46-47, 65, 84, 91.

31. John J. Brock, "The Theory and Practice of the Union of the Russian People," (Unpublished Ph. D. dissertation, University of Michigan, 1972), pp. 261-262, 266, 207, 8, 272.

NOTES TO CHAPTER VI

1. Kokovtsov, *Out of My Past*, pp. 124, 126.

2. The Russian financial situation and the international loan are discussed in Witte's and Kokovtsov's memoirs, in Margaret Miller's *The Economic Development of Russia, 1905-1914*, and in articles by B. V. Ananich in *Vnutrenniaia politika tsarizma (Seredina XVI-Nachalo XX v.)* (The Internal Politics of Tsarism from the Mid-Sixteenth to the Beginning of the 20th Century), and Olga Crisp, "The Russian Liberals and the 1906 Anglo-French Loan to Russia," *Slavonic Review*, 39: (1960-1961), pp. 497-511. For a detailed study of the economic and foreign policy aspects of the loan see James William Long's Ph. D. dissertation, "The Economics of the Franco-Russian Alliance, 1905-1906," (University of Wisconsin, 1968).

3. Witte, TN II, pp. 193, 297.

4. Witte, TN II, pp. 98, 291-292, 184-185, 77; "Zapiski A. F. Redigera o 1905 god," p. 90; Sidney Harcave, *Years of the Golden Cockerel* (New York, 1968), p. 372.

5. Bing, *Secret Letters*, p. 211.

6. In his study, "P. N. Durnovo as Minister of Internal Affairs in the Witte Cabinet," Wayne Santoni largely discounts Witte's complaints about Durnovo's favored position with the sovereign. Santoni emphasizes the areas of policy agreement between the two ministers and judges their frequent cooperation to be more significant than the personal rivalry of which Witte complained so bitterly.

7. Santoni, *Ibid.*, p. 635; *Vtoroi period revoliutsii*, January-April, 1906, Vol. I, Part II, pp. 76-77.

8. T. von Laue, "Count Witte and The Russian Revolution of 1905," p. 40.

9. Bing, *Secret Letters*, p. 205; the document on the Vladivostok incident is in *Krasnyi Arkhiv* 11-12; Leningrad, 1925), p. 436; Nicholas, *Dnevnik*, p. 232.

10. Witte's letter of April 14, 1906 is on pp. 294-296 of the second volume of his memoirs. Bulatsel's warning was quoted from *Russkoe Znamia* in J. Brock's dissertation, "The Theory and Practice of the Union of the Russian People," p. 254; Baring, *A Year in Russia*, pp. 184-185.

11. The statement made at the Congress of Representatives of the Nobles' Associations is quoted in Sergei M. Dubrovskii's *Stolypinskaia zemelnaia reforma (Stolypin Land Reforms)*, (Moscow, 1963), p. 102; Shipov, *Vospominaniia*, pp. 408-409.

12. Nicholas, *Dnevnik*, p. 238. Polovtsov, "Dnevnik," *Krasnyi Arkhiv* 4: (Leningrad, 1923), p. 102; Gurko, *Figures and Features of the Past*, p. 458.

13. Witte, TN I, p. 280; Iswolsky, *Memoirs*, 29; Joseph O. Baylen, "The Tsar's 'Lecturer-General'," Research Paper No. 23, July, 1969 (Georgia State College, Atlanta, Georgia), p. 57.

14. Baylen, *Ibid.*, p. 42.

15. Bing, *Secret Letters*, p. 220; Bernard Pares, ed., *Letters of the Tsar to the Tsaritsa* (London, 1923), p. 29.

16. Mark Aldanov, "Count Witte," *Russian Review* 1: (November, 1941), p. 56.

17. *Rech*, April 23, 1906, (St. Petersburg, 1906).

18. Kokovtsov, *Out of My Past*, pp. 127, 124.

19. After a reorganization in 1905, the official title for that post was the Head of the Chief Administration of Land Organization and Agriculture. For the sake of brevity and clarity the term Minister of Agriculture will be used in this study.

20. *Rech*, April 23 and April 28, 1906; Witte, TN II, p. 245.

21. Gurko, *Figures and Features of the Past*, pp. 505, 459-460; Iswolsky, *Memoirs*, pp. 91-92.

22. For Stolypin's appointment see Mary E. Schaeffer's Ph. D. dissertation, "The Political Policies of P. A. Stolypin," (University of Indiana, 1964), pp. 41-43; Trepov's report is in Vladimir P. Semennikov, ed., *Revoliutsiia 1905 goda i samoderzhavie (The Revolution of 1905 and the Autocracy)*, (Moscow-Leningrad, 1928), pp. 100-101; Kryzhanovskii, *Vospominaniia*, p. 209.

23. Kokovtsov, *Out of My Past*, p. 150; Sir Bernard Pares, *The Fall of the Russian Monarchy* (New York, 1961), p. 94; Harcave, *Years of the Golden Cockerel*, p. 298; Gurko, *Figures and Features of the Past*, p. 75; A. F. Rediger, "Iz zapisok A. F. Redigera (1906)," (From the Notes of A. F. Rediger About 1906), *Krasnyi Arkhiv*, 60: (Leningrad, 1933), p. 116.

24. Witte's proposals are discussed in Mehlinger and Thompson, *Count Witte*, pp. 314-316, and Hosking, *The Russian Constitutional Experiment*, pp. 18-19. See also Gurko, *Figures and Features of the Past*, p. 452, and the reports of the Council of Minister's meetings in January and February of 1906 in V. V. Veselovskii, ed., *Agrarnyi vopros v sovete ministrov (1906 g.)*

(The Agrarian Question in the Council of Ministers: 1906) (Moscow-Leningrad, 1924). Gessen's statement is cited in Judith E. Zimmerman's Ph. D. dissertation, "Between Revolution and Reaction," pp. 213-214; *Rech*, April 6, 1906.

25. Kokovtsov, *Out of My Past*, p. 124; Gurko, *Figures and Features of the Past*, p. 459.

26. Kokovtsov, *Ibid.*, p. 129.

27. This account of the reception comes from Polovtsov, "Dnevnik," p. 99; Alexander, Grand Duke of Russia, *Once a Grand Duke*, pp. 226-227; Gurko, *Figures and Features of the Past*, p. 470; Kryzhanovskii, *Vospominaniia*, p. 81; Elizabeth Narishkin-Kurakin, *Under Three Tsars* (New York, 1931), p. 190; Marie, Grand Duchess of Russia, *The Education of a Princess* (New York, 1932), p. 84. Tagantsev, *Perezhitoe*, p. 35; Nicholas's speech is printed just before the stenographic record of the opening meeting of the First Duma.

28. Samuel N. Harper, *The Russia I Believe In* (University of Chicago Press, 1945), p. 35. The document containing the reaction of the Dowager-Empress is in *Krasnyi Arkhiv*, 15: (Leningrad, 1926), p. 214; *Rech*, April 28, 1906.

29. Baylen, "The Tsar's 'Lecturer-General'," p. 71.

NOTES TO CHAPTER VII

1. A. A. Mukhanov, *Pervaia gosudarstvennaia duma* (First State Duma) (St. Petersburg, 1907), Part I, pp. 190-192; *Rech*, April 28, 1906.

2. For the amnesty issue and Duma strategy in general see the Ph. D. dissertations of Judith Zimmerman, "Between Revolution and Reaction," and George N. Rhyne, "The Constitutional Democratic Party."

3. Baring, *A Year in Russia*, pp. 191-193; Iswolsky, *Memoirs*, pp. 88-89; B. Pares, *Russia and Reform* (London, 1907), p. 550; Kryzhanovskii, *Vospominaniia*, pp. 81-82.

4. The Soviet scholar S. M. Sidelnikov included a careful analysis of the Duma membership in Chapter VI of his *Obrazovanie i deiatelnost pervoi gosudarstvennoi dumy*. It is based on his own estimates, as well as a review of earlier studies. See also Mukhanov's *Pervaia gosudarstvennaia duma* and Zimmerman's "Between Revolution and Reaction." For the platform statements of most of the major parties see Dmytryshyn's *Imperial Russia: A Source Book*. The Octobrist statement is in Menashe's "Alexander Guchkov and the Origins of the Octobrist Party."

5. J. F. Hutchinson, "The Octobrists in Russian Politics: 1905-1917," (Ph. D. dissertation, University of London, 1966), pp. 60-61; Iswolsky, *Memoirs*, p. 108.

6. Michael H. Voskobiynyk's unpublished Ph. D. dissertation, "The Nationalities Question in Russia in 1905-1907: A Study in the Origin of Modern Nationalism, with Special Reference to the Ukrainians," (University of Pennsylvania, 1972) contains a wealth of material about the deputies belonging to the national minorities. I am indebted to him for much of the following discussion. See pages 240-241 for the program of the Union of Autonomists.

7. Quoted in *Ibid.*, p. 257.

8. Pares, *Russia and Reform*, p. 541.

9. This point was well taken by J. Zimmerman in "Between Revolution and Reaction"; For Kadet dominance of the First Duma see Zimmerman in *Ibid.*, pp. 192-194, 198-199.

10. Miliukov, *Memoirs*, p. 96.

11. Thomas Riha, *A Russian European* (University of Notre Dame Press, 1969), p. 113; Miliukov, *Memoirs*, pp. 98-99.

12. Kryzhanovskii, *Vospominaniia*, p. 97; Iswolsky, *Memoirs*, pp. 108, 103-104.

13. Kokovtsov, *Out of My Past*, p. 101; Witte, TN II, pp. 298-299, 91.

14. Quoted in Riha, *A Russian European*, p. 112.

15. Witte, TN I, pp. 295-296.

16. Thomas Riha, "Constitutional Developments in Russia," in Theofanis G. Stavrou, ed., *Russia Under the Last Tsar* (University of Minnesota Press, 1969), p. 98.

17. PSZRI, Number 27, p. 479.

18. Sergei Pushkarev, *The Emergence of Modern Russia: 1801-1917*, trans. by R. H. McNeal and Tova Yedlin (New York, 1966), p. 241; Riha, *A Russian European*, p. 147; Harcave, "Jewish Political Parties," p. 72; *Vtoroi period revoliutsii*, January-April, 1906, Vol. I, Part I, p. 648.

19. Mukhanov, *Pervaia gosudarstvennaia duma*, Part I, p. 53.

20. From an article by Hans Rogger in *The European Right*, ed. by Hans Rogger and Eugen Weber (University of California Press, 1965), p. 488. The 1905 platform statement of the Union of the Russian People is in Dmytryshyn's *Imperial Russia: A Source Book*.

21. Nicholas, *Dnevnik*, p. 229.

22. Curtiss, *Church and State in Russia*, pp. 240-241, 202-203.

23. Pares, *Russia and Reform*, p. 543; Kryzhanovskii, *Vospominaniia*, pp. 77-80.

24. Kryzhanovskii, *Ibid.*, p. 85.

25. Gurko, *Figures and Features of the Past*, p. 471.

NOTES TO CHAPTER VIII

1. For Rodichev's proposal see SO, pp. 21-25; Baring, *A Year in Russia*, p. 195.

2. Anikin's and Aladin's remarks, SO, pp. 25-26; Baring, *A Year in Russia*, p. 199; Iswolsky, *Memoirs*, p. 190; Miliukov, *Memoirs*, p. 100.

3. Iswolsky, *Memoirs*, p. 190.

4. Gurko, *Figures and Features of the Past*, pp. 453; SO, pp. 30-31.

5. Riha, *A Russian European*, pp. 127-128; Mukhanov, *Pervaia gosudarstvennaia duma*, Part I, pp. 85-87, 90.

6. Miliukov, *Memoirs*, p. 100.

7. Sidelnikov, *Obrazovanie i deiatelnost pervoi gosudarstvennoi dumy*, p. 212; Rhyne, "The Constitutional Democratic Party," pp. 313-314; Rhyne's dissertation contains a good discussion of the background and debates about the Address to the Throne.

8. Kryzhanovskii, *Vospominaniia*, p. 83.

9. Mikhanov, *Pervaia gosudarstvennaia duma*, Part I, pp. 170-171.

10. See the recollections of his father throughout Vladimir Nabokov's beautiful memoirs, *Speak, Memory* (New York, 1966); Pares, *Russia and Reform*, pp. 547-548. The draft proposal of the address appears in SO, pp. 74-76; there is an English translation of the final version in George Rhyne's dissertation on the Constitutional Democrats.

11. Iswolsky, *Memoirs*, p. 169; Kokovtsov, *Out of My Past*, pp. 459, 135.

12. Miliukov, *Memoirs*, p. 104.

13. See the discussion about the extraordinary laws at a special ministerial commission which met on February 10, 1905 as reprinted in A. K. Drezin, ed., *Tsarism v borbe s revoliutsiei 1905-1907 gg. (Tsarism in Its Struggle With Revolution, 1905-1907)* (Moscow, 1936).

14. Zimmerman, "Between Revolution and Reaction," pp. 226-227; SO, pp. 241-243.

15. Voskobiynyk, "The Nationalities Question," pp. 268, 263-264.

16. Quoted from a May 5, 1906 letter of Samuel Harper by Zimmerman in *Ibid.*, p. 227.

17. "Iz rezoliutsii Nikolaia II," ("Among the Resolutions of Nicholas II"), *Byloe*, 12: (June, 1918), p. 142; For the Duma's response to Nicholas' snub see Rhyne "The Constitutional Democratic Party," pp. 330-333; Riha, *A Russian European*, p. 121; SO, pp. 245-248.

18. Baring, *A Year in Russia*, pp. 208-209; Iswolsky, *Memoirs*, p. 169; Mukhanov, *Pervaia gosudarstvennaia duma*, Part I, p. 120.

19. Kokovtsov, *Out of My Past*, p. 137; Mukhanov, *Pervaia gosudarstvennaia duma*, Part I, pp. 61-62.

20. Gurko, *Figures and Features of the Past*, pp. 471-472; Kokovtsov, *Out of My Past*, pp. 139-140.

21. Goremykin's statement is on pages 321-327 of the stenographic records of the First Duma. There is an English translation in *The Russian Review* 2: 2 (London, 1913), pp. 165-172. This account of Goremykin's appearance is based on the following sources: Iswolsky, *Memoirs*, p. 170; Pares, *Russia and Reform*, p. 549; Kokovtsov, *Out of My Past*, p. 140; Gurko, *Figures and Features of the Past*, p. 473. Goremykin's program was similar in its general outline to the one Witte presented to the Tsar before his resignation. However, the bills necessary to implement it were not included, and most of them were never sent to the Duma, as had been Witte's intent.

22. Iswolsky, *Memoirs*, pp. 170-171; Kokovtsov, *Out of My Past*, p. 140; Baring, *A Year in Russia*, p. 213; Nabokov's remarks are on pages 327-328 of the stenographic record of the First Duma.

23. Kokovtsov, *Out of My Past*, pp. 140-141; V. A. Maklakov, *The First State Duma* (Mary Belkin, trans., Indiana University Press, 1964), pp. 98-99; SO, pp. 342-343.

24. For Geiden's statement see SO, pp. 349-350; Zhilkin's resolution is discussed in Rhyne's "The Constitutional Democratic Party," pp. 338-339, and Zimmerman's "Between Revolution and Reaction," pp. 230-231; SO, pp. 351-354.

25. Baring, *A Year in Russia*, p. 215; Miliukov, *Memoirs*, p. 106; Kokovtsov, *Out of My Past*, p. 141; Iswolsky, *Memoirs*, p. 171.

26. *Rech*, May 14, 1906; Polovtsov, "Dnevnik" in *Krasnyi Arkhiv* 4: (Leningrad, 1923), p. 112; Kokovtsov, *Out of My Past*, pp. 142-143.

NOTES TO CHAPTER IX

1. See Zimmerman, "Between Revolution and Reaction," pp. 231-232.

2. Sidelnikov, *Obrazovanie i deiatelnost pervoi gosudarstvennoi dumy*, p. 224. The telegram excerpts which follow are from *Pravitelstvennyi Vestnik*, May 5, 1906.

3. Maklakov, *The First State Duma*, pp. 115, 167.

4. Baring, *A Year in Russia*, p. 234; Iswolsky, *Memoirs*, p. 172.

5. The Duma statute is in F. D. Kalinychev's *Gosudarstvennaia duma v Rossii;* See articles 33, 58-60 on pages 118, 122; Alfred Levin, *The Second Duma*, p. 90.

6. For the interpellation about the telegrams see Maklakov, *The First State Duma*, pp. 167-171; See Rhyne, "The Constitutional Democratic Party," pp. 352-356; See Zimmerman, "Between Revolution and Reaction," pp. 240-241; SO, pp. 369-370, 389-391, 639-640, 969-970, 1704.

7. See Rhyne, "The Constitutional Democratic Party," pp. 349-352, 288; For a list of the interpellations see pages 252-301 of the index to the stenographic records of the First Duma; Maklakov, *The First State Duma*, p. 157; Mukhanov, *Pervaia gosudarstvennaia duma*, Part II, p. 10.

8. Mukhanov, *Ibid.*, pp. 9-10; Part I, p. 91; See Rhyne, "The Constitutional Democratic Party," pp. 351, 291; See Zimmerman, "Between Revolution and Reaction," p. 245.

9. See SO, pp. 951-958, 1125, 1133-1141, 1196. The issue is covered in Zimmerman's "Between Revolution and Reaction," pp. pp. 111-119; Rhyne's "The Constitutional Democratic Party," pp. 357-361; and Voskobiynyk's "Nationalities Question in Russia in 1905-1907," pp. 489-498. There is an English translation of Urusov's speech in M. Baring's *A Year in Russia*, pp. 250-257.

10. *Vtoroi period revoliutsii*, May-September, 1906, Vol. II, Part I, p. 583. This account of the Duma reaction to the Riga sentences comes from: Maklakov, *The First State Duma*, pp. 145-149, 152-159; Sidelnikov, *Obrazovanie i deiatelnost pervoi gosudarstvennoi dumy*, pp. 245-246, 249; See Rhyne, "The Constitutional Democratic Party," pp. 362, 365; See Zimmerman, "Between Revolution and Reaction," pp. 229-230, 235-238; SO, p. 294.

11. Mukhanov, *Pervaia gosudarstvennaia duma*, Part I, pp. 222-226. The formal response to the interpellation about the Riga sentences, along with two others of a similar nature, came from Chief Military Prosecutor-General V. P. Pavlov on June 1. Pavlov informed the First Duma that officials had no choice but to invoke the statute on capital punishment while it was still in effect. He denied that ministers had any right to suggest to governor-generals or military commanders that such sentences not be confirmed. Shouts of "hangman" greeted his statement and the Duma expressed its "deep indignation" at the unsatisfactory reply. Sidelnikov, *Obrazovanie i deiatelnost pervoi gosudarstvennoi dumy*, pp. 249-250; SO, pp. 900-901, 915.

12. For the matter of legislative initiative in the Duma see Serge L. Levitsky, "Legislative Initiative in the Russian Duma." *American Slavic and East European Review*, 3: (October, 1956),

pp. 313-324; See Zimmerman, "Between Revolution and Reaction," pp. 212-215; See Rhyne, "The Constitutional Democratic Party," pp. 294-295.

13. For the July 19, 1906 session see Maklakov, *The First State Duma*, pp. 176-177; Mukhanov, *Pervaia gosudarstvennaia duma*, Part I, pp. 256-258; SO, pp. 1469-1484.

14. In December, 1906 Nicholas was to veto a measure advocated by P. Stolypin which would have eliminated many of the legal disabilities against the Jews. Schaeffer, "The Political Policies of P. A. Stolypin," p. 58.

15. SO, pp. 378-379, 1006-1008, 1010-1013, 1074, 1096; Miliukov, *Memoirs*, p. 99. See Voskobiynyk's dissertation, "The Nationalities Question" for samples of contributions to the debates by minority deputies, pp. 272-277.

16. See Zimmerman, "Between Revolution and Reaction," pp. 205, 207.

17. Mukhanov, *Pervaia gosudarstvennaia duma*, Part II, pp. 12-13.

18. Kokovtsov, *Out of My Past*, p. 143; See Zimmerman, "Between Revolution and Reaction," pp. 213-214; Maklakov, *The First State Duma*, pp. 122-123. See the index to the stenographic records for a list of all proposals presented to the First Duma and a summary of the action taken upon them.

19. Gurko, *Figures and Features of the Past*, pp. 473-474. The *Rech* statement is cited in Zimmerman, "Between Revolution and Reaction," p. 214.

20. Kokovtsov, *Out of My Past*, p. 143; See an entry for July 25, 1906 in *Osobye zhurnali sovetov ministrov*, Vol. I *(Special Journals of the Council of Ministers)* (St. Petersburg, 1907).

21. For the famine relief issue see Zimmerman, "Between Revolution and Reaction," pp. 261-263 and the article by Peter Dolgorukii in the third section of Mukhanov's *Pervaia gosudarstvennaia duma*; Gurko, *Figures and Features of the Past*, p. 481; Stolypin's remarks, SO, pp. 1241-1244.

22. Dolgorukii's comments, Mukhanov, *Pervaia gosudarstvennaia duma*, Part III, pp. 135-136; See Zimmerman, "Between Revolution and Reaction," p. 297.

23. For Stolypin's political ideas see Schaeffer, "The Political Policies of P. A. Stolypin," pp. 185, 189, 272.

24. Kokovtsov, *Out of My Past*, p. 143; Mukhanov, *Pervaia gosudarstvennaia duma*, Part III, p. 143.

25. Mukhanov, *Ibid.*, Part I, p. 250. For the famine relief bill see SO, pp. 1449-1451, 1656-1662, 1665, 1684-1691, 1708-1709. For the State Council action on the measure see Oleh W. Gerus' Ph. D. dissertation, "The Reformed State Council, 1905-1917," (University of Toronto, 1970), p. 124.

NOTES TO CHAPTER X

1. For general descriptions of Russian agriculture see Launcelot A. Owen, *The Russian Peasant Movement, 1906-1917* (New York, 1963); George Pavlovsky, *Agricultural Russia on the Eve of the Revolution* (London, 1930); Geroid T. Robinson, *Rural Russia Under the Old Regime;* and Sergei Pushkarev, *The Emergence of Modern Russia, 1801-1917.*

2. Margaret S. Miller, *The Economic Development of Russia,* p. 55.

3. See Pushkarev's *The Emergence of Modern Russia* for charts and an analysis of land ownership, pp. 206-210.

4. Mukhanov, *Pervaia gosudarstvennaia duma,* Part III, pp. 18-19.

5. The party positions on the land issue are found in the following works: Social Revolutionaries; Dmytryshyn, *Imperial Russia,* pp. 336-337: Social Democrats; *Ibid.,* p. 330: Constitutional Democrats; Harcave, *First Blood,* pp. 297-298: Octobrists; Menashe, "Alexander Guchkov and the Origins of the Octobrist Party," p. 219.

6. *Polnoe sobranie rechei Nikolaia II,* pp. 70-72.

7. For the efforts of the administration towards handling the agricultural problem see: George L. Yaney, "The Imperial Russian Government and the Stolypin Land Reform," (Ph. D. dissertation, Princeton University, 1961), pp. 88-90, 102; Mehlinger and Thompson, *Count Witte,* pp. 182-187.

8. The text of Witte's report is in V. V. Veselovskii, *Agrarnyi vopros v sovete ministrov, 1906 (The Agrarian Question in the Council of Ministers, 1906)* (Moscow-Leningrad, 1924). In that report Witte mentioned a project of his Minister of Agriculture (as of May, 1905 the post's formal title was Director of the Department of Land Organization and Agriculture) which included a recommendation that large estates be expropriated in areas of acute need, or where peasants were already renting the land. The recommendation was only a minor part of a broad plan for agrarian reform. Its author, N. N. Kutler, lost his ministerial post in early February of 1906. Yaney, "The Imperial Russian Government and the Stolypin Land Reform," pp. 124-126. Kokovtsov, *Out of My Past,* pp. 100-102.

9. Yaney, "The Imperial Russian Government and the Stolypin Land Reform," pp. 101, 109, 111; Gerschenkron, *Continuity in History,* pp. 231-233.

10. Yaney, "The Imperial Russian Government and the Stolypin Land Reform," p. 111.

11. Dubrovskii, *Stolypinskaia zemelnaia reforma,* pp. 93-94; The exchange between Goremykin and Witte is in TS (April), pp. 231-236.

NOTES TO CHAPTER XI

12. SO, pp. 241, 328.
13. SO, p. 248-251; The English text of the project is in Rhyne, "The Constitutional Democratic Party," pp. 478-480. See his and Zimmerman's dissertations for detailed discussions of it.
14. Project of the 104, SO, pp. 560-562; Project of the 33, SO, pp. 1088, 1153-1156; Sidelnikov, *Obrazovanie i deiatelnost pervoi gosudarstvennoi dumy*, pp. 302-303.
15. A good discussion of the minority deputies' positions on the land reform issue is found on pages 281-288 of Voskobiynyk's dissertation, "The Nationalities Question in Russia in 1905-1907."
16. Zimmerman, "Between Revolution and Reaction," pp. 207-209, 249, 232-235; Mukhanov, *Pervaia gosudarstvennaia duma*, Part III, pp. 8, 12-14; Pares, *Russia and Reform*, p. 555. Rhyne, "The Constitutional Democratic Party," pp. 284-285.
17. May 19, 1906 session: Stishinskii, SO, pp. 509-517; Gurko, SO, pp. 517-523; May 23, 1906 session: Gurko, SO, pp. 566-567; Stishinskii, SO, pp. 568-569; Mukhanov, *Pervaia gosudarstvennaia duma*, Part II, pp. 19, 16-17.
18. Gurko, *Figures and Features of the Past*, pp. 477; Polovtsov, "Dnevnik" in *Krasnyi Arkhiv*, 4: (Leningrad, 1923), p. 112.
19. Iswolsky, p. 176; SO, p. 1213; Zimmerman, "Between Revolution and Reaction," p. 214; See the text in Aleksander N. Brianchaninov's *Rospusk gosudarstvennoi dumy (The Dissolution of the State Duma)* (Pskov, 1906), Part II, pp. 34-50.
20. Text in *Ibid.*, pp. 51-56.
21. Iswolsky, *Memoirs*, p. 177; Brianchaninov, *Rospusk gosudarstvennoi dumy*, Part I, pp. 41-44; Zimmerman, "Between Revolution and Reaction," pp. 269-270; Rhyne, "The Constitutional Democratic Party," pp. 415-419; SO, pp. 1953-1956.
22. Pares, *Russia and Reform*, pp. 558-559; Zimmerman, "Between Revolution and Reaction," pp. 258, 270; Rhyne, "The Constitutional Democratic Party," pp. 420-422.
23. The records of the June 6, 1906, and June 7, 1906, sessions of the First Duma were printed in a "korrektura" (Supplement) to the rest of the stenographic record. The June 6 session is on pages 2015-2082 of that supplement.

NOTES TO CHAPTER XI

1. PSZRI, Number 28103; Kokovtsov, *Out of My Past*, pp. 126, 136-137.

2. The numerous accounts by participants in these negotiations are ably summarized in the article of Robert L. Tuck, "Paul Miliukov and the Negotiations for a Duma Ministry, 1906," *American Slavic and East European Review* 10: (June, 1951), pp. 117-129.

3. My views on Nicholas' decision to dissolve the First Duma were clarified during a long conversation with Stephen Bensman, graduate student in history at the University of Wisconsin, who has done extentive research on the agrarian question in the First Duma.

4. See the accounts of that evening in Kokovtsov's *Out of My Past*, pp. 151-153; and Iswolsky's *Memoirs*, pp. 197-198.

5. Nicholas, *Dnevnik*, p. 244.

6. Rediger, "Iz zapisok A. F. Redigera," *Krasnyi Arkhiv* 60: (Leningrad, 1933), pp. 116-118; S. Valk, ed., "Iz pravitelstvennykh nastroenii v epokhy I-i gosudarstvennoi dumy," (Regarding the Mood of the Government During the Era of the First Duma), *Krasnyi Arkhiv* 15: (Leningrad, 1926), p. 214.

7. *Vtoroi period revoliutsii*, May-September, 1906, Vol. II, Part I, p. 586; Polovtsev, "Dnevnik," *Krasnyi Arkhiv* 4: (Leningrad, 1923), p. 117; Gurko, *Figures and Features of the Past*, p. 484; Kokovtsov, *Out of My Past*, pp. 154-156.

8. Brianchaninov, *Rospusk gosudarstvennoi dumy*, Part I, p. 54; Text of the manifesto, PSZRI, Number 28105.

9. Zimmerman, "Between Revolution and Reaction," pp. 249, 252-253.

10. B-ov, M. and Dan, F., *Rabochie deputaty v pervoi gosudarstvennoi dume (The Workers' Deputies in the First State Duma)* (St. Petersburg, n.d.), p. 166; Miliukov, *Memoirs*, p. 129; Riha, *A Russian European*, p. 133; Zimmerman, "Between Revolution and Reaction," pp. 275-277.

11. Kokovtsov, *Out of My Past*, p. 155.

12. The text of the Vyborg Manifesto is in Brianchanonov's *Rospusk gosudarstvennoi dumy*, Part II, p. 60. Riha, *A Russian European*, pp. 133-134; Zimmerman, "Between Revolution and Reaction," pp. 276-285. The exact number of the signatories to the Vyborg Manifesto is in doubt, since there was more than one copy circulated. The copy recognized as official by the government had 170 signatures, including 10 who signed after the meeting in Finland. Some Kadet accounts claim over 200 signers.

13. Pares, *A Wandering Student*, p. 140; Harper, *The Russia I Believe In*, p. 51; Samuel Kucherov, *Courts, Lawyers, and Trials Under the Last Three Tsars* (New York, 1953), pp. 239-243. Of just under 170 deputies eventually tried, all but two were sentenced to three months in prison, along with permanent loss of their political rights. The charge—participation in a *conspiracy to distribute* a revolutionary manifesto—was deliberately selected.

Had they been prosecuted merely for signing such a document, loss of political rights would not have been among the prescribed penalties.

14. Baring, *A Year in Russia*, p. 287; Brianchaninov, *Rospusk gosudarstvennoi dumy*, Part I, pp. 59, 61.

15. Riha, *A Russian European*, pp. 135, 137-138; Miliukov, *Memoirs*, p. 132.

16. Riha, *A Russian European*, p. 131.

17. Mukhanov, *Pervaia gosudarstvennaia duma*, Part I, pp. 5-6, 117, 186.

18. *Vtoroi period revoliutsii*, May-September, 1906, Vol. II, Part I, pp. 54, 52; Zenzinov, *Perezhitoe*, pp. 340-341.

19. Bing, *Secret Letters*, p. 212; Iswolsky, *Memoirs*, p. 206.

20. Harper, *The Russia I Believe In*, p. 51; Clement S. Masloff, "Violence and/or Land Reform: The Russian Peasant and the Duma, 1906-07." Paper delivered at the Midwest Slavic Conference at Cleveland State University, May 1975, p. 5, f.n. 24.

21. Pushkarev, *The Emergence of Modern Russia*, pp. 20, 249; Paul Avrich, *The Russian Anarchists* (Princeton University Press, 1967), p. 64.

22. Gurko, *Figures and Features of the Past*, pp. 497-498; Kokovtsov, *Out of My Past*, p. 159, 164-165; Maria P. von Bok, *Reminiscences of My Father, Peter A. Stolypin*, trans. by Margaret Patoski (Metuchen, New Jersey, 1970), pp. 150-156.

23. Nicholas, *Dnevnik*, p. 251; Bing, *Secret Letters*, pp. 215, 216-218; Zenzinov, *Perezhitoe*, p. 351.

24. *Vtoroi period revoliutsii*, May-September, 1906, Vol. II, Part II, p. 589; Kokovtsov, *Out of My Past*, p. 160.

25. Bing, *Secret Letters*, pp. 218-219; Nicholas' letter to Dubasov, *Krasnyi Arkhiv*, 11-12: (Leningrad, 1925), p. 442.

26. Schaeffer, "The Political Policies of P. A. Stolypin," p. 76; Anatoly Marchenko, *My Testimony*, trans. by Michael Scammel (New York, 1969), pp. 15-16.

27. For these measures see: George L. Yaney's Ph. D. dissertation; Gerschenkron, *Continuity in History and Other Essays*, pp. 233-241; Ben-Cion Pinchuk, "The Octobrists in the Third Duma 1907-1912," (Ph. D. dissertation, University of Washington, 1969), pp. 77-79. For the development of Stolypin's views on land reform see Mary E. Schaeffer's Ph. D. dissertation.

28. Kokovtsov, *Out of My Past*, p. 167.

NOTES TO CHAPTER XII

1. Nicholas, *Dnevnik*, p. 231.

2. Reiger, "Zapiski A. F. Redigera o 1905 g." *Krasnyi Arkhiv* 45: (Leningrad, 1931), p. 90.

3. Narishkin-Kurakin, *Under Three Tsars*, p. 189.

4. Gilliard, *Thirteen Years at the Russian Court*, p. 206.

5. From Kennan's article in the symposium volume edited by Richard Pipes: *Revolutionary Russia* (Garden City, N.Y., 1969), p. 11.

6. The quotes by Miliukov are in Riha's *A Russian European*, pp. 135, 121; "Iz zapisok A. F. Redigera, (1906)," *Krasnyi Arkhiv* 60: (Leningrad, 1933), pp. 114-115; Miliukov, *Memoirs*, p. 134, 141-142.

7. There is an English translation of the Nobles' Associations' May of 1906 address in George W. Simmond's Ph. D. dissertation, "The Congress of Representatives of the Nobles' Associations, 1906-1916" (Columbia University, 1964).

8. Nabokov, *Speak, Memory*, p. 96.

9. For the April decree on religious toleration see Curtiss' *Church and State in Russia*; The laws on labor were nicely summarized by Michael O. Gately in a paper delibered at Sir George Williams University in Montreal in May of 1971 entitled "The Legislative Response to the Labor Problem in Russia, 1905-1914."

10. Voskobiynyk, "The Nationalities Question in Russia," pp. 222, 131, 138-140.

11. For a concise survey of the new press regulations see Jacob Walkin's article, "Government Controls Over the Press in Russia, 1905-1914," *Russian Review* (July, 1954), pp. 203-209.

Bibliography

The items in this bibliography are arranged according to subject, with the exception of the newspapers, and certain documentary collections.

I. DOCUMENTARY COLLECTIONS AND NEWSPAPERS

Crown Councils (1905-1906): Proceedings:
"Petergofskoe soveshchanie o proekte gosudarstvennoi dumy: sekretnye protokoly." Berlin, n.d. (The minutes of the July, 1906 sessions.)

"Tsarskoselskiia soveshchaniia: Protokoly." Printed in three parts. December sessions: *Byloe*, 3: St. Petersburg, 1917, pp. 235-265; February sessions: *Byloe*, 5-6: St. Petersburg, 1917, pp. 289-318; April sessions: *Byloe*, 4: St. Petersburg, 1917, pp. 188-245.

Dmytryshyn, Basil, ed. *Imperial Russia: A Source Book, 1700-1917*. New York, 1967.

Fundamental Laws of 1906. *Krasnyi Arkhiv*, 11-12: Leningrad, 1925, pp. 121-142. The text of the draft presented to the April, 1906 crown council by the Council of Ministers is included.

Kalinychev, F. I. *Gosudarstvennaia duma v Rossii v dokumentakh i materialakh*. Moscow, 1957.

Osobye zhurnali soveta ministrov. Volume I, St. Petersburg, 1906.

Pankratova, A. M., ed. *Revoliutsiia 1905-1907 gg. v Rossii: Dokumenty i materialy.* A multi-volume work begun in connection with the 50th anniversary of the 1905 Revolution. Volumes useful to this study include:

Vserossiiskaia politicheskaia stachka v Oktiabre 1905 goda. Moscow-Leningrad, 1955.

Vyshi podem revoliutsii 1905-1907 gg: Vooruzhennye vosstaniia. 3 volumes. Moscow-Leningrad, 1955-1956.

Vtoroi period revoliutsii: 1906-1907 gody. January to April, 1906, Volume I, Parts I and II. Moscow-Leningrad, 1957-1959: May to September, 1906, Volume II, Parts I, II, III. Moscow-Leningrad, 1961-1963.

Pravitelstvennyi Vestnik. The official administration daily, published in St. Petersburg from 1855 to 1918.

Raeff, Marc. *Plans for Political Reform in Imperial Russia, 1730-1905.* Englewood Cliffs, N.J., 1966.

Rech. The central organ of the Kadet Party, published in St. Petersburg from February, 1906 to 1917.

Russia: Gosudarstvennaia duma. *Opis del arkhiva kantseliarii gosudarstvennoi dumy.* St. Petersburg, 1914.

Russia: Gosudarstvennaia duma. *Stenograficheskie otchety 1906 god: sessiia pervaia.* St. Petersburg, 1906.

Russia: Gosudarstvennaia duma. *Materialy k stenograficheskim otchetam 1906 g. Korrekturnye ottiski po zasedaniiam 39 i 40 (6 i 7 Iulia).* St. Petersburg, 1907.

Russia: Gosudarstvennaia duma. *Ukazatel k stenograficheskim otchetam 1906 god.* St. Petersburg, 1907.

Russia: *Polnoe sobranie zakonov Rossiiskoi Imperii.* Sobranie tretie: March 1, 1881-December 31, 1913. 33 volumes. St. Petersburg, 1885-1916.

Russia: *Svod zakonov rossiiskoi Imperii.* Volume I, Parts I and II. St. Petersburg, 1906.

II. NICHOLAS II, THE IMPERIAL FAMILY, AND THE COURT

Alexander, Grand Duke of Russia. *Once a Grand Duke.* Garden City, New York, 1932.

Baylen, Joseph O. "The Tsar's 'Lecturer-General': W. T. Stead and the Russian Revolution of 1905." Research Paper No. 23, July 1969. Georgia State College, Atlanta, Georgia.

Buxhoeveden, Baroness Sophie. *The Life and Tragedy of Alexandra Feodorovna, Empress of Russia.* New York, 1929.

Gilliard, Pierre. *Thirteen Years at the Russian Court.* New York, 1921.

Goremyka, Anton, ed. *Nikolai II: ego lichnost, intimnaia zhizn, i pravlenie.* London, 1905.

"Iz pravitelstvennykh nastroenii v epokhu I-i gosudarstvennoi dumy." *Krasnyi Arkhiv* 15: Leningrad, 1926, p. 214.

"Iz rezoliutsii Nikolai II." *Byloe* 12: Petrograd, 1918, pp. 142-147.

"Iz zapisnoi knizhki arkhivista: Nikolai II v 1905 gody." *Krasnyi Arkhiv* 11-12: Leningrad, 1925, pp. 434-439.

Marie, Grand Duchess of Russia. *Education of a Princess.* New York, 1932.

Massie, Robert K. *Nicholas and Alexandra.* New York, 1967.

Mossolov, A. A. *At the Court of the Last Tsar.* Translated by E. W. Dickes. London, 1935.

Narishkin-Kurakin, Elizabeth. *Under Three Tsars.* Translated by Julia E. Loesser. New York, 1931.

Nicholas II. *Archives secretes de l'empereur Nicholas II.* Edited by Vladimir A. Lazarevskii. Paris, 1928.

———. *Dnevnik Imperatora Nikolaia II. 1890-1906.* Berlin, 1923.

———. *The Letters of the Tsar to the Tsaritsa, 1914-1917.* Translated by A. L. Hynes. New York, 1929.

———. "Pisma Nikolaia II k Dubasovy." *Krasnyi Arkhiv* 11-12: Leningrad, 1925, pp. 440-442.

———. *Polnoe sobranie rechei Imperatora Nikolaia II: 1894-1906.* St. Petersburg, 1906.

———. *The Secret Letters of the Last Tsar.* Translated by Edward J. Bing. New York, 1938.

Pares, Bernard, ed. *The Letters of the Tsaritsa to the Tsar, 1914-1916.* London, 1923.

Vyrubova, Anna A. *Memoirs of the Russian Court.* New York, 1923.

III. THE REVOLUTION OF 1905

American Committee for Liberation from Bolshevism, Inc. *The Revolution of 1905 as Reported in the Russian Press 50 Years Ago.* Compiled by Vladimir S. Varsavsky. November, 1955.

Baring, Maurice. *A Year in Russia.* New York, 1907.

Baynac, Jacques *et al. Sur 1905.* Paris, 1974.

Broido, Eve. *Memoirs of a Revolutionary.* Translated by Vera Broido. New York, 1967.

Chermenskii, E. D. *Burzhuaziia i tsarizm v revoliutsii, 1905-1907 gg.* Moscow-Leningrad, 1939.

Erman, L. K. "Demokraticheskaia intelligentsiia rossii v revoliutsii, 1905-1907 gg." *Voprosy Istorii* 12: Moscow, 1966, pp. 23-38.

———. *Intelligentsiia v pervoi russkoi revoliutsii.* Moscow, 1966.

Harcave, Sidney. *First Blood: The Russian Revolution of 1905.* New York, 1964.

Hough, Richard. *The Potemkin Mutiny.* Englewood Cliffs, New Jersey, 1963.

Kaplan, Simon. *Once A Rebel.* New York, 1941.

Khrustalev-Nosar, George. "The Council of Workmen Deputies." *Russian Review* 2: 1 London, 1913, pp. 89-100.

Lenin, Vladimir I. *Selected Works.* Volume III. *The Revolution of 1905-1907.* International Publishers, New York, n.d.

Mintslov, Sergei R. *Peterburg v 1903-1910 godakh.* Riga, 1931.

Nevinson, Henry W. *The Dawn in Russia.* London, 1906.

Pankratova, Anna M. *Pervaia russkaia revoliutsiia 1905-1907 gg.* Moscow, 1951.

Pethybridge, Roger. *Witness to the Russian Revolution.* New York, 1967.

Sablinsky, Walter. "The All-Russian Railroad Union and the Beginning of the General Strike in October, 1905" in Alexander and Janet Rabinowitch (eds.). *Revolution and Politics in Russia*. Indiana University Press, 1972.

Savinkov, Boris. *Memoirs of a Terrorist*. New York, 1931.

———. *What Never Happened*. Translated by Thomas Seltzer. New York, 1917.

Schwarz, Solomon M. *The Russian Revolution of 1905*. University of Chicago Press, 1967.

Sef, S. E. *Burzhuaziia v 1905 godu*. Moscow-Leningrad, 1926.

Spector, Ivar. *The First Russian Revolution: Its Impact on Asia*. Englewood Cliffs, New Jersey, 1962.

Taylor, Patrick R. "The Trans-Siberian Railroad and the Russian Revolution of 1905." Unpublished Ph. D. dissertation, University of Tennessee, 1969.

Trotsky, Leon. *1905*. Translated by Anya Bostock. New York, 1972.

Wolfe, Bertram. *Three Who Made A Revolution*. Boston, 1955.

Woytinsky, Wladimir S. *Stormy Passage: A Personal History Through Two Russian Revolutions to Democracy and Freedom*. New York, 1961.

Zenzinov, Vladimir. *Perezhitoe*. New York. 1953.

III. THE ADMINISTRATION OF NICHOLAS II AND THE CRISIS OF 1905-06

Aldanov, Mark. "Count Witte." *Russian Review* 1: November, 1941, pp. 56-64.

———. "P. N. Durnovo—Prophet of War and Revolution." *Russian Review* 2: November, 1942, pp. 31-45.

Astrov, N. I., and Gronsky, Paul P. *The War and the Russian Government*. New Haven, 1929. (Pages 3-25 contain an intelligent analysis of the Fundamental Laws of 1906.)

Byrnes, Robert F. "Pobedonotsov on the Instruments of Russian Government." *Continuity and Change in Rus-*

sian and Soviet Thought. Edited by Ernest J. Simmons. Harvard University Press, 1955.

―――. *Pobedonostsev: His Life and Thought.* Indiana University Press, 1968.

Chuloshnikov, A. "K istorii manifesta 6 avgusta 1905 goda." *Krasnyi Arkhiv* 15: Leningrad, 1926, pp. 262-270.

de Enden, M. N. "The Roots of Witte's Thought." *Russian Review* 29: January, 1970, pp. 6-24.

Dillon, E. J. "Two Russian Statemen." *Quarterly Review* 236: London, 1921, pp. 402-417.

Drezen, A. K., ed. *Tsarizm v borbe s revoliutsiei 1905-1907 gg.* Moscow, 1936.

Dubrovskii, Sergei M. *Stolypinskaia zemelnaia reforma.* Moscow, 1963.

Eroshkin, Nikolai P. *Ocherki istorii gosudarstvennykh uchrezhdenii dorevoliutsionnoi rossii.* Moscow, 1960.

Gerus, Oleh Walter. "The Reformed State Council, 1905-1917: A Phase in Russian Constitutionalism." Unpublished Ph. D. dissertation, University of Toronto, 1970.

Gurko, Vladimir. *Figures and Features of the Past: Government and Opinion in the Reign of Nicholas II.* Translated by Laura Matveev. Stanford, California: Stanford University Press, 1939.

Iswolsky, Alexander P. *The Memoirs of Alexander Iswolsky.* Translated by Charles L. Seeger. London, 1920.

"K istorii manifesta 17 oktiabria 1905 goda." *Byloe* 14: Leningrad, 1919, pp. 108-111.

Kokovtsov, Vladimir N. *Out of My Past.* Translated by Laura Matveev. Stanford University Press, 1935.

Kryzhanovskii, Sergei E. *Vospominaniia.* Berlin, n.d.

Lopukhin, A. A. *Otryvki iz vospominanii.* Moscow, 1923.

Levin, Alfred. "Peter Arkadevich Stolypin: A Political Appraisal." *Journal of Modern History* 37: December, 1965, pp. 445-463.

―――. "Russian Bureaucratic Opinion in the Wake of the 1905 Revolution." *Jahrbücher für Geschichte Osteuropas* 11: April, 1963, pp. 1-12.

Long, James William. "The Economics of the Franco-Russian Alliance, 1904-1906." Unpublished Ph. D. dissertation, University of Wisconsin, 1968.

Mehlinger, Howard D. and John M. Thompson. *Count Witte and the Tsarist Government in the 1905 Revolution.* Indiana University Press, 1972.

———. "Count Sergei Iu. Witte and the Problems of Constitutionalism in Russia, 1905-1906." Unpublished Ph. D. dissertation, University of Kansas, 1964.

Miliukov, P. "Sergei Iu. Witte." In *Entsiklopedicheskii slovar.* Granat, Moscow, 1911.

Nevskii, V., ed. "K istorii manifesta 17 oktiabria." *Krasnyi Arkhiv* 4: Leningrad, 1923, pp. 411-416.

Polovtsev, A. A. "Dnevnik A. A. Polovtseva 1905 g." *Krasnyi Arkhiv* 4: Leningrad, 1923, pp. 63-128.

Pares, Bernard. "Conversations with Mr. Stolypin." *Russian Review* 2: 1: London, 1913, pp. 101-110.

———. "The Peterhof Conference." *Russian Review* 2: 3: London, 1913, pp. 87-120.

Pobedonostsev, Konstantin P. *Reflections of a Russian Statesman.* University of Michigan Press, 1965.

Rediger, A. F. "Iz zapisok A. F. Redigera, (1906)," *Krasnyi Arkhiv* 60: Leningrad, 1933, pp. 92-133.

———. "Zapiski A. F. Redigera o 1905 g." *Krasnyi Arkhiv* 45: Leningrad, 1931, pp. 86-111.

Santoni, Wayne D. "P. N. Durnovo as Minister of Internal Affairs in the Witte Cabinet: A Study in Suppression." Unpublished Ph. D. dissertation, University of Kansas, 1968.

Schaeffer, Mary E. "The Political Policies of P. A. Stolypin." Unpublished Ph. D. dissertation, University of Indiana, 1964.

Semennikov, V. P., ed. *Revoliutsiia 1905 goda i samoderzhavie.* Moscow-Leningrad, 1928.

Snow, George E. "Vladimir Nikolaevich Kokovtsov: Case Study of an Imperial Russian Bureaucrat, 1904-1906." Unpublished Ph. D. dissertation, University of Indiana, 1970.

Stolypin, Peter. "Vsepoddaneishii otchet saratovskogo gubernatora P. Stolypina za 1904 god." *Krasnyi Arkhiv* 17: Leningrad, 1926, pp. 83-87.

Szeftel, Marc. "The Legislative Reform of August 6, 1905," in A. Marongiu, ed. *Mélanges: Etudes presentées à la*

311

Commission Internationale pour L'Histoire des Assemblées d'Etats. Palermo, Italy, 1967.

_____. "Nicholas II's Constitutional Decisions of October 17-19, 1905 and Sergei Witte's Role" in *Album J. Balon.* Namur, Belgium, 1968.

Tagantsev, Nikolai S. *Perezhitoe: uchrezdenie gosudarstvennoi dumy v 1905-1906 gg.* Petrograd, 1919.

Tamarov, I., ed. "Manifest 17 Oktiabria." *Krasnyi Arkhiv* 11-12: Leningrad, 1925, pp. 39-96.

Veselovskii, V. V., ed. *Agrarnyi vopros v sovete ministrov (1906).* Moscow-Leningrad, 1924.

von Bock, Maria Petrovna. *Reminiscences of My Father, Peter A. Stolypin.* Translated by Margaret Patoski. Metuchen, New Jersey, 1970.

von Laue, Theodore. "Count Witte and the Russian Revolution of 1905." *American Slavic and East European Review* 17: February, 1958, pp. 25-46.

Witte, Sergei. "Doklad S. Iu. Witte." *Krasnyi Arkhiv* 11-12: Leningrad, 1925, pp. 149-150.

_____. "Doklad S. Iu. Witte ob osnovnykh zakonakh." *Krasnyi Arkhiv* 11-12: Leningrad, 1925, pp. 115-116.

_____. "Graf Witte v borbe s revoliutsiei." *Byloe.* St. Petersburg, 1918, pp. 3-10.

_____. "Interviu S. Iu. Witte s predstaviteliami pechati." *Krasnyi Arkhiv* 11-12: Leningrad, 1925, pp. 99-105.

_____. "O karatelnoi okspeditsii v Pribaltiiskom krae." *Ibid.,* pp. 150-151.

_____. *The Memoirs of Count Witte.* Translated by Abraham Yarmolinsky. Garden City, New York, 1921.

_____. "O revoliutsionnom dvizhenie v Finliandii." *Krasnyi Arkhiv* 11-12: Leningrad, 1925, pp. 145-149.

_____. *Vospominaniia: Tsarstvovanie Nikolaia II.* Volumes I and II. Berlin, 1922.

_____. "Zapiska Vitte ot 9 oktiabria." *Krasnyi Arkhiv* 11-12: Leningrad, 1925, pp. 51-61.

Yaney, George L. "The Concept of the Stolypin Land Reform." *Slavic Review* 23: June, 1964, pp. 275-293.

_____. "The Imperial Russian Government and the Stolypin Land Reform." Unpublished Ph. D. dissertation, Princeton University, 1961.

IV. POLITICAL PARTIES AND THE DUMA

Bohon, John. "Reactionary Politics in Russia: 1905-1909." Unpublished Ph. D. dissertation, University of North Carolina, 1967.

Boiovich, Milan M. *Chleny gosudarstvennoi dumy, Portrety i biografii.* Pervyi sozyv. Moscow, 1906.

B-ov, M. and Dan, F. *Rabochie deputaty v pervoi gosudarstvennoi dume.* St. Petersburg, n.d.

Brianchaninov, A. N. *Rospusk gosudarstvennoi dumy.* Pskov, 1906.

Brock, John J. Jr. "The Theory and Practice of the Union of the Russian People: 1905-1907." Unpublished Ph. D. dissertation. University of Michigan, 1972.

Chasle, Pierre. *Le Parlement russe.* Paris, 1910.

Freeze, Gregory L. "A National Liberation Movement and the Shift in Russian Liberalism." *Slavic Review* 28: March, 1969, pp. 81-91.

Guchkov, Alexander I. "The General Political Situation and the Octobrist Party." *Russian Review* 3: 1: London, 1914, pp. 141-158.

Haimson, Leopold H. "The Parties and the State: The Evolution of Political Attitudes." In Black, Cyril E. *The Transformation of Russian Society.* Cambridge: Harvard University Press, 1960.

Harcave, Sidney S. "Jewish Political Parties and Groups and the Russian State Dumas from 1905 to 1907." Unpublished Ph. D. dissertation. University of Chicago, 1943.

Harper, Samuel N. "The Budget Rights of the Russian Duma." *Journal of Political Economy* 16: March, 1908, pp. 152-156.

_____. *The New Electoral Law for the Russian Duma.* University of Chicago Press, 1908.

Harrison, W. "The Octobrists and the Russian Revolution of 1905." *Durham University Journal* 24: March, 1963, pp. 49-59.

Hutchinson, J. F. "The Octobrists in Russian Politics, 1905-1917." Unpublished Ph. D. dissertation, University of London, 1966.

Ivanovich, V. *Rossiiskiia partii, souizy i ligi*. St. Petersburg, 1906.

Keep, J. L. H. "Russian Social Democracy and the First State Duma." *Slavonic and East European Review* 34: December, 1955, pp. 180-199.

Levin, Alfred. *The Second Duma*. Second edition. Hamden, Conn.: Archon Books, 1961.

———. *The Third Duma, Election and Profile*. Hamden, Conn.: Archon Books, 1973.

Levitsky, Serge L. "Legislative Initiative in the Russian Duma." *American Slavic and East European Review* 15: October, 1956, pp. 313-324.

Maklakov, Vasili A. *The First State Duma*. Translated by Mary Belkin. Indiana University Press, 1964.

Masloff, Clement S. "Violence and/or Land Reform: The Russian Peasant and the Duma, 1906-07." Paper delivered at the Midwest Slavic Conference at Cleveland State University, May 1975.

Menashe, Louis. "Alexander Guchkov and the Origins of the Octobrist Party: The Russian Bourgeois in Politics, 1905." Unpublished Ph. D. dissertation, New York University, 1966.

———. "A Liberal With Spurs." *Russian Review* 26: January, 1967, pp. 38-53.

Miliukov, Paul. *Political Memoirs 1905-1912*. Translated by Carl Goldberg. University of Michigan Press, 1967.

———. *God borby*. St. Petersburg, 1907.

———. "The Representative System in Russia." In Duff, J. D. *Russian Realities and Problems*. Cambridge University Press, 1917.

———. *Russia and Its Crisis*. Chicago, 1905.

Mukhanov, A. A. *Pervaia gosudarstvennaia duma*. St. Petersburg, 1907. (Volumes I, II, and III are bound into one book.)

Pinchuk, Ben-Cion. "The Octobrists in the Third Duma." Unpublished Ph. D. dissertation, University of Washington, 1969.

"Pismo kn. E. N. Trubetskogo Nikolaiu Romanovu po povodu rospuska 1 gosudarstvennoi dumy." *Krasnyi Arkhiv* 10: Leningrad, 1925, pp. 300-304.

"Proekt tronnoi rechi." *Krasnyi Arkhiv* 11-12: Leningrad, 1925, pp. 142-143.

Radkey, Oliver H. *The Agrarian Foes of Bolshevism.* Columbia University Press, 1958.

Recouly, Raymond. *La Tsar et la Douma.* Paris, 1906.

Rhyne, George N. "The Constitutional Democratic Party from its Origins Through the First State Duma." Unpublished Ph. D. dissertation, University of North Carolina, 1968.

Riha, Thomas. *A Russian European: Paul Miliukov in Russian Politics.* University of Notre Dame Press, 1968.

Rodichev, F. "The Liberal Movement in Russia (1891-1905)." *Slavonic and East European Review* 2: December, 1923, pp. 249-262.

Rogger, Hans and Webber, Eugen. *The European Right.* University of California Press, 1965.

———. "The Formation of the Russian Right." *California Slavic Studies* 3: pp. 66-94. University of California Press, 1964.

———. "Was There a Russian Fascism: The Union of the Russian People." *Journal of Modern History* 36: December, 1964, pp. 398-415.

Sergeev, A., ed. "Pervaia gosudarstvennaia duma v Vyborge." *Krasnyi Arkhiv* 57: Leningrad, 1933, pp. 85-99.

Shipov, Dimitri N. *Vospominaniia i dumy o perezhitom.* Moscow, 1918.

Sidelnikov, Stepan M. *Obrazovanie i deiatelnost pervoi gosudarstvennoi dumy.* Moscow, 1962.

Sobranie rechei deputatov gosudarstvennoi dumy. Ist and IInd sessions. St. Petersburg, 1908.

Smith, Nathan. "The Constitutional Democratic Movement in Russia, 1902-1906." Unpublished Ph. D. dissertation, University of Illinois, 1958.

Szeftel, Marc. "The Representatives and Their Powers in the Russian Legislative Chambers (1906-1917)," in *Liber Memorialis Sir Maurice Pawicke: Studies Presented to the International Commission for the History of Representative and Parliamentary Institutions,* XXVII. Louvain, 1965.

Treadgold, Donald. "The Constitutional Democrats and the

Russian Liberal Tradition." *American Slavic and East European Review* 10: June, 1951, pp. 85-94.

Tuck, Robert L. "Paul Miliukov and the Negotiations for a Duma Ministry, 1906." *American Slavic and East European Review* 10: June, 1951, pp. 117-129.

Tyrkova-Williams, Ariadna. "The Cadet Party." *Russian Review* 12: July, 1953, pp. 173-186.

————. "Russian Liberalism." *Russian Review* 10: January, 1951, p. 3-14.

Vodovozov, Vasili V. *Sbornik programm politicheskikh partii v rossii.* St. Petersburg, 1905.

Voskobiynyk, Michael H. "The Nationalities Question in Russia in 1905-1907: A Study in the Origins of Modern Nationalism, With Special Reference to the Ukrainians." Unpublished Ph. D. dissertation, University of Pennsylvania, 1972.

Vyborgskii protsess. St. Petersburg, 1908.

Walsh, Warren B. "The Composition of the Dumas." *Russian Review* 8: April, 1949, pp. 111-116.

————. "Political Parties in the Dumas." *Journal of Modern History* 22: June, 1950, pp. 114-150.

Zimmerman, Judith E. "Between Revolution and Reaction: The Russian Constitutional Democratic Party, October 1905-June 1907." Unpublished Ph. D. dissertation, Columbia University, 1967.

V. GENERAL BACKGROUND INFORMATION

Most of the works of broad scope included in this section are those which have been cited in the text.

A. *Books*

Avrich, Paul. *The Russian Anarchists.* Princeton University Press, 1967.

Beckman, George M. *The Making of the Meiji Constitution.* University of Kansas Press, 1957.

Charques, Richard. *The Twilight of Imperial Russia.* London, 1958.

Curtiss, John S. *Church and State in Russia.* Columbia University Press, 1940.

Dillon, Emile J. *The Eclipse of Russia.* New York, 1918.

Fischer, George. *Russian Liberalism from Gentry to Intelligentsia.* Harvard University Press, 1958.

Fisk, Otis H. *Germany's Constitutions of 1871 and 1919: Texts With Notes and Introductions.* Cincinnati, Ohio, 1924.

Florinsky, Michael. *The End of the Russian Empire.* New York, 1961.

———. *Russia: A History and Interpretation.* Volume II. New York, 1955.

Gelai, Shmuel. *The Liberal Movement in Russia: 1900-1905.* Cambridge University Press, 1973.

Gerschenkron, Alexander. *Continuity in History and Other Essays.* Harvard University Press, 1968.

Gessen, Iosif V. "Reminiscences." An English translation, in typescript, of I. V. Gessen's memoirs. In the Hoover Archives, n.d.

Harcave, Sidney. *Years of the Golden Cockerel.* New York, 1968.

Harper, Paul V., ed. *The Russia I Believe In: The Memoirs of Samuel N. Harper, 1902-1941.* University of Chicago Press, 1945.

Hosking, Goeffrey A. *The Russian Constitutional Experiment: Government and Duma, 1907-1914.* Cambridge University Press, 1973.

Kalmykow, Andrew D. *Memoirs of a Russian Diplomat: Outposts of the Empire 1893-1917.* Yale University Press, 1971.

Katkov, George. *Russia 1917: The February Revolution.* New York, 1967.

Keep, J. L. H. *The Rise of Social Democracy in Russia.* Oxford University Press, 1963.

Kerensky, Alexander. *The Crucifixion of Liberty.* New York, 1934.

———. *Russia and History's Turning Point.* New York, 1965.

Kovalevsky, Maxime. *Russian Political Institutions.* University of Chicago Press, 1902.

Kucherov, Samuel. *Courts, Lawyers, and Trials Under the Last Three Tsars.* New York, 1953.

Lyaschenko, Peter I. *History of the National Economy of Russia to the 1917 Revolution.* Translated by L. M. Herman. New York, 1949.

Mavor, James. *An Economic History of Russia.* Volume II. London, 1925.

Maynard, Sir John. *Russia in Flux: Before October.* New York, 1962.

Miller, Margaret S. *The Economic Development of Russia, 1904-1914.* New York, 1967.

Nabokov, Vladimir. *Speak, Memory.* New York, 1966.

Nakano, Tomio. *The Ordinance Power of the Japanese Emperor.* John Hopkins University Press, 1923.

Oldenburg, S. S. *Tsarstvovanie Imperatora Nikolaia II.* Volumes I and II. Belgrade, 1939; Munich, 1949.

Owen, Launcelot A. *The Russian Peasant Movement, 1906-1917.* New York, 1963.

Pares, Bernard. *The Fall of the Russian Monarchy.* New York, 1961.

Pares, Bernard. *My Russian Memoirs.* London, 1931.

———. *Russia and Reform.* London, 1907.

———. *A Wandering Student.* Syracuse University Press, 1948.

Pavlovsky, George. *Agricultural Russia on the Eve of the Revolution.* London, 1930.

Pipes, Richard. *Struve: Liberal on the Left, 1870-1905.* Harvard University Press, 1970.

Postgate, R. W., ed. *Revolution from 1789-1906: Documents Selected and Edited with Notes and Introductions.* New York, 1962.

Pushkarev, Sergei. *The Emergence of Modern Russia, 1801-1917.* Translated by R. H. McNeal and Tova Yedlin. New York, 1966.

Quigley, Harold S. *Japanese Government and Politics.* New York, 1932.

Robinson, Geroid T. *Rural Russia Under the Old Regime.* University of California Press, 1967.

Schapiro, Leonard B. *Revolution and Nationalism in Rus-*

sian Nineteenth Century Political Thought. Yale University Press, 1967.

Seton-Watson, Hugh. *The Russian Empire, 1801-1917.* Oxford University Press, 1967.

Simmonds, George W. "The Congress of Representatives of the Nobles' Associations, 1906-1916." Unpublished Ph. D. dissertation, Columbia University, 1964.

Stavrou, Theofanis G. *Russia Under the Last Tsar.* University of Minnesota Press, 1969.

Timberlake, Charles, ed. *Essays on Russian Liberalism.* University of Missouri Press, 1972.

Treadgold, Donald W. *The Great Siberian Migration.* Princeton University Press, 1957.

_____. *Lenin and His Rivals.* New York, 1955.

Urussov, S. D. *Memoirs of a Russian Governor.* Translated by Herman Rosenthal. London, 1908.

von Laue, Theodore H. *Sergei Witte and the Industrialization of Russia.* New York, 1963.

Walkin, Jacob. *The Rise of Democracy in Pre-revolutionary Russia: Political and Social Institutions Under the Last Three Czars.* New York, 1962.

White, John A. *The Diplomacy of the Russo-Japanese War.* Princeton University Press, 1964.

Williams, Harold W. *Russia of the Russians.* New York, 1914.

Wright, Herbert F. *The Constitutions of the States at War: 1914-1918.* Washington, D.C., 1919.

Yaney, George L. *The Systematization of Russian Government.* University of Illinois Press, 1973.

B. *Articles*

Crisp, Olga. "The Russian Liberals and the 1906 Anglo-French Loan to Russia." *Slavonic Review* 39: June, 1961, pp. 497-511.

Hodgson, John H. "Finland's Position in the Russian Empire, 1905-1910." *Journal of Central European Affairs* 20: July, 1960, pp. 158-173.

Harper, Samuel N. "Exceptional Measures in Russia." *Russian Review* 1: 4: London, 1912, pp. 92-105.

Karpovich, Michael. "Two Types of Russian Liberalism: Maklakov and Miliukov." In Simmons, Ernest J. *Continuity and Change in Russian and Soviet Thought.* Harvard University Press, 1955.

Kennan, George F. "The Breakdown of the Tsarist Autocracy." In Pipes, Richard. *Revolutionary Russia.* Harvard University Press, 1968.

Pares, Bernard. "The Reform Movement in Russia." *Cambridge Modern History,* Volume XII. New York, 1910.

Rigsberg, Benjamin. "Tsarist Censorship Performance, 1894-1905." *Jahrbücher für Geschichte Osteuropas* 17: March, 1969, pp. 59-76.

Riha, Thomas. "Riech: Portrait of a Russian Newspaper." *American Slavic and East European Review* 22: December, 1963, pp. 663-682.

Rimlinger, G. V. "Autocracy and the Factory Order." *Journal of Economic History* 20: March, 1960, pp. 67-92.

Robinson, James H. "Constitution of the Kingdom of Prussia" in *Supplement to the Annals of the American Academy of Political and Social Science,* September, 1894, pp. 198-249.

Rogger, Hans. "Reflections on Russian Conservatism, 1861-1905." *Jahrbücher für Geschichte Osteuropas* 14: June, 1966, pp. 195-212.

Szeftel, Marc. "The Form of Government of the Russian Empire Prior to the Constitutional Reforms of 1905-1906." In Curtiss, John S. *Essays in Russian and Soviet History.* Columbia University Press, 1963.

Szeftel, Marc. "Personal Inviolability in the Legislation of the Russian Absolute Monarchy." *American Slavic and East European Review* 17: February, 1958, pp. 1-24.

Tidmarsh, K. "The Zubatov Idea." *American Slavic and East European Review* 19: September, 1960, pp. 335-346.

von Laue, Theodore. "The Chances for Liberal Constitutionalism." *Slavic Review* 24: March, 1965, pp. 34-46.

———. "Factory Inspection under the Witte System." *American Slavic and East European Review* 19: October, 1960, pp. 347-362.

————. "Of the Crises in the Russian Polity." In Curtiss, John S. *Essays in Russian and Soviet History.* Columbia University Press, 1963.

————. "Russian Labor Between Field and Factory." *California Slavic Studies* 3: pp. 33-66. University of California Press, 1964.

————. "Russian Peasants in the Factory." *Journal of Economic History* 21: March, 1961, pp. 61-81.

————. "Tsarist Labor Policy, 1895-1903." *Journal of Modern History* 34: June, 1962, pp. 135-145.

Walkin, Jacob. "The Attitude of the Tsarist Government Towards the Labor Problem." *American Slavic and East European Review* 13: June, 1954, pp. 163-184.

————. "Government Controls Over the Press in Russia, 1905-1914." *Russian Review* 13: July, 1954, pp. 203-209.

Yaney, George L. "Some Aspects of the Imperial Russian Government on the Eve of the First World War." *Slavonic and East European Review* 43: December, 1964, pp. 68-90.

INDEX

Address to the Throne: analysis of, 182-187, 232-233; administration response to, 183, 187-196, 197-199, 211

Agrarian measures: *ukazs* of; November, 1905, 56-57, 230-231, 271; March, 1903 and August, 1904, 230; March, 1906, 231; Stolypin sponsored measures (1906), 231, 259-261, 271; administration policy towards, 185, 190-191, 216-220 *passim*, 224, 226-232, 236-240, 244, 247, 260, 270; opposition proposals, 185, 223-226. See also appropriate listings under Stolypin, peasants, First Duma, as well as under the major political groups of that assembly.

Akchurian, Joseph, 129

Aladin, Aleksei, 176-177, 188, 194, 210

Alexander II, 9, 51

Alexander III, 42-43, 45, 50

Alexander Mikhailovich, Grand Duke, 39

Alexandra Feodorovna, Tsarritsa, 42-44, 77

Alexis Nikolaievich, Tsarevich, 43, 150-151, 263

Amnesty: demands for; 19, 21, 29-30, 53, 54, 268; decree of October 21, 1905; 55-56, 58; issue in First Duma, 152-155, 174-178, 183, 191, 198

Anikin, Stepan, 176-177, 194, 209

Army: revolutionary disorders in, 33-34, 63-64, 68-69, 136, 246; discontent in 24, 33-34, 36; concessions to, 70; annual recruit levy, 120, 122, 279

Article 87 (45), 119, 121, 257, 259, 277

Associations, *ukaz* of March 4, 1906, 169-171, 272

Baring, Maurice: comments of, 15-16, 57, 71, 137, 155, 177, 188, 195, 199, 250-251

Belostok Pogrom: issue in Duma, 203-206, 247-248

Birzhevye vedomosti (The Stock Market Journal), 54

Bobrinskii, Count A.A., 85

Bobrinskii, Count V.A., 96

Bolsheviks, 10, 158

Broido, Eva, 63

Bulatsel, Paul, 137

Bulygin, Alexander, 22, 48, 78-79, 87, 88, 91

Bulygin Duma: statute, 78-80, 82-83, 89-91; electoral law, 76-77, 83-89, 90-91, 100-102, 125; public reaction to, 24, 48, 93-94

Bund. See Jewish Bund

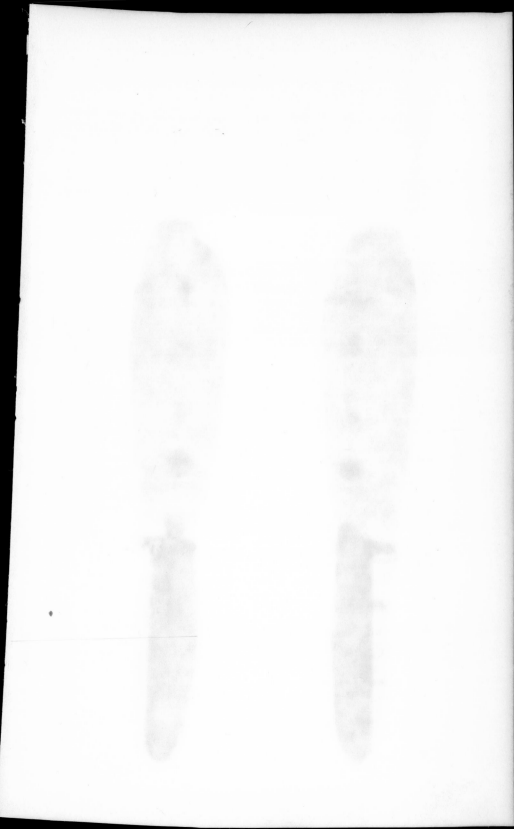

DATE DUE	

GAYLORD   PRINTED IN U.S.A.